Young Children's Foreign Language Anxiety

PSYCHOLOGY OF LANGUAGE LEARNING AND TEACHING
Series Editors: Sarah Mercer, *Universität Graz, Austria* and
Stephen Ryan, *Waseda University, Japan*

This international, interdisciplinary book series explores the exciting, emerging field of Psychology of Language Learning and Teaching. It is a series that aims to bring together works which address a diverse range of psychological constructs from a multitude of empirical and theoretical perspectives, but always with a clear focus on their applications within the domain of language learning and teaching. The field is one that integrates various areas of research that have been traditionally discussed as distinct entities, such as motivation, identity, beliefs, strategies and self-regulation, and it also explores other less familiar concepts for a language education audience, such as emotions, the self and positive psychology approaches. In theoretical terms, the new field represents a dynamic interface between psychology and foreign language education and books in the series draw on work from diverse branches of psychology, while remaining determinedly focused on their pedagogic value. In methodological terms, sociocultural and complexity perspectives have drawn attention to the relationships between individuals and their social worlds, leading to a field now marked by methodological pluralism. In view of this, books encompassing quantitative, qualitative and mixed methods studies are all welcomed.

All books in this series are externally peer-reviewed.

Full details of all the books in this series and of all our other publications can be found on http://www.multilingual-matters.com, or by writing to Multilingual Matters, St Nicholas House, 31-34 High Street, Bristol BS1 2AW, UK.

PSYCHOLOGY OF LANGUAGE LEARNING AND TEACHING: 15

Young Children's Foreign Language Anxiety

The Case of South Korea

Jieun Kiaer, Jessica M. Morgan-Brown and Naya Choi

MULTILINGUAL MATTERS
Bristol • Blue Ridge Summit

DOI https://doi.org/10.21832/KIAER1609
Library of Congress Cataloging in Publication Data
A catalog record for this book is available from the Library of Congress.
Names: Kiaer, Jieun, author. | Morgan-Brown, Jessica M., author. | Choi, Naya, author.
Title: Young Children's Foreign Language Anxiety: The Case of South Korea/Jieun Kiaer, Jessica M. Morgan-Brown and Naya Choi.
Description: Bristol; Blue Ridge Summit: Multilingual Matters, 2021. | Series: Psychology of Language Learning and Teaching: 15 | Includes bibliographical references and index. | Summary: 'This book presents original research on the effects of foreign language anxiety (FLA) on young language learners. It includes suggestions for alleviating FLA and encouraging foreign language enjoyment which will ultimately facilitate more effective language learning and support children's psychosocial wellbeing' – Provided by publisher.
Identifiers: LCCN 2021004689 | ISBN 9781800411593 (paperback) | ISBN 9781800411609 (hardback) | ISBN 9781800411616 (pdf) | ISBN 9781800411623 (epub) | ISBN 9781800411630 (kindle edition)
Subjects: LCSH: Second language acquisition – Psychological aspects. | English language – Study and teaching (Elementary) – Korea (South) | English language – Study and teaching (Elementary) – Korean speakers.
Classification: LCC P118.2 .K525 2021 | DDC 418.0071 – dc23
LC record available at https://lccn.loc.gov/2021004689

British Library Cataloguing in Publication Data
A catalogue entry for this book is available from the British Library.

ISBN-13: 978-1-80041-160-9 (hbk)
ISBN-13: 978-1-80041-159-3 (pbk)

Multilingual Matters
UK: St Nicholas House, 31-34 High Street, Bristol BS1 2AW, UK.
USA: NBN, Blue Ridge Summit, PA, USA.

Website: www.multilingual-matters.com
Twitter: Multi_Ling_Mat
Facebook: https://www.facebook.com/multilingualmatters
Blog: www.channelviewpublications.wordpress.com

Copyright © 2021 Jieun Kiaer, Jessica M. Morgan-Brown and Naya Choi

All rights reserved. No part of this work may be reproduced in any form or by any means without permission in writing from the publisher.

The policy of Multilingual Matters/Channel View Publications is to use papers that are natural, renewable and recyclable products, made from wood grown in sustainable forests. In the manufacturing process of our books, and to further support our policy, preference is given to printers that have FSC and PEFC Chain of Custody certification. The FSC and/or PEFC logos will appear on those books where full certification has been granted to the printer concerned.

Typeset by Riverside Publishing Solutions.
Printed and bound in the UK by the CPI Books Group Ltd.
Printed and bound in the US by NBN.

Contents

Figures and Tables	vii
Acknowledgements	ix
Abbreviations	x

1 Introduction — 1
  1.1 Rationale for Young Children's Foreign Language Anxiety — 1
  1.2 Who is this Book Intended For? — 3
  1.3 Structure and Content of the Book — 3

2 Foreign Language Anxiety and Foreign Language Enjoyment — 5
  2.1 Research in Language Classroom Psychology from FLA to FLE — 5
  2.2 The Psychology of Anxiety in Language Learning — 10
  2.3 Conclusion — 15

3 Foreign Language Anxiety in Children — 16
  3.1 Metrics and Research on Child Classroom Anxiety — 16
  3.2 Psychology of Anxiety in Children — 24
  3.3 Conclusion — 27

4 Foreign Language Anxiety in the South Korean Context — 29
  4.1 English Fever — 30
  4.2 State of FLA Research in South Korea — 39
  4.3 Lingual Frenectomies — 41
  4.4 Applicability to a Wider Context/Target Audience — 42
  4.5 Conclusion — 44

5 Sources of Increased FLA Among Young Children — 46
  5.1 Myths — 46
  5.2 East Asian Language Anxiety, Understanding Asian Mentalities — 54
  5.3 Parental Influence in Language Learning — 59
  5.4 Conclusion — 62

6	Case Study: Factors Affecting Young Children's FLA: Kindergarten vs. English Immersion Institution	63
	6.1 Method	63
	6.2 Results	69
	6.3 Discussion	82
7	Effects of Innovative Language Learning on Foreign Language Anxiety and Foreign Language Enjoyment	86
	7.1 Effects of FLA and FLE	87
	7.2 Technological Methods	88
	7.3 Task-based Language Teaching (TBLT)	91
	7.4 Case Study: Young Korean Children's L2 Vocabulary Learning Through Cooking	93
	7.5 Conclusion	107
8	Towards a More Ethical Learning Environment	109
	8.1 Warning Signs and Detection of Children's Anxiety	109
	8.2 Practical Solutions for Alleviating Anxiety	112
	8.3 Creating a Welcoming Environment	119
	8.4 The Importance of Awareness	123
	Conclusion	125
	Implications for Practice	129
	Reflections for Further Research	132
	Appendix A: Anxiety Metrics	137
	Appendix B: Kindergarten vs. Immersion English Parent Surveys	141
	References	150
	Index	171

Figures and Tables

Figures

6.1	Likert scale used for evaluating English and Korean language proficiency	64
6.2	The five impulsiveness scale items	65
6.3	The four items of the anticipatory worry scale	65
6.4	Child variables by institution	71
6.5	Family education level by institution	73
6.6	Family income and English ability by institution	73
6.7	Family experience in English-speaking countries by institution	74
6.8	Student-teacher ratio by institution type	75
6.9	Language use by institution type	76
6.10	Language rule by institution type	77
6.11	FLA by institution type	77
7.1	Test and task procedures	96
7.2	Different learning experiences in the during-task step of mixing ingredients – Photo Group (PG) vs. Object Group (OG)	97
7.3	Using PowerPoint (PPT) in the class	97
7.4	Productive and receptive test results	100
8.1	The cognitive triangle of interactions that are the focus of cognitive behavioural therapy	118

Tables

6.1	Descriptive statistics of children	64
6.2	Descriptive statistics of children attending kindergarten	69
6.3	Descriptive statistics of children attending English immersion institution	70
6.4	Comparison of child variables between the kindergarten and English immersion institution	71

6.5	Comparison of family variables between the kindergarten and English immersion institution	72
6.6	Comparison of institutional variables between the kindergarten and English immersion institution	74
6.7	Comparison of English education hours	75
6.8	The predictors (child variables) of children's FLA (kindergarten)	78
6.9	The predictors (child variables) of children's FLA (English immersion institution)	79
6.10	The predictors (family variables) of children's FLA (kindergarten)	80
6.11	The predictors (child variables) of children's FLA (English immersion institution)	80
6.12	The predictors (institution variables) of children's FLA (kindergarten)	81
6.13	The predictors (institution variables) of children's FLA (English immersion institution)	82
7.1	Participants by group	95
7.2	Marking range	98
7.3	Mean differences (standard deviation) for productive tests through ANOVA	99
7.4	Mean differences (standard deviation) for receptive tests through ANOVA	100
7.5	T-test and mean scores of vocabulary knowledge	101
7.6	Mean differences between pre- and immediate post-test of productive skills	101
7.7	Mean differences between pre-test and delayed post-test of productive skills	101
7.8	Mean differences between pre-test and immediate post-test of receptive skills	102
7.9	Mean differences between pre-test and delayed post-test of receptive skills	102
7.10	Answers to 'Do you like cooking? If so, are there any reasons?'	103
7.11	Answers to 'Does a cooking activity help you learn English words? If so, how did it help you?'	103
7.12	Answers to 'Which activity would you prefer to do: cooking with real objects or photos of food? In either case, why do you think it is more fun?'	104
7.13	Answers to 'Was the dish you made any good? What did you like? (OG)' 'What did you like? (PG)'	104

Acknowledgements

We would like to acknowledge the wide range of people who have helped us in the process of completing this book project. We would like first and foremost to thank all the teachers, parents and children involved in the research for this book's case studies. Without their openness and participation, we would not have been able to investigate firsthand the effects that South Korean language classrooms can have on early childhood anxiety.

We would also like to give a special acknowledgement to children's counselor NanDee Walker, NCC, LPC, RPT for her consultations on therapeutic interventions for childhood anxiety, as well as to counseling psychologist Dr Ka Yan Danise Mok for her insights into adult anxiety and its manifestations.

Additionally, we would like to thank Dr Sujeong Kang for helping us collect and analyze the data from the many kindergartens, and Sangeun Lee for organizing the data and helping to correct the manuscript.

Our gratitude goes out to Amena Nebres for all of her editorial help, as well as to Toby Bladen for his helpful edits and suggestions on the earlier drafts of this manuscript. Furthermore, we would like to express gratitude to all of the reviewers, editors, copyeditors, and others who looked over the manuscripts and offered invaluable suggestions for its improvement during the publication process, especially Laura Longworth whose patience was endless and whose help was invaluable.

Finally, above all, we would like to thank our families and friends for all their support, love and encouragement throughout this process. Thank you Ian, Sarah and Jessie. Thank you Garett and Aelwyn. Thank you Alex and Daniel.

Abbreviations

AI	Artificial Intelligence
CBT	Cognitive Behavioural Therapy
CLIL	Content and Language Learning
CPH	Critical Period Hypothesis
EE	Extramural English
EFL	English as a Foreign Language
EMI	English Medium Instruction
FLA	Foreign Language Anxiety
FLCA	Foreign Language Classroom Anxiety
FLE	Foreign Language Enjoyment
FNE	Fear of Negative Evaluation
KEDI	Korean Education Development Institute
L1	First Language
L2	Second Language
NS	Native Speaker
OAPE	Organization Against Private-sector Education
OG	Object Group
OLAT	One Language at a Time
PG	Photo Group
SAD	Social Avoidance and Distress
SD	Standard Deviation
SES	Socioeconomic Status
SLA	Second Language Acquisition
TBLL	Task-Based Language Learning
TBLT	Task-Based Language Teaching
TEFL	Teaching English as a Foreign Language
TESOL	Teaching English to Speakers of Other Languages
TL	Target Language
YLL	Young Language Learners

1 Introduction

Societies across the globe are becoming increasingly interwoven at an unprecedented speed and with an impressively wide scope. In this process of globalization, the role of English as Lingua Franca (ELF) is becoming ever more crucial not only in business/trade and education but in every societal sector. So-called 'English fever' (Park, 2007) is found in most countries, particularly in the places for which Kachru (1985) famously coined term the 'Expanding Circle', including most of the East Asian countries (e.g. mainland China, Japan and Korea). In these places, English, while not a historical or governmental language, is considered as one of the most valuable forms of social capital and is therefore widely acquired and used: good English means good career prospects and, beyond this, enables individuals to operate on local, national and international levels, making them more competitive and positioning them for financial and social success. Though we focus on South Korean case studies in this book, most observations are also applicable to Japanese and Chinese cases.

1.1 Rationale for Young Children's Foreign Language Anxiety

Within this context of English as a global lingua franca, the English learning boom is unsurprising. Believing the oft-cited trope of 'the younger the better' when it comes to language learning, fervent parents have been introducing English language education to their youngsters at earlier and earlier stages of their lives, at times even before the babies have been exposed to their mother tongue. In extreme cases, expectant mothers sometimes start playing English stories to their babies in the womb as part of their *taegyo* – prenatal education (see Chapter 3) – or even enrol in prenatal English classes. This zeal, however, has had significant side effects on young children, their families and society as a whole, as we shall unfold in this book. Our main aim is to shed light on young children's foreign language anxiety (FLA). Many parents and educators believe that children will absorb English effortlessly if they are merely exposed to English – just because they are young. In order to maximize these expected language learning outcomes, English-only total immersion is often chosen as a default method, particularly through enrolment in expensive *Yeongeo yuchiwon* 'English kindergartens'. However, numerous children experience distress due to the onset of foreign language anxiety, which not only negatively affects their language learning, but also their overall mental wellbeing. Nevertheless, thus far, little attention has been given to improving the situation, and parents and educators continue to put more emphasis on the need to increase the amount of immersive exposure to English.

However, within these English-only classrooms, many of the pedagogical methodologies used to teach language to very young children are underdeveloped. Others have been replicated from methodologies meant for teaching older children who have passed Penfield and Roberts' proposed critical language period (Penfield & Roberts, 1959). Combined with the sparseness of well-researched, theoretically founded pedagogical practices, FLA often enters the picture. When not recognized or addressed, FLA can have detrimental effects not only on a child's language acquisition but also on the child's overall psychosocial wellbeing. Much of the existent research on FLA focuses on adult language learners or on students in the age range 12–18. Little work has been done on children at the youngest tiers of education. Therefore, in this book, we compile research on the topic of FLA, particularly as it relates to childhood education and, more specifically, language education. Examining case studies alongside analyses of childhood anxiety in general, this book aims to show the status quo of young children's FLA and the need to consider ways to decrease FLA in young children's English education. Furthermore, we aim to offer possible solutions to create more ethical environments where young children can feel safe and explore language without feeling anxious. We assert that, when children are educated in such an environment, they not only enjoy learning but will also flourish in their learning targets.

As background for this book, to illustrate the causes and effects of FLA in real world situations, we use the early childhood English education sector in South Korea. The current environment in South Korea is one in which children are placed in English education classrooms starting at a very young age, sometimes to the detriment of their academic, psychosocial and physical wellbeing (Park, 2007). The highly competitive nature of Korean society has caused the education industry in the country to become what it is today. In fact, in the South Korean educational sector, English language acquisition stands out as one of the most worrying social phenomena that young Koreans encounter. This is the case not only for older but also for younger children. In this book, we will look at the current state of English education in South Korea and its problems, offering practical solutions that could make the English education industry more effective and healthier for students. Although we examine specifically the early childhood English education situation in South Korea, many of the findings in South Korea can be applied to other East Asian contexts and global situations as well. As the drive for English language acquisition continually increases all over the world, understanding how best to simultaneously educate children and guard their psychosocial wellbeing is key.

1.2 Who is this Book Intended For?

This book is intended to inform, foster awareness and offer language classroom solutions for parents, teachers, policymakers and school administrations who operate with in the field of early childhood language education. Even if, as Dewaele *et al.* (2018) have noted, teachers are generally not the main cause of FLA in classrooms, they can play an integral role in spotting and alleviating it. In the case of L1 users of English teaching in South Korea, they can also employ cultural sensitivity to avoid needlessly increasing FLA in students within specific cultural environments. Teachers additionally are an important part of fostering Foreign Language Enjoyment (FLE) (Dewaele & MacIntyre, 2014), which, while not the antithesis of FLA, can help to promote healthy learning environments. Therefore, it is important for teachers to both be aware of FLA in their classrooms and promote FLE among their students (Dewaele & Dewaele, 2020). In highlighting these two important features of language learning, this book can be used in conjunction with teacher training in order to help teachers become aware of the signs of FLA in their students as well as methods for its alleviation. While the book focuses on the South Korean context, the problems and difficulties experienced in South Korean classrooms are not unique to the country. Therefore, educators, researchers and policymakers in other similar language classroom situations may also use this book as a guide for creating a safe language learning environment for young children.

1.3 Structure and Content of the Book

This book can be divided into three rough sections. Chapters 2 to 4 are foundational in that they lay the groundwork of the current situation as it stands regarding FLA and the research thereof. In Chapter 2, we give an overview of the current research on FLA, focusing on Foreign Language Classroom Anxiety (FLCA) as proposed by Horwitz *et al.* (1986). As part of this analysis, we incorporate Dewaele and MacIntyre's recent research on Foreign Language Enjoyment (FLE) (2014, 2016), and how positive psychology research has affected views of FLA/FLCA (MacIntyre & Mercer, 2014; MacIntyre *et al.*, 2016). We also discuss the psychological effects of anxiety in general, and more specifically FLA. In Chapter 3, we narrow our focus to FLA in young children, focusing in on the specific ways in which FLA manifests itself and various factors that contribute to FLA and classroom anxiety, more generally, in children. Finally, in Chapter 4, we set forth the specific situation in South Korea, describing the current state of the perception of an 'English Fever' phenomenon in South Korea and the ensuing rise in FLA among young children. While staying focused on the Korean situation, we make sure to emphasize the applicability of certain South Korean issues within a wider global context.

The second section, comprising Chapters 5 and 6, outlines the problems and challenges associated with FLA and early childhood English education. Chapter 5 centres on the sources of FLA among young children and also looks at common myths surrounding language education that, while widely accepted by the general public, have very little foundation in application when it comes to the language education of young children. Such myths include immersion teaching methods, emphasis on 'native-speaker pronunciation' over communicative function, rote learning methods and various supposed dangers of bilingual education. We also note the dangers of passive solutions to these problems, such as the Korean government's decision to stop offering early childhood English education, which in turn drove parents into the less-regulated private education sector. Chapter 6 includes case studies regarding FLA in Korean Early English Education Centres conducted by Choi and Kiaer.

In the final section of this book, we offer solutions to the problems and challenges outlined in the previous two sections. In Chapter 7, we propose the use of innovative language learning in early English classrooms including Task-based Language Teaching (TBLT) and translanguaging pedagogical practice involving the comfortable use of multiple language repertoires in the English classroom. In the final chapter, we outline some existing proposals by other authors regarding childhood anxiety and alter the models to fit a classroom context. As young children often lack the vocabulary and psychosocial awareness to express their experiences with FLA, we also provide a description of the various signs of FLA in young children. Educators may use this description to identify students who are suffering and then apply FLA alleviation techniques, which are also discussed. We offer theoretically founded suggestions for creating a safe learning environment, taking advantage of this early period of language learning by activating young children's minds rather than raising affective filters through FLA.

Research on the best methodology for teaching language to children in a psychologically safe space is difficult to undertake due to various ethical hurdles that must be overcome. The safety of the children must be ensured throughout the entire study. Nevertheless, it is important that educators, researchers and policymakers alike do whatever is ethically possible to determine the best practices for safely teaching foreign languages to young children. This book aims to provide a base on which future research can build in order to increase the depth of knowledge on the issue of FLA in young language learners.

2 Foreign Language Anxiety and Foreign Language Enjoyment

2.1 Research in Language Classroom Psychology from FLA to FLE

Before diving into the background literature on Foreign Language Anxiety (FLA) and its effects on young children, it is important at the beginning of this book to acknowledge that each language learner, whether they are 3 years old or 93 years old, is different. Dörnyei (2005), echoing theory and research from Gardner (1985) onwards, asserted that each language learner differs with regard to personality, temperament, mood, aptitude, motivation, learning/cognitive style, learning strategies and self-regulation. We additionally wish to emphasize that the descriptions of anxiety and suggestions for its alleviation within this book are general. As many researchers before us have indicated, they will not be universally applicable to everyone. These descriptions and recommendations are nonetheless useful in that they paint a general picture of FLA that can inform the creation of language teaching methodology, which should then be adapted by educators and parents to suit their individual students/children.

Anxiety is a complex issue that has been much discussed in the Second Language Acquisition (SLA) field since the 1980s. Good reviews of the existing FLA research can be found in Dewaele *et al.* (2018), Dörnyei (2005), Horwitz *et al.* (1986), MacIntyre (1999), Oxford (1999) and Young (1999). For one of the most comprehensive outlines of research that has taken place regarding FLA, see Horwitz (2010), in which she gives a timeline of all the seminal research that has been done on the subject from 1972 to 2010. Horwitz dates the beginnings of focused FLA research from a 1972 article about the effects of moderate alcohol consumption on second language ability. The main conclusion of this study, which is applicable to a discussion of FLA in all ages, was that, in a relaxed state, a student's language production ability increased (Guiora *et al.*, 1972). Subsequent studies by Chastain (1975), Kleinmann (1977) and Dulay and Burt (1977) all attempted to investigate the effects of FLA on learners. However, they all lacked a consistently accepted metric by which to measure FLA and the variables that affect it.

Answering a call from Scovel (1978) to create a tool for consistent measurement of FLA, the study of anxiety in the language classroom became more empirical in the 1980s. Various metrics for quantifying a student's Foreign Language Classroom Anxiety (FLCA) were introduced, most notably the Foreign Language Classroom Anxiety Scale (FLCAS). This metric, which was introduced by Gardner (1985) and Horwitz *et al.* (1986), used a 5-point Likert scale to measure self-perceptions of anxiety in second language learners. In the case of Gardner (1985), he carried out investigations into anxiety's role in the language classroom through his work on the affective variables of language learning in English-speaking students in French language classrooms. It was through this work that significant variables were noted and the idea of individual differences in the experience of FLA was expanded. Gardner also introduced a basic metric for measuring FLA, though it was not intended to be universally applicable. Horwitz *et al.* (1986) then built on Gardner's study. Through observation, Horwitz and her colleagues noticed that students who suffered from FLA used avoidance techniques in their language production, making many preventable errors and showing an inability to participate in spontaneous conversations. On the other hand, students that were more relaxed exercised more creativity in their linguistic expression in the second language and were more interpretive. With these observations, the researchers defined five psycho-physiological symptoms of FLA (tenseness, trembling, perspiring, palpitations and sleep disturbances), using these as a foundation for the 33-item FLCAS metric. Variations of this scale have been utilized in SLA classrooms around the world in studies throughout the last three decades.

Horwitz's (2010) outline of FLA research also discusses the expansion of FLA research across the affective variables pointed out by Gardner. Studies focus on students in non-European language settings (Aida, 1994; Elkhafaifi, 2005; Liu & Jackson, 2008; Saito & Samimy, 1996; Spitalli, 2000), of different ages, different language abilities, varying language aptitudes (Sparks & Young, 2009) and personality traits. Studies have also broken language learning down into its component parts (reading, writing, listening and speaking) to investigate where FLA enters into the learning process more commonly (Oh, 1992; Young, 1990). Articles have additionally focused on methodology and pedagogy for creating low-anxiety classrooms in order to decrease the negative effects of FLA (Horwitz, 1996; Horwitz *et al.*, 2009; Koch & Terrell, 1991; Young, 1991). Research continues along this trend with very few alterations to Gardner's (1985) and Horwitz *et al.*'s (1986) foundational research in FLA.

While some variation exists in the definition of FLA, it is generally accepted that, while trait anxiety[1] can contribute to the likelihood a language learner will experience FLA, FLA itself is a form of state anxiety or 'specific anxiety reaction' that is situational and not a consistent part of a person's psychology (Horwitz *et al.*, 1986: 125;

Dörnyei, 2005: 198). Consequently, it is the environment, situation and stressors of language learning that cause the learner to experience FLA. Much of the research on FLA finds its foundations in the theory of affective filters in SLA, first put forward by Dulay and Burt (1977), then widely disseminated through the work of Krashen in the early 1980s (Krashen, 1982: 30–31). Anxiety, alongside motivation and self-confidence, is posited as one of the variables that influences affective filters. A decrease in anxiety is hypothesized to lower these affective filters that block the learners' ability both to produce in a second language, as well as negatively affecting their ability to process input.

More recently, a new thread of research regarding the emotional vulnerability of students in the foreign language classroom has come into focus. Dewaele (2018: 677), building off almost a decade of his own work and that of colleagues, cites an 'emotional deficit' in the field of SLA research. The same author advocates the adoption of positive psychology in SLA research as put forward by MacIntyre and Mercer (2014) and MacIntyre et al. (2016). Positive psychology, as the name would imply, focuses on the positive components and strengths of individuals in a situation, encouraging the amplification of these components in the attempt to decrease effects of negative components in a given situation. Building on a focus on positive emotions, Dewaele puts forward the idea of Foreign Language Enjoyment (FLE) as something that should be considered in conjunction with FLA. In multiple studies, Dewaele and his colleagues have shown that FLA and FLE are not opposite ends of a spectrum, but rather two emotional components of language learning that should both be given attention in the creation of effective educational methodologies. In a 2018 study, Dewaele et al. showed that 'enjoyment and anxiety are separate dimensions' (Dewaele et al., 2018: 690). Someone with high FLE can also have high FLCA, so a heightened FLE does not necessarily indicate a low level of FLCA. In their title for a 2016 chapter, Dewaele and MacIntyre even referred to FLE and FLCA as 'The right and left feet of the language learner' (Dewaele & MacIntyre, 2016: 215). Building on this work, throughout this book, we will also emphasize the necessity of creating environments that allow heightened levels of FLE within the classroom. This aims to facilitate improved language acquisition. Much of Dewaele's research does not delve into the relationship between FLE and language attainment, as most of his studies are carried out in British schools with highly motivated students. However, more recently, he has worked closely with Li, who carried out research that showed the links between FLCE, FLE and actual vs. perceived achievement within the context of Chinese high school students (Li, 2019). Dewaele, with various colleagues, most notably MacIntyre, also studies the effects of 'positive psychology' on the language learning experiences of individual students and their attitudes and comfort levels within the foreign language classroom. Recently, his work with Li analysing and adapting a FLE scale for the context of Chinese secondary school students (Li *et al.*, 2018) as well as his research with Jiang looking at the effects of FLA outside of the classroom (Jiang & Dewaele, 2020) have expanded the geographic scope of FLA and FLE research, but have not expanded the age range of students being observed.

While a substantial amount of empirical evidence regarding FLA has been acquired in the Western world, Dewaele has tried to branch out somewhat in his research to include non-European languages and language learners (Jiang & Dewaele, 2020; Li *et al.*, 2018; Yan & Dewaele, 2018, 2020). Yet, as he readily admits, because he continues to carry out the majority of his empirical studies in Europe, it is difficult to truly assess how the typological distance between home and target languages and their associated characteristics affects both FLE and FLCA. However, in a 2010 paper, he hypothesized that language learners will exhibit higher levels of confidence and therefore heightened levels of enjoyment when the target language is typologically related to either their mother tongue or another language in their linguistic repertoire (Dewaele, 2010; Dewaele & MacIntyre, 2014). From this, we may thus infer the converse: when the languages that compose a learner's repertoire are not typologically related to the target language, a decrease in self-confidence among students might be seen, which would lead to a decrease in FLE. In recent years, scholars have been looking at these effects of FLA in the context of Chinese secondary school English classrooms, particularly in connection with emotional intelligence (Li, 2019; Li & Xu, 2019). As this book's focus is mainly the situation in South Korea, this concept of decreased enjoyment due to typological distance between mother tongue and other known languages and target languages is particularly pertinent. Due to the distance between English and Korean from a typological standpoint (grammar, orthography, lexicon and syntax are all unrelated), the FLE of students may naturally be lower, even without a variety of other factors that affect enjoyment in the language classroom.

Dewaele and MacIntyre's 2014 study looks at the effect of multiple language repertoires on a student's FLE and FLCA. It was noted that the higher the number of languages within a student's repertoire the lower their exhibited FLCA. However, between those languages, students tend to show higher FLCA levels with the languages they have learned later/learned less proficiently. This corroborates research showing that proficiency, especially in relation to the other students in one's class, is significantly correlated with levels of FLCA (Dewaele *et al.*, 2018: 680). In fact, in Dewaele *et al.*'s (2018) research among British secondary school students, it was shown that only four of the investigated independent variables were positively correlated with levels of FLCA to a statistically significant extent, namely: gender; foreign language level; relative standing among peers; and attitude towards the foreign language. Quite surprisingly, and in contrast to other studies done on the same topic, the variable of age, while significantly correlated to levels of FLE, was not significantly associated with increased or decreased levels of FLCA. As we show in Chapter 6, however, in studies carried out in the South Korean context, age was shown to be a significant variable in FLA research carried out with Young Language Learners (YLLs).

Another stance consistent across most existing FLA research is that a no-anxiety language learning environment is as undesirable as an environment that fosters excessive anxiety. Various researchers have shown that a certain amount of anxiety within a learning environment can actually drive successful language acquisition (Dörnyei, 2005; MacIntyre, 2002; Scovel, 2001; Sonstroem & Bernardo, 1982). However, the 'right' level of anxiety to achieve peak language learning is both difficult to determine and different for every language learner. In Dewaele *et al.*'s 2018 study, one component the authors examined was the time spent operating in the Target Language (TL). Although the authors did not discover any significant effects of proportionate TL speaking time on FLCA, they did find a significant correlation between the levels of FLE in relation to the percentage of time spent speaking in the TL. They noted that the more the students had the opportunity to speak in the TL, the more enjoyment they felt. However, this enjoyment peaked around the 60 per cent mark of class time spent operating in the target language, even among the more proficient language learners (Dewaele *et al.*, 2018: 692), suggesting that a translanguaging approach to language teaching – an approach that allows for the presence of multiple languages in the language learning classroom – may foster increased FLE (see Chapter 8 for more on translanguaging pedagogy). Dewaele *et al.* (2018) additionally showed that certain stressful situations, such as being expected to operate in the TL, encouraged FLE and did not significantly affect students' levels of FLCA. Therefore, it is important to create an environment that is both aware of students FLA levels, but also does not try to relax students so much that all stressors disappear completely, stagnating possible development. In addressing this, Dewaele *et al.* (2018) again advocate the application of positive psychology, citing research from MacIntyre and Gregersen (2012), who introduced the concept of positive psychology to SLA research, as well as earlier research by Krashen (1982) and Frederickson (2003). This prior research points out the potentially detrimental effects of negative psychology, focusing on FLA, and the positive effects of focusing on increasing FLE and other positive emotions within the language classroom. This positive psychology-inspired research, however, does not endorse an exclusive focus on positive emotions. As shown earlier, research has demonstrated that a certain amount of anxiety, a negative emotion, can be useful in language learning.

Horwitz's 2010 timeline of prior FLA research also shows the expansion of FLA to cover a variety of variables. Yet, none of the seminal studies listed in her timeline investigate the effects of FLA on young language learners (YLLs). Given the position of English as the global lingua franca and the drive around the world to acquire proficient English abilities, the age at which students are beginning to learn foreign languages in educational settings is decreasing. Given that FLE research is in even more of a nascent state than FLA research, there is almost no existent research that has investigated the presence and effectiveness of positive psychology in the YLL classroom. Thus, in Chapter 3 of this book, we investigate the limited research that has been done on FLA specifically in YLLs, associating them with applicable research in related fields. In later sections of the book, we additionally analyse the applicability of positive psychology and FLE within YLL environments. We offer suggestions for future research that could broaden our understanding of the best ways to facilitate successful and healthy early childhood SLA. In the next section of this chapter, we analyse the general psychological effects of anxiety on people, narrowing in on possible long-term effects of FLA on language learners, highlighting differences and similarities between FLA and general anxiety.

2.2 The Psychology of Anxiety in Language Learning

As discussed in the previous review of the existent literature, there have been several approaches to viewing the relationship between anxiety and language learning. Scovel (1978) clarified that anxiety comes from second language learners using different measurements and conceptualizations of anxiety. He showed that increased anxiety occurred in correspondence to the difficulty level of task. Horwitz *et al.* (1986) showed that language anxiety is, as opposed to trait anxiety, situation specific (state anxiety). They suggested a Foreign Language Classroom Anxiety Scale (FLCAS), a self-report measurement to assess anxiety in the language classroom. Following Horwitz *et al.*'s work, MacIntyre and Gardner (1991) further clarified differences between FLA and other kinds of anxiety: trait anxiety (a personality trait), state anxiety (an emotional state) and situation-specific anxiety (anxiety in a well-defined situation) – this can also be seen as a subcategory of state anxiety – with second language learning anxiety belonging to the third category (Liu & Chen, 2013).

In determining the level of a person's anxiety, there are three key measurement methodologies that are generally employed: self-rating by participants, behavioural observation and physiological assessment (Zheng, 2008). Causes of anxiety in language learning situations have also been shown to be multi-variable. As mentioned earlier in the discussion of Horwitz *et al.*'s 1986 study, the main three causes that contribute to FLA are: communication apprehension, fear of negative evaluation and test anxiety.

Beyond measurement methods and these general causes, various scholars have also inquired into the relationship between language anxiety and psychiatric state. Coinciding with incidences of FLA, learning disabilities have been reported such as reading disorders (dyslexia), developmental arithmetic disorder (dyscalculia), disorders of written expression (dysgraphia) and other nonverbal learning disorders. The association between speech disorders and psychiatric disorders have also been reported through various studies throughout the 1980s (Baker & Cantwell, 1982, 1987a, 1987b, 1987c; Beitchman *et al.*, 1988; Beitchman *et al.*, 1989). Some of these psychiatric disorders have been reported more in children with speech or/and language disorders, compared to controls (Camarata *et al.*, 1988; Cohen *et al.*, 1989; Cohen *et al.*, 1993). Some psychiatric disorders were found more in different developmental stages (Beitchman *et al.*, 2001; Johnson *et al.*, 1999). Thus, those with diagnosed learning disabilities or other psychological conditions may be at a heightened risk for experiencing FLA in their language classrooms.

2.2.1 Anxiety and learning: Socioeconomic status as a lens

Another way to analyse FLA is by looking at it as a form of stress. We must therefore look at the ways in which stressors such as FLA can affect the brain itself. One way to understand how stress affects brain development can be adopted from environmental factor theory (Grandgeorge *et al.*, 2009; McEwen, 2012; Nölle *et al.*, 2020). For instance, Socioeconomic Status (SES) contributes to environmental factors that have a psychological impact resulting in differences in brain development. SES is a measurement of a person's personal experience in terms of economic (family's financial income) and social (education, occupation, family chaos) factors. By assessing a combination of main contributing factors (income, education, occupation), a person's SES can be graded into high SES, middle SES and low SES. Recently, researchers have been applying this concept to investigations seeking to explain human behaviour over the long term. Griskevicius and Kenrick (2013) explain some examples of how we can understand human behaviour by looking at childhood SES. According to them, a person who experienced low SES in their childhood would choose the 'fast track' to success for their life. On the other hand, a person whose childhood SES was high would choose the 'slow track', or secure/guaranteed track, to success for their life. We can predict these two individuals' decisions when we give them mortality cues. A person of low SES would follow fast track, whilst the other person of high SES would follow the slow one. Specifically, the low SES person chooses a '50% chance of 20 USD' whereas the high SES person chooses '10 USD for sure' (Griskevicius *et al.*, 2011). This indicates that a low SES person prefers 'bigger' and 'faster' success, whereas a high SES person prefers 'higher certainty' and 'slow' decisions. Thus, as the authors of this research insist, environmental factors, which cover the subject's childhood experience, should be considered for understanding human decision making. Like the effects of one's childhood SES affecting them throughout adulthood, other social stressors, including FLA might have similar long-term effects.

Recently, research regarding SES has been expanding to the field of neuroscience. Researchers have examined or discussed the effects of SES in terms of executive function (Hook *et al.*, 2013; Romer *et al.*, 2009), prefrontal cortical thickness (Lawson *et al.*, 2013) and brain or neural development (Hackman & Farah, 2009; Hackman *et al.*, 2010; Raizada & Kishiyama, 2010). For example, childhood SES displayed significant correlations with the thickness of the prefrontal cortex, and parental education was shown to be correlated with the right anterior cingulated gyrus and the left superior frontal gyrus (Lawson *et al.*, 2013). In addition, according to Hook *et al.* (2013), the development of executive function is dependent upon 'a long period of post-natal development' (Casey *et al.*, 2000). Investigations of the long-term effects of SES on the brain indicate that stress can have long lasting physiological effects affecting cognitive ability and academic achievement. As FLA, along with other education-related anxieties, is a form of psychological stress, it is important to carry out investigations on the long-term cognitive effects of prolonged FLA experienced in early childhood as well as the positive effects, if any, of FLE.

Certain studies on SES have also shown that there is a relationship between SES and language attainment, even with regards to one's first language (L1). Lower SES students have been shown to have lower language attainment in their native language, which can then become a factor in lower academic performance (Gayton, 2010; Ginsborg, 2006; Khansir *et al.*, 2016; Kormos & Kiddle, 2013; Letts *et al.*, 2013; Schuele, 2001; Schwab & Lew-Williams, 2016). If SES affects L1 and academic performance, it will most likely also affect the acquisition of another language in the foreign language classroom, especially as it requires a certain SES level in order to facilitate certain experiences that can help boost language acquisition – e.g. private academies, tutoring or study abroad. In later chapters, we will look at this factor specifically as it relates to foreign language anxiety and language acquisition in South Korean early childhood English programs.

2.2.2 Perfectionist tendencies and anxiety

Learning represents the acquisition of new skills that bring new information to the social experience, academic ability and personal identity of that individual. FLA is a well-documented form of anxiety that has been investigated for decades, but, as shown throughout this and proceeding chapters, fewer books and research articles have been published specifically targeting this form of anxiety in young children, despite the rise in language instruction directed at increasingly younger children. A common characteristic that can lead to anxiety in all aspects of life, but notably in education, is perfectionism. Gregersen and Horwitz (2002) listed the symptoms of perfectionist tendencies taken from Brophy (1999: 112) as follows:

(1) performance standards that are impossibly high and unnecessarily rigid;
(2) motivation more from fear of failure than from pursuit of success;
(3) measurement of one's own worth entirely in terms of productivity and accomplishment;
(4) all-or-nothing evaluations that label anything other than perfection as failure;
(5) difficulty in taking credit or pleasure, even when success is achieved, because such achievement is merely what is expected;
(6) procrastination in getting started on work that will be judged; and
(7) long delays in completing assignments, or repeatedly starting over on assignments, because the work must be perfect from the beginning and continue to be perfect as on goes along (Gregersen & Horwitz, 2002: 563).

Students categorized as having 'perfectionist' tendencies are at an increased risk for developing FLA, as well as low performance levels in the foreign language classroom (Gergersen & Horwitz, 2002: 563). Again, the three cardinal pillars of FLA include (1) communication apprehension, (2) fear of negative evaluation and (3) test anxiety. Using a newly acquired language to express oneself can cause great anxiety for students with perfectionist traits as using unfamiliar grammatical rules and vocabulary alongside applying contextual linguistic knowledge and terms carries a risk of making errors. This possibility of error making represents a major source of anxiety as it may evoke negative evaluation from their teachers or peers, as well as their own negative self-evaluations. Perfectionist language learners display many of the following symptoms: remaining silent until they are reassured that their sentences will be flawless – known as a 'silent period' – setting an unrealistic expectation for themselves; fearing negative evaluation. Together these symptoms create a perfect environment in which anxiety might brew. Studies have indicated that there is a correlation between perfectionism and FLA (Baran-Łucarz, 2013; Dewaele, 2017; Gregersen & Horwitz, 2002; Pishghadam & Akhondpoor, 2011) and a study by Baran-Łucarz (2013) has suggested that, when a teacher uses language that emphasizes perfectionism, it has the potential to impose a perfectionist mindset on students, thereby predisposing them to acquiring foreign language anxiety.

Perfectionist tendencies are global; however, these tendencies can be exacerbated on a societal level in the East Asian context. In South

Korea, among other places, numerical test scores, rather than more hands-on practical applications of knowledge and skills, are considered one of the most valuable indications of one's abilities, and perfectionist tendencies drive education towards the achievement of high test scores. Assessments of language ability are no different – though this is not unique to South Korea – in that a person's ability to speak English is not based on their ability to communicate with another person using that language's semiotic and syntactic repertoire, but is rather based on the score a person receives on an internationally recognized standardized test such as the TOEFL, IELTS, TOEIC or Cambridge tests. This form of numerical perfectionism in turn affects teaching methodologies – often rote memorization and direct language instruction – and ultimately the psychosocial wellbeing of the students.

These exam scores are highly emphasized in job applications, and before students even face the job market, they have the *Suneung* – the primary university entrance examination in South Korea – looming over them at the end of their high school careers. Although some universities have been reassessing their admission practices, predominately for admission into South Korea's top universities, students are judged mainly on their *Suneung* scores, which assess skills in English, Korean language, mathematics and optionally social studies, sciences, vocational education or foreign languages (Kwon *et al.*, 2017: 8). Thus, in all secondary education leading up to this important exam, students are being prepared solely to take this test, meaning that education leading to communicative competence is often thrown aside in the name of social mobility through exam scores, which evaluate test-taking ability in English more than English language production competency. Emphasis on scoring high on these various tests leads to perfectionist tendencies in other aspects of life as well and ultimately hinders the development of communicative competence in English. This is also partly influenced by the perceived relevance of communicative competence in the South Korean social sphere. In the United Kingdom or the United States, communicative competence in English is imperative in most employment opportunities and the majority of social spaces; however, in Korea, English is seen more often as a tool to aid a student in getting into a good school or finding a good job. This view of English, although changing, is still common in much of Kachru's 'expanding circle' – countries in which English is introduced as a subject in schools and universities, the use of which is geared towards communication with the inner and outer circles (Kachru, 1985: 243). In Korea, as the communicative aspect of English is not always immediately exercisable, the acquisition of English becomes norm dependent. Testing grounds become more important than actual communication, and tests demand perfection as defined by this norm dependent orientation in English acquisition that focuses the 'perfect' English on the norm-defining 'inner circle' counties where English is the primary language. In South

Korea – and many other parts of the world – people's lives, experiences, intelligence and language ability are being reduced to numbers, numbers attempting to measure things that were never quantifiable to begin with.

2.3 Conclusion

As we have seen, anxiety can have a variety of correlated psychological and physiological effects. Many factors can determine the intensity of these effects, such as socioeconomic status, parental education level, pre-existing learning disabilities and perfectionism. These are some factors that can also contribute to the exacerbation of FLA. However, FLA can be experienced by any person of any age. The research cited in the first part of the chapter has shown that shifting the focus away from anxiety to enjoyment may be a good method in alleviating many of the psychological stressors that lead to the negative effects of FLA, leaving the positive effects of low levels of FLA that can challenge students to attain high levels of language acquisition.

In the next chapter, we will look specifically at forms of anxiety related to education, their causes and their effects on the young children who experience them. We look at research that has been done on language anxiety in children, as well as research that has been conducted on math anxiety, which we posit to be closely related to foreign language anxiety in that they are both situational classroom anxieties acquired in the process of learning to navigate situations or problems using new codes. Keeping in mind the general anxiety research from this chapter, we will now focus on anxiety in children in depth.

Note

(1) Trait anxiety is anxiety that is a part of the person's general personality/character, not dependent on any specific situation. Though it can more commonly be triggered in certain situations, it is generally thought to always be lying underneath the surface, unlike state anxiety which disappears when the situation disappears.

3 Foreign Language Anxiety in Children

3.1 Metrics and Research on Child Classroom Anxiety

As mentioned in Chapter 2, little research has been carried out on the causes and effects of FLA specifically in YLLs. To give background to the research in this book, in this chapter, we look at research on measuring children's anxiety, the effectiveness of early childhood language education, anxiety in early childhood and education-related anxiety. We draw parallels between FLCA and math anxiety, pointing out similarities in the effects on working memory and possible long-term consequences. Finally, we outline briefly certain myths about language learning that have contributed to causing FLCA, which we will look into more deeply in Chapter 5.

3.1.1 Metrics for measuring FLA in children

While no metrics currently exist to measure FLA specifically in young children, we propose that they could be created based on the following models of anxiety measurement in young children combined with Horwitz *et al.*'s (1986) Foreign Language Classroom Anxiety Scale (FLCAS) and the use of modern technology designed to measure general anxiety.

La Greca *et al.* (1988) proposed a simplified form of Reynolds and Richmond's (1978) Revised Children's Manifest Anxiety Scale (RCMAS) called the Social Anxiety Scale for Children (SASC) designed to measure the anxiety of young children in social situations. This is applicable to FLA in young language learners as education constitutes a social situation. Their scale is based on a 10-item self-report measure based on two main factors: Fear of Negative Evaluation (FNE) and Social Avoidance and Distress (SAD). While this metric examines levels of social anxiety, which is a type of trait rather than state anxiety, elements may be present in a state anxiety like FLCA as well. The presence of a state anxiety such as FLCA may additionally exacerbate the social avoidance and distress of students who also have social anxiety. This scale uses a combination of self-reporting and peer reporting to determine a child's 'group' within their social structure, which may not be as useful to implement in a FLA-specific metric. However, other elements of the measuring methods may be useful in determining to what extent social factors affect a student having FLCA.

Delving into education-related anxiety metrics, Wren and Benson (2004) constructed a tool for measuring test anxiety in children, the *Children's Test Anxiety Scale* (CTAS). They created a model that asks young children about their activities and thoughts during tests. While the model was shown to be relatively reliable, it only started with students in grade 3 – US grade 3 is ages 8–9 years old. Studies have shown that test anxiety increases a lot in grades 3–5. Yet we have few to no metrics to measure those younger than grade 3, as most of the metrics are not designed for young children who may not yet be literate and therefore cannot self-report in the same manner an older child would. Therefore, in order to determine the level of test-taking and other classroom-related anxieties in young children, a metric accounting for younger grades is equally important. Wren and Benson also point out how a learner's reading level is really important to factor into any metric if you want your results to be reliable. In any anxiety metric administered to young children, especially those who have not yet learned to read, the administration process must be carefully considered. Will all of surveys be conducted verbally? If that is the case, then administrators need to account for the comfort levels of the students when answering questions. One suggestion is making sure that parents deliver the survey and that they do it in one sitting and in a specific environment. As with any survey, variable control will be one of the biggest hurdles. However, this could also complicate results as parental expectations can also be a causal factor in anxious children.

Metrics for measuring FLA could also be adapted from the math anxiety scale used by Ramirez *et al.* (2013). The study examined the effects of math anxiety on the working memory of first- and second-grade students. The metric used, the Child Math Anxiety Questionnaire (CMAQ), is a truncated version of Suinn *et al.*'s (1988) Math Anxiety Rating Scale (MARS). The CMAQ takes into account the attention span of younger children and reduces the number of questions. Whereas similar metrics for older students and adults commonly contain between 26 and 95 items, the CMAQ was reduced to a more age-appropriate eight-item scale. The measurement of feeling is also based on a sliding scale of increasingly nervous-looking faces. To institute this type of metric in FLA research in young children, items from Horwitz *et al.*'s (1986) FLCAS could be reduced and adapted in a similar manner to give a cursory assessment of a child's FLCA. Those children who exhibit signs of heightened FLCA through this metric could then be subjected to more stringent measurements. Modern technology, such as testing kits for heightened levels of cortisol or wrist monitors that track heart rate and perspiration, could be used in conjunction with these metrics to determine to what extent a child is experiencing FLCA. These technologies are further explored in Chapter 8. These tests and metrics are all non-invasive, although they may have a certain degree of stress associated with their administration that will also need to be taken into account. The metrics mentioned in this chapter, as well as the metric that we used for our own measurement of FLA anxiety in young children (Chapter 6) are included in the appendices.

3.1.2 General research on anxiety in children

While early childhood education-related research may be limited, there is much existent research on the causes and effects of general anxiety in children which can be used as a foundation on which to carry out future FLA research with YLLs. In this section, we outline some of the research that has been carried out in this general sector that we think will best inform YLL FLA research.

In their 1998 paper, Chorpita and Barlow (1998) assert that lack of control in early development may lead to a vulnerability towards anxiety in the future. Various environmental factors lead children to feel like they have lost control over their lives and choices, which then leads to feelings of anxiety. Applying this to the language classroom, in an English-only classroom, limiting children's semiotic repertoires may result in children feeling a loss of control, leading to anxiety. This then has the potential to worsen over time if left unaddressed, possibly resulting in a chronic trait anxiety condition affecting the rest of their lives. According to Kagan and Snidman (1999), roughly 20% of children have an innate temperamental bias that predisposes them to anxiety, especially when certain environmental factors enter into play. This is something that teachers should be aware of. In Chapter 8, we outline signs that teachers can look for in order to assess students for existent anxiety. If teachers can determine which students might be more prone to anxiety in certain situations, they can more easily alleviate it when it arises.

While signs of anxiety in students in the second language classroom have not yet been adequately compiled in the existing research, Dadds *et al.* (1997) conducted a study on how to prevent and intervene early in anxiety disorders in children. The proposed intervention was both cognitive and behavioural, involving a family-based approach. The article showed an improvement in the intervention group compared to the control group, signifying that identification of anxiety in children is important in order to intervene early enough to prevent future anxiety disorders from appearing. The study also highlights the importance not only of teachers' involvement in identifying students who suffer from anxiety in the classroom, but also the importance of family involvement. Such involvement can alleviate the detrimental effects of anxiety and prevent as much as possible its increase over time.

Building on the importance of the role of family, McLeod *et al.* (2007) emphasize the importance of asserting the role of parenting in discussions of childhood anxiety. Parental control was shown to be strongly associated with childhood anxiety. Just as Chorpita and Barlow put forward in 1998, the factor of control and feeling out of control in one's environment lead to anxiety. This is most likely a factor in foreign language classrooms, where students do not know when they are going to be called on. Fear of being unable to express themselves rises and, in English-only classrooms, students are often severed from most of their ability to comprehend and express themselves. Also, regarding language learning, motivation is a huge factor. Gardner and MacIntyre (1991) assert that both instrumental (extrinsic) and integrative (intrinsic) motivation for language learning produce greater results when there is an incentive for learning, e.g. a prize or monetary reward. Yet, when there is no incentive, students with integrative motivation continue to study longer than those who are only instrumentally motivated. If students are only learning English because they are forced to by their parents, they probably derive more anxiety from the situation due to their lack of intrinsic/integrative motivation – and in some cases students being forced by their parents lack even instrumental motivation, as there is not really any incentive other than not getting scolded by their parents. Having an integrative motivation for language acquisition may allow students to overcome some of their anxieties, as exhibited in the 2018 research of Dewaele *et al.* on highly motivated language students in British secondary schools.

As mentioned earlier, La Greca *et al.* (1988, 2010) note that there are two main factors that go into the evolution of anxiety in children: Fear of Negative Evaluation (FNE) and Social Avoidance and Distress (SAD). Neglected children and children in 'lower' social group 'classes' have been shown to exhibit the most anxiety. Such anxiety will then exhibit itself in avoidance of social situations and various other physiological symptoms of anxiety. La Greca *et al.*'s research results showed that FNE was actually a more potent determiner of whether or not a child had social anxiety. Thus, fear of evaluation – testing or teacher feedback, or judgement of peers in the language classroom in the case of SLA – can be a large determining factor in whether a child will experience increased anxiety.

Finally, in looking at the long-term effects of anxiety in early childhood, Shonkoff *et al.* (2012) cite the long-term effects that stress can have on children, claiming that it can cause predispositions for certain conditions and diseases both physical and psychological ones. These predispositions are usually tied into poverty, discrimination or maltreatment. Education plays a role in this, as well as the environment in which children grow up. Thus, anxiety can have a major impact on psychosocial, physical and emotional wellbeing. Anxiety can also become a predictor for future socioeconomic standing and success. In light of previous research on the possibly long-ranging damage of anxiety and stress experienced in early childhood, it is important to understand and alleviate its causes. In the realm of education, it is important to try to gear classrooms in general – and more specifically language classrooms – toward a positive psychology approach, as previously outlined in Chapter 2.

3.1.3 Math anxiety and its overlaps with FLA

The notable lack of research on the anxiety of young children in learning situations is not limited to the language classroom. Although research on math anxiety has been carried out since the 1970s, only recently have educators and psychologists started to look at the math anxiety experienced by young children specifically. While math anxiety and FLA may not be exactly the same thing, we believe that as they are both state anxieties that manifest themselves in educational settings requiring the acquisition of new codes, particularly in production/testing situations when children are under heightened pressure, there might be similarities found and helpful research that might overlap.

In the existing research on math anxiety, it is generally well accepted that this form of state anxiety affects working memory. This was first indicated in the research of Ashcraft and Kirk (2001), which showed that those who had math anxiety performed worse on tasks requiring working memory. Ashcraft asserts that this is consistent with research that has been carried out on general anxiety:

> General anxiety is hypothesized to disrupt ongoing working memory processes because anxious individuals devote attention to their intrusive thoughts and worries, rather than the task at hand. (Ashcraft, 2002: 183)

Linguistic research has shown that working memory is also integral in the acquisition and use of languages (Baddley, 2003). Thus, if math anxiety has detrimental effects on working memory, which then affects a student's ability to correctly determine mathematical solutions, it would stand to reason that FLA would similarly affect working memory in linguistic situations. If so, this could make accurate/coherent language production more difficult for those experiencing FLA.

Research determining the effects of math anxiety on working memory, and consequently on educational motivation and attainment in mathematics, has mostly been carried out on older students aged 12 and higher. This is much like the case of FLA research. However, in recent years, researchers have started paying closer attention to the math anxiety experienced by children at the very beginning of their educational careers. A study by Ramirez *et al.* (2013) investigated the effects of math anxiety on first and second grade children. The results of this study showed that math anxiety in young children affects working memory capacity in the same way it does in older children and adults. Furthermore, this study showed that students with higher working memory were actually more affected by math anxiety than those with lower working memory who also experienced math anxiety. This result is particularly important in that working memory is closely linked with critical thinking and problem-solving skills and abilities. If anxiety is disabling a student's ability to access their high working memory, then a student, who in actuality has a heightened potential for high-level performance in math, would be evaluated as having low competence. Thereafter, they may be discouraged either implicitly or explicitly from continuing to pursue the study of math in later years, as future avoidance has also been shown to be a consequence of unaddressed math anxiety. As learning English in early childhood becomes just as prevalent as learning math in many East Asian countries, these same anxieties which lead to the disabling of working memory and the associated consequences may be seen in the foreign language classroom as well.

Other research on math anxiety highlights the effects of teachers' anxiety on their students. Teachers who are not confident in their own abilities often pass on their anxieties to the children. A study among early childhood educators showed that many of the (predominately female) teachers were not confident in their own math abilities, most likely due to their own math anxiety causing them to avoid math as soon as they were allowed. This lack of confidence showed in the classroom and then passed on anxieties to impressionable students. Beilock *et al.*'s (2010) study showed that the combination of teacher anxiety and the general belief that boys are better at math than girls contributed to heightened levels of math anxiety among female students in early childhood. This in turn affected their math achievement. While research has shown that FLA is not as gendered as math anxiety, the effects that anxious teachers can have on students are transferable. The research done on math anxiety corroborates FLA studies carried out by Horwitz (1992, 1993, 1996) that showed that many foreign language teachers also experience anxiety, and this anxiety can impact classroom instruction. In one of these studies, Horwitz (1996) showed the following:

> Subjects who reported higher levels of anxiety were significantly less likely to actually anticipate using the more innovative and language-intensive teaching practices, even though they had previously rated these activities equally as positively as their less anxious peers. (Horwitz, 1996: 368)

Anxious teachers may opt not to use the Target Language (TL) in their classroom, which limits language input, thereby decreasing the number of neural connections created in students' neural language networks. They also may opt for older, less effective methodologies with which they are more familiar, perhaps because it is how they were taught, rather than trying newer methodologies that could positively affect children's language learning processes. This is significant to note in creating solutions for alleviating FLA in early childhood classrooms, as any innovative solutions will also need to address the possible anxiety of educators in implementing them.

Finally, Geist (2010) asserts that math anxiety disproportionately affects at-risk populations and females. According to his summary of the existing research, negative attitudes towards math are passed down to children through parents, teachers and society. These inherited negative attitudes will then further affect these children's scholastic performance. This research on inherited attitude in math supports the research that we discuss in Chapter 5 about mothers' roles in the process of early childhood language learning in South Korea.

As state anxieties brought about by heightened pressure in classroom situations, the effects and consequences of math anxiety and FLA can be assumed to have a certain amount of overlap. This is particularly the case as language learning at a very young age becomes more and more of a requirement in many parts of the world. Additionally, math anxiety and FLA are similar in that mathematical learning and language acquisition both place much pressure on working memory, which has been shown to be adversely affected by the presence of anxiety.

3.1.4 Myths that contribute to early childhood FLA

Contributing to the prevalence of foreign language anxiety among children in language classrooms worldwide are common misconceptions about the necessity of learning a language in childhood in order to attain fluency. For decades, linguists, psychologists, cognitive scientists and educators have been debating whether or not the Critical Period Hypothesis (CPH) applies in Second Language Acquisition (SLA). The CPH states that after a certain point somewhere between age 5 and the onset of puberty, acquiring language becomes more difficult and success is far less likely (Penfield & Roberts, 1959). Various case studies have shown some support for this hypothesis within the realm of first language acquisition (Curtiss, 1977, 1989; Johnson & Newport, 1989). However, within the field of SLA, debate continues to rage, with numerous case studies having contradicted the hypothesis (Genesee, 1987; Rivera, 1998; Snow & Hoefnagel-Höhle, 1978). Indeed, most psycholinguists now believe that success in acquiring a second language is not dependent solely on age, but rather on a variety of linguistic, cognitive, and social factors (Bialystok & Hakuta, 1994; Marinova-Todd *et al.*, 2000).

Despite much research to the contrary with regard to SLA, many parents still ascribe to what was originally put forth by neurologists Penfield and Roberts (1959), younger equals better. However, this original research was mostly based on neurological research that showed the increased ability of children to overcome language-related problems in their first language after a brain injury compared to adults who had suffered similar injuries (Lenneberg, 1960). Subsequently, many researchers analysed various other situations in which children overcame language deprivation or difficulties when adults in the same situation could not. This is explained by the physiological changes that have been purported to take place in the brain at a certain point in adolescence which decrease the flexibility of the brain, making language learning and other parts of social development more difficult (Lenneberg, 1967; Long, 1990).

While the CPH has been fairly well received when it comes to first language acquisition – although debate still remains even here – when it comes to SLA, the reception has been much rockier. As stated earlier, there is little proof that someone who has already acquired a first language cannot successfully acquire a second after the end of the 'critical period' (Pfenninger & Singleton, 2019). There are countless examples of people who have successfully learned languages far into adulthood. A longitudinal study by researchers at the University of Amsterdam in the 1970s uncovered data that refutes the hypothesis outright by showing that, over the course of a year, the Dutch language acquisition of 8- to 15-year-old English speakers was ranked far higher than that of the 3- to 5-year-olds who had been learning for the same amount of time (Snow & Hoefnagel-Höhle, 1978). This study from the 1970s hints that the CPH is not supported in second language acquisition situations. Further research has been done since then, many with results supporting that of Snow and Hoefnagel-Höhle (1978), including Bongaerts *et al.*'s (1997) study on the distinguishability of accent between highly advanced late second language learners and English L1 speakers. In this study, English L2s were rated in the same range as English L1s, showing that phonetic production is not constrained by age. Marinova-Todd *et al.* (2000) concluded:

> Although older learners are indeed less likely than young children to master an L2, a close examination of studies relating age to language acquisition reveals that age differences reflect differences in the situation of learning rather than the capacity to learn. They do not demonstrate any constraint of the possibility that adults can become highly proficient, even nativelike, speakers of L2s. (Marinova-Todd *et al.*, 2000: 9)

According to these authors, it is life situation rather than cognitive ability that might prevent adults from acquiring an L2 to the extent that a child might. Marinova-Todd *et al.* (2000) also point out various reasons why existing research has misled many adults into thinking that only children can acquire languages to advanced levels: (1) facts regarding speed of acquisition have been misinterpreted; (2) the differences in language ability across age groups has been wrongly attributed to neurological factors and decreased cognitive capacity in adulthood; and (3) the research has emphasized unsuccessful cases of language acquisition in adults rather than successful ones (Marinova-Todd *et al.*, 2000: 11). Numerous other studies lay out how age affects language learning. Many also outline the necessity for successful first language acquisition to take place in order for the elements for successful SLA to exist (Vanderplank, 2008). It is worth noting, however, that this ignores the successful language acquisition of children who grow up functionally bilingual, i.e. those with multiple first languages.

Various other myths have been circulated that have contributed to the levels of FLA among early childhood language learners. These include myths of total immersion, the necessity of native speaker-like pronunciation, the dangers of using the first language in the second language classroom and the effectiveness of rote learning. Many of these myths are compounded by the critical period hypothesis which convinces parents and teachers that all methods must be tried in fostering successful second language acquisition in children or they will miss their chance to become the 'perfect speaker' of a second language. These compounding myths will be further discussed in Chapter 5 as we investigate the problems and challenges in childhood second language acquisition.

One of the effects of this pervasive misinformation in the field of second language acquisition is that it results in children being placed in language classrooms earlier and earlier. This stems from parents' belief that their children will not be able to successfully acquire the Target Language (TL) when they are older and more entrenched in their education. In East Asia in particular, this has led to the aforementioned 'English Fever', resulting in a massive industry of early childhood English education programmes. We discuss such programmes in further depth in Chapter 4.

3.2 Psychology of Anxiety in Children

3.2.1 Young children's anxiety symptoms

Anxiety is one of the most common psychiatric disorders among young people. It has a high probability of lifelong psychiatric disturbance, alongside adverse impacts on educational achievement and leisure activities. Young children are less likely to present themselves independently and are often brought to a doctor by their parents. As discussed previously, childhood psychiatric disorders that go unaddressed often have chronic consequences. Since many of the symptoms of paediatric anxiety disorders are non-specific, it is important to have a low threshold of suspicion when it comes to recognizing symptoms of anxiety, as well as other disorders, in a child.

The World Health Organization (WHO) listed anxiety as one of the most common mental disorders globally. Depending on different parameters (e.g. character of feelings experienced during the episode of anxiety, impact on mood, severity), anxiety disorders can be divided into five categories, which are: panic disorders, generalized anxiety disorder (GAD), social anxiety disorder, post-traumatic stress disorder (PTSD) and obsessive-compulsive disorder (OCD). It is important to note that even within these five categories of anxiety disorders, there are further subcategories, of which foreign language anxiety is one (World Health Organization, 2017). Symptoms of anxiety that are common to each type entail loss of interest, decreased energy, difficulty in concentrating; physiological symptoms include palpitations and sweating (Horwitz et al., 1986).

3.2.2 How children's early experience shapes mental wellbeing

Fear and anxiety are recognized and experienced by children as young as 6–12 months old. As the child grows older, their cognitive and social skills develop, enabling them to distinguish between usual and unpredictable events. As children get better at recognizing unpredictable events, their fears slowly vanish, with the exception of traumatic situations such as maltreatment and threatening circumstances. As the child grows, their mental wellbeing is constantly affected by their experiences. Emotion and learning are the two major areas affected by prolonged exposure to anxiety. In the developing brain itself, anatomically the prefrontal cortex, which entails functions associated with memory and cognitive functions, is affected by increased stress. Stress is a subjective experience that can manifest itself in different forms: negative stimuli such as situations that instil doubt into one's reality, occurrence of errors, and loss of control trigger increased levels of stress hormones (e.g. catecholamine), which interfere with higher-order ability such as working memory and attention regulation. The effects of stress on human cognitive function are well documented through both research and actual events. For example, one notable event was highly skilled pilots crashing their planes in World War II due to mental errors made in highly stressful situations. In this way, stress can contribute to the impairment of prefrontal cortex structure and function (Arnsten, 2009).

Gadye (2018) compared anxiety to fear as two related psychological reactions to stimuli. He wrote that 'fear is an immediate response to a specific threatening stimulus. Anxiety, on the other hand, is less intense but more sustained response to anxiety-inducing sources that may be known'. Long-term anxiety affects much the brain, as anxiety involves multiple parts of the brain in its low-level activation of the 'fear network' (Gadye, 2018). This network involves both the cognitive brain and the emotional brain as anxiety creates complex interactions between regions in the frontal lobe and the amygdala. The logical/cognitive part of the brain associates a situation with a particular stimulus that causes fear, the amygdala then starts sending signals that would be an appropriate response to this stimulus. This causes increased brain 'chatter' which can then manifest itself in the various symptoms of anxiety. In FLA, the frontal lobe would recognize the potential for making a mistake that would lead to negative teacher or peer evaluation. The amygdala and other emotion-related brain regions would then activate and increase their chatter, making it more difficult for a student to concentrate on the task at hand. Anxiety is a normal response to stimuli; however, if the anxiety persists for a long time, interfering with the normal functioning of the brain, resulting in 'inappropriate or irrational behaviors' (Gadye, 2018) this can interfere with a person's ability to function normally and become hugely problematic.

Childhood experiences of anxiety predispose an individual to acquiring psychiatric disorders in adulthood, therefore posing a significant risk for developing poor mental health as an adult. Childhood experiences have the potential for long-lasting negative impacts that manifest later on in adulthood. This indicates that some children might not naturally outgrow their fear responses over time, but rather are affected by them for as long as they continue to go unaddressed. The damage done to the child's mental wellbeing by fear and anxiety is not always environmentally dependent. Instead it has the possibility of sticking with the child until interventions are made to assist the child in overcoming the initial and consequent traumatic experiences.

3.2.3 Effects of anxiety in early stages of young children's cognitive development

Neural plasticity is the brain's ability to reshape and rewire itself under the influence of pathological and environmental changes (Huttenlocher, 2002). Consequently, neural plasticity allows the brain to develop and acquire new functions, maintaining a resilient attitude towards hostile environments or guarding against structural damage to the brain (Huttenlocher, 2002: 2). Children naturally have more neural plasticity as they grow and develop, meaning that a child's brain is extremely malleable (Colombo, 1982). This malleability is invaluable as children learn physical skills and how to recognize and express emotion, as well as developing social skills, the acquisition of which is important for their ability to function within society in the future.

Psychologists have documented that the interaction between young children and their environment has a huge impact on their development, and negative experiences (e.g. anxiety) tend to have a greater impact than positive experiences, thus anxiety-inducing environments have the possibly of having serious repercussions on children's functioning abilities when they mature (Post et al., 1998). Unstable bonds between parenting figures and children suggest a weak foundation for children's development, with research having suggested this also has an impact on children's ability to learn and manage emotion when they grow up (Denham, 2003; Pollak et al., 2000; Salisch, 2001). Although neural plasticity is high in the early stages of children's development, timing is a determining factor in the feasibility of this change. Early intervention for any childhood negative experience proves to be effective in preventing any chronic consequences.

From a biological perspective, the chronic stimulus of stress exacerbates the body's capacity to cope with stress, thereby disrupting the efficiency of the brain circuitry to develop (Miller *et al.*, 2011). Such disruption could ultimately lead to permanent physical and psychological damage (López *et al.* 1999). It is therefore imperative to address/alleviate stress and anxiety in these formative years in order to avoid the development of these chronic issues and to take advantage of the malleability of the childhood brain for positive developmental and educational purposes.

3.2.4 Child psychiatry – a struggling field

As previously mentioned, early intervention is important for preventing long-term effects associated with stress and anxiety in early childhood. However, a career in paediatric psychiatry is not one of the more popular career choices made by medical students; in 2016, only 70 applicants applied for the 68 posts in the United Kingdom (Burden, 2016). This is not a UK-specific finding; difficulty in recruitment is documented in the United States and various European countries as well, the main reasons being the length of the training period required and the lack of funding for research (Revet *et al.*, 2018; Russett *et al.*, 2019). Obtaining qualifications in paediatric psychiatry entails a long period of academic training, followed by further rigorous clinical placements. The paediatric psychiatry service is under ever-increasing pressure, caused by increasing public demand and decreasing public funds allotted to support and maintain the essential infrastructure and human resources needed to deliver a safe and efficient system to care for paediatric patients.

The shortage of psychiatrists being recruited is a global problem; developing countries throughout Africa and South America do not hit the target of one psychiatrist per 10,000 population that is set by the World Health Organization (WHO) (Shields *et al.*, 2017). The World Psychiatry Association (WPA) has identified some push and pull factors that repel or attract medical students from choosing psychiatry as their specialty, namely the demographics of the profession (i.e. there are more female psychiatrists than male ones) and the stigma and status of psychiatry within the medical profession (Shields *et al.*, 2017). To ensure an increase in the availability of medical personnel qualified to treat paediatric psychiatry patients, these funding and stigma issues will first need to be overcome.

3.3 Conclusion

Anxiety has the potential to affect children for the rest of their lives if not noticed and addressed early enough. Yet the research on anxiety in young children, particularly in educational settings, is still lacking. This lack of research is mirrored in the medical field by the lack of child psychologists and the even greater lack of paediatric psychiatrists. Combined, these shortages lead to a lack of understanding of the extent to which anxiety affects young children as well as a lack of resources for treating suspected cases of anxiety.

The focus of this book is the anxiety experienced by young South Korean children in the foreign language classroom and the possible effects that it can have on the rest of their lives if left unaddressed. It is therefore important to consider cultural differences that may also affect the psychology of these young language learners. These cultural factors must also be taken into account when developing strategies for addressing the alleviation of FLA in the East Asian context, as well as encouraging FLE in language classrooms for young children.

One such factor is that Asian communities typically adopt a more collectivist culture than many of their Western counterparts, which translates into meaning an individual identity is at least partially determined by its interconnectedness with others. Some behaviours of Asian children may be attributed to the effects of the 'Asian parenting model', which is adopted by many parents and is often seen as authoritarian, characterized by low support and high control (Chao, 1995; Kim & Wong, 2002; Lui & Rollock, 2013; Park et al., 2010; Pong et al., 2010). This fuels the perfectionist tendencies of many students from East Asia in order to please parents while simultaneously enhancing fear of negative evaluation by teachers and peers, both factors in the promotion of foreign language anxiety.

Compounded with this increased potential for anxiety among children in East Asia is the lingering stigma attached to seeking treatment for mental health conditions. A study by Jang et al. (2018) showed that while 5.8% of Korean adults surveyed admitted to depressive feelings, only 16% of that number had sought any consultation with a healthcare professional. Since children cannot seek professional care on their own for mental health struggles, they have to wait for a parent or adult caregiver to refer them for help in a society where many adults are reluctant to approach mental health professionals. While the stigma has shown some alleviation over time, and young adults are more likely to seek care than older adults (Jang et al., 2018: 2), in both South Korea and the rest of the world, progress still needs to be made in removing stigma and providing adequate resources for those suffering from mental health struggles.

In the next chapter of this book, building on what we have introduced about FLA and anxiety in children, we focus on the situation in South Korea specifically, looking at the perceived cultural phenomenon of 'English Fever' and the trends and policies governing early childhood English education.

4 Foreign Language Anxiety in the South Korean Context

In South Korea, there is a saying that the success of a child's English education depends on three things: (1) grandparents' assets, (2) mothers' information and (3) fathers' indifference. If one's grandparents have the economic means to pay for classes and language learning experiences, one's mother has the background in English to support the language acquisition at home, and one's father stays out of the process by not interfering in how the child is being educated, then the child will be successful in acquiring English at a young age. In South Korea, and in much of the world in general, learning English has become less of an option and more of a necessity, leading to the impression of a fervour for English education. As such, children are starting to learn English at younger and younger ages. Based on recent research that the language acquisition process begins in prenatal stages (Gervain, 2018; Moon *et al.*, 2013; Utako *et al.*, 2017), even prenatal English programs have been launched in various countries. In South Korea specifically, many children are enrolled in immersion English schools and expected to operate in English starting at a very young age, sometimes to the detriment of their academic, psychosocial, and physical wellbeing (Park, 2007). The South Korean zeal for English Education, often termed 'English Fever', has become heightened such that at any given time over 100,000 Korean students are studying abroad (Ock, 2016). This is the case not only for older students but also for younger children. Unfortunately, as study abroad in early childhood is not a government sanctioned activity, it is impossible to acquire completely reliable statistics on the number of South Korean children currently studying abroad. In this chapter, we will look at the current state of English education in South Korea, as well as the state of FLA research regarding anxiety experienced throughout the English education process. We will then extrapolate these South Korean norms to a wider East Asian and global context.

4.1 English Fever

4.1.1 Origins and government response

The perception of a South Korean 'English Fever' has been a hot topic on the peninsula for the past few decades. However, while the specific focus on English education is a newer phenomenon in Korea, the zeal for education in general has been a distinctive part of Korean society and culture for centuries, derived from the Confucian belief which puts an emphasis on education, believing that the true self can be realized through learning. Traditionally, this was limited to the upper classes. However, since the end of the Chosŏn dynasty (1897) and the consequent slow move towards democracy, education has come to be seen as a way that anyone, through their own effort, might advance themselves to a higher social level (Park, 2009b: 51). Throughout childhood, education is seen as paving a path towards an elite university, graduation from which will guarantee future job prospects and economic stability. Thus, parents are willing to go to great lengths to ensure that their children have a chance to enter into one of the top three Korean universities, also referred to as the SKY universities (Seoul National University, Korea University, Yonsei University), or to study at an elite overseas institution. Korea is a highly educated society in general, with 69.9% of 25- to 34-year-olds having received some sort of tertiary education as of 2017, a number which has been consistently increasing over the last decade according to OECD (2017) statistics.

Among Koreans, it is commonly said that, because South Korea is such a small and mountainous country, their natural resources are limited. Therefore, they must make the most of their human resources by investing in education. Thus, investment in education is often seen in the light of investing in human capital (Hultberg *et al.*, 2017). However, often in a cost-benefit analysis, taking into account the over-saturation of qualified candidates in a competitive job market, the investment in higher education is not worth its cost. Nonetheless, Korean families continue to become indebted in order to secure private education for their children in the hope of their future success (Hultberg *et al.*, 2017).

Since the end of the Japanese occupation of the Korean peninsula (1910–1945) and the consequent installation of American military troops in the South, proficiency in English has been seen as one of the skills that will most ensure one's ability to get ahead. English proficiency is also viewed as an important way to make the nation as a whole more competitive on an international level. Therefore, English is a major component of the Korean college entrance exam (수능, *Suneung*) and many classes at the university level are taught using English as the medium of instruction (EMI), especially at the more prestigious universities. Many companies judge potential job candidates based largely on their English alongside the skillset required for the work. As previously stated, most parents desire to help their children secure a good future, and thus spare no expense in providing every opportunity they can to allow their children to learn English, hoping that this will help them on the college entrance exam, which will then springboard them into a good university and a promising career.

This parental desire for the success of their children has led many to invest thousands of dollars each year into private education for their children, leading to an abundancy of cram schools, or hagwon. These are run after school, and typically focus on English, mathematics and Korean language skills (the primary topics on the *Suneung* exam), though there are also hagwon for music and other extracurricular subjects. Because the majority of students attend hagwon, which starts after school and sometimes does not finish until late in the evening, teachers often teach as if students are all getting help outside of school. This makes more parents feel pressured to send their children to hagwon, for fear of falling behind. Thus, in Korea, a child whose only formal schooling is at the local government-funded school is seen as the exception rather than the norm. In 2018, parents' spending on their children reached a record high, according to the Ministry of Education and Statistics Korea. Total spending on private education was 19.5 trillion won, or roughly $17 billion dollars, marking a 4.4% increase on the previous year. The same survey also revealed that 82.5% of elementary school children were receiving private education. Parents spent more on English education than on any other subject – a total of 5.7 trillion won (Kim, 2019). With the amount of money that is poured into the Korean English education system, one would expect the results to be astonishing. On the contrary, most Korean people are highly dissatisfied with the returns on their investment. According to the 2018 *Test and Score Data Summary for TOEFL iBT Tests*, South Korea had a mean TOEFL score of 84 (out of 120). The global average was 82 for males, and 83.1 for females, putting the Korean mean slightly above the global average. However, out of 168 countries, almost all of which do not invest nearly as much into English education as South Korea, Korea's average TOEFL score was only higher than roughly 50% of other nations' mean scores (ETS, 2018: 14–15). Though this is an improvement over the last decade – they ranked in the 37th percentile in 2005 (Park, 2009b: 51) – it is still much lower than what many South Koreans would expect based on the amount of money that pours into English language education. Why is it that despite the vast economic investment into the nation's English education, they are only able to achieve slightly above average rankings? Of course, score results are not a perfect indicator of the success or failure of the South Korean English education industry, but it does point at some degree of ineffectiveness in the system. So, what is the cause of the system's ineffectiveness? There is no one single answer to this question, but we can perhaps highlight some contributing factors.

Although the parents and teachers show great interest, there is currently no systematic program provided by the Ministry of Education in South Korea for early childhood English education. Most of the English teaching in early ages is done by kindergartens in the private sector (Ma, 2007). As of 2010, learning English in government-funded public schools starts at the third-grade level. The government tried lowering this level to the first and second grade in 2007, but this was not continued (Yi, 2009). The current government under President Moon Jae-in has recently adopted a special law to ban early childhood English education in kindergartens and schools that receive government funding. One of President Moon's election pledges was to protect young children's human rights by giving them the right to resist English education. However, people greatly worry whether this will reinforce more private-sector-driven education. Hence, the implementation of this measure was delayed (Kim, 2018).

The age at which English education begins for Korean children is continually decreasing. According to a 2014 report by the OAPE (the Organisation Against Private-sector Education, 사교육없는세상, sagyoyung ŏmnŭn sesang), 3.2% of students then in high school had started to learn English by the age of three. In contrast, among young children at that time, 35.29% had started to learn English at the age of three. Most Korean parents agree that teaching English to their children at an early age is a priority, particularly those from higher socioeconomic backgrounds (OAPE & Yu, 2014). According to a survey from Park (2015), over 90.5% of parents were supportive of early English education, as they deemed it the most effective means of ensuring successful English language acquisition. However, organizations like the OAPE seek to reverse extreme trends in private education in South Korea, attempting to highlight the ill effects and heavy burden of private education on South Korean children. Through these activities, they aim to produce a system where state education can be sufficient to prepare children for further schooling and life. According to statistics from OAPE, in the recent government policy under Education Minister Eun-hye Yu, 71.9% of parents were supportive of early English education being included as part of the national early childhood curriculum (OAPE, 2014a).

According to Kang and Choi (2010) and Kim *et al.* (2014), about 80 per cent of teachers also expressed the view that teaching English in early childhood is necessary. In 51.7% of these cases, the reason was to expose young children to English in their daily lives. Twenty percent of the teachers surveyed said that the reason was that in the future all people will be required to speak English. Only 11.5% of those teachers surveyed said that early education is more efficient (Kang & Choi, 2010). Kim *et al.* (2014) showed that younger children show more of an interest in learning language, claiming that that is why English should be taught to young children. However, the people who thought that early language teaching is not necessary listed the following reasons: (1) 30.9% said that English learning at an early age would disturb the learning of the mother language, Korean, and (2) 29.1% said that the existent curriculum for English is not appropriate. However, in direct response to this first reason, Song *et al.* (2011) showed that teaching English in early childhood is effective because children find it interesting and engaging at an early age. They showed that learning English at an early age does not interfere with learning the mother tongue, Korean, nor does it interrupt young children's identity formation, findings that are contrary to previous work by Wu *et al.* (2002).

4.1.2 English teaching institutions, methodologies and staff

Currently, there are two general types of day care institutions in South Korea where parents can leave their children prior to reaching school age: nurseries (ŏlinichip) – ages 0–5 – and kindergartens (yuch'iwŏn) – ages 3–5. Nurseries and kindergartens are subdivided, again, into two categories: public and private. On top of this, there is the English kindergarten which does not belong to either of these categories. The term has no legal/administrative definition but is a general term for the cram schools that teach preschool-aged children English. It is often difficult to gather statistics on the number of English kindergartens in operation due to this lack of legal definition and the tendency of some English kindergartens to go by other names.

According to Kim (2008) and Ma (2008), kindergartens that teach English have greatly increased. In the 1980s, only 30% taught English. In the 1990s, this increased to 50%. In 2000, 60–70% taught English and in 2008 over 90% taught English. English teaching as an extracurricular activity is the most popular among extracurricular activities in kindergarten (Jun, 2009). In this case, there are about ten children in one class. For young children in non-English specific kindergartens, teaching usually takes place four times a week, about 20 to 30 minutes each time (Kim & Yu, 2012). According to one investigation of the part-time English kindergartens in 2014, they teach their children English on average 5575 minutes per month. This was at least 12 times more than the 'special activity' programs of nurseries and other kindergartens (OAPE, 2014b). One investigation of 11 English kindergartens in Seoul revealed that they were teaching subjects like math, natural science, history and geography in English with British, American and Canadian textbooks (OAPE, 2015). Most places teach English once or twice a week to children who are younger than three years old (Bae & Seo, 2011). In contrast to these early childhood programs in nurseries and kindergartens, in English kindergartens, teaching is done in units of 40 minutes, five times a day, and for four or five hours daily. According to OAPE and Yu (2014), the average hours taught in an English kindergarten in Seoul are 4 hours and 57 minutes each day.

As of 2015, according to the Korean Education Development Institute (KEDI), there were 339 English kindergartens. These are concentrated in big cities such as Seoul (26.8%) and Busan (14.5%). According to OAPE and Yu (2014), there are 224 English kindergartens in Seoul, and most of them are in Gangnam (41 places). The numbers of young children attending English kindergartens are rapidly increasing. The reason why parents chose to send their children to English kindergartens was that they believed it provided a better learning environment. This seems to be the case regardless of the socioeconomic status (SES) of parents (KEDI, 2015). The number of students in proportion to teachers is small, also making this setting preferable.

For older children, there are various after school 'cram schools' or hagwon, as well as 'English villages' that provide immersion experiences for students. In extreme cases, parents might send their children to study abroad for a year or two in an English-speaking country. Many of the parents who choose to take their children abroad to learn English do so because they are dissatisfied with the perceived quality of English education in Korea. Alternatively, such parents may ascribe to the belief that complete immersion in English at a young age is the best and fastest way to become truly fluent. The most recent available statistics put the number of elementary school students studying overseas at 27,349, which was a decrease from preceding years, owing to the declining birth rate and diminishing means of the Korean middle class (ICEF, 2013). Along with those studying in English-speaking countries, this number also includes those students studying abroad in China, roughly 13.2% of the total (Bae, 2013: 418). When taking into account the fact that sending children to study abroad, whether accompanied by their families or not, is technically illegal in South Korea (Park, 2009b: 54), these numbers are staggering. In these early childhood study abroad cases, the child is usually accompanied by their mother while the father stays behind in Korea alone to work, resulting in a phenomenon that South Korea has dubbed 'wild goose fathers' (*gireogi appa*). This zeal for English education has had many effects on Korean families, both physical and psychological. A study by Heo (2013) showed that many of the fathers left behind suffer from malnutrition (77%) and depression (70%), and a number of them (30%) also succumb to alcoholism. Mothers also expressed difficulties experienced in raising their children by themselves in a foreign country. One mother in Park's (2007) study expressed that she found it hard to discipline her children, and that her son's behaviour in particular had worsened due to separation from his father's influence.

In recent years, many books have been published that show how mothers can teach their children English. However, this method presents some difficulties, because many South Korean mothers have been taught English through a direct, grammar-centred approach, whereas current second language acquisition methodology centres on teaching children through a variety of communicative approaches. Thus, mothers often feel inferior when speaking English because of their non-native pronunciation. As a result, instead of talking with their children, they tend to play songs or stories using audiotapes (Yi & Yi, 2015). Numerous studies have shown that teaching a language through audio and video clips is not as effective in comparison to actual real-world exposure to and human interaction in another language. In a study conducted with students in the Flemish-speaking region of Belgium, Kuppens (2010) showed that watching English television with subtitles has been shown to improve vocabulary acquisition and test scores in older students; however, in infants and younger students who are not yet literate in English, this kind of media-only exposure to a second language has been shown to be predominantly unsuccessful (Conboy *et al.*, 2015; Kuhl *et al.*, 2003). The ineffectiveness is especially true regarding the acquisition of phonological systems. Kuhl *et al.*'s (2003) study showed that in very early childhood, human presence is required for language learning (Kuhl *et al.*, 2003: 9100). Many Korean mothers are subjecting their children to English media with the hope that it will help them with acquiring English's phonological system. Lack of success following the use of media in turn leads parents to enrol their children in many of the aforementioned English language programs.

4.1.2.1 Programme fee information

As mentioned at the beginning of this chapter, one of the main determining factors for a student being able to successfully learn English in South Korea is said to be one's grandparent's assets. KEDI (2015) reported that a full-day kindergarten program costs 1,237,000 KRW (1013.88 USD)[1] per month, whereas a half-day kindergarten costs 797,000 (653.24 USD) per month. According to KEDI (2015), even for after school programs where students are only taught for an hour or so each day, tuition fees can be considerably expensive. For example, tuition for English academies was around 231,800 KRW (189.99 USD) per month.

Prices have continued to be maintained at this high level (Lee, 2018). This article listed the average monthly cost of an English kindergarten in Seoul between 688,000 KRW (563.90 USD) and 797,000 KRW (653.24 USD) for a half day kindergarten, with some schools in more desirable neighbourhoods charging as much as 1,625,000 KRW (1331.89 USD) for their half day programs. Full day programs were also reported to range from an average of 1,000,000 KRW (819.63 USD) to 1,760,000 KRW (1442.54 USD) depending on the Seoul neighbourhood in which the kindergarten is located. These tuition costs are higher than those of Seoul National University, the most prestigious university in South Korea (Seoul National University, 2019).

4.1.2.2 Teaching staff

In publicly funded nurseries and kindergartens, laws exist to favour bilingual Korean-English speakers with Korean nationality as teachers (Park, 2015). However, no such laws exist governing the teaching staff of English kindergartens. While the situation has seen a lot of improvement over the past decade, many of these English kindergartens hire native-English-speaking teachers, generally from North America, who are not trained in early childhood education. Instead, these staff are hired mostly based on their native speaker English ability, with the minimum requirement of holding a bachelor's degree and a passport from an English-speaking country. This stems from the 'native speaker fantasy' that pervades much of the English education sector in South Korea.

In government regulated institutions, according to KEDI (2015), there are growing demands for the necessity of regulating the qualifications of foreign teachers, such as more stringent checking of criminal and medical records. The thing that parents like most about Korean teachers is their understanding of their children's education (44.9% of respondents) and their reliability (26.4%), whereas the reason they like foreign teachers is because of their unique and effective methodology of teaching English (50%). Parents cited the increased price as the biggest negative of foreign English teachers (47.2%). Due to the amount the schools must expend to hire, relocate, and house foreign staff, prices for classes and programs taught by foreign teachers can be very expensive compared to those taught by Korean teachers. Also, according to statistics cited by KEDI, in most English kindergartens that employ foreign teachers, 73.5% of the time the teaching in English kindergartens is done by a foreign teacher and a Korean teacher together. In these cases, half of the teaching is done by the Korean teacher and the other half of the time students are instructed by the foreign teacher. In other situations, 9.1% of the time classes are taught solely by the foreign teacher, and 4.5% of the time the Korean teacher is the main teacher and is only supported by the foreign teacher.

In order to appear to be a school that teaches 'true English' (i.e. American English), many English nurseries/kindergartens, English villages and cram schools hire monolingual native speakers, generally from North America, to come to Korea and teach. Song *et al.* (2011) showed that parents prefer Western teachers most, followed by pair teaching done by one Westerner and one Korean and then Koreans who majored in English. Parents cited a preference for Westerners based on their desire for their children to improve their interest in the English language itself, alongside acquiring 'native-like' pronunciation and a wider vocabulary through basic communication with a native speaker. However, as stated before, for these native speaker teachers, a bachelor's degree is a requirement, but there is no standard dictating that the degree must be related to English or any kind of educational training. Teachers with English or teaching backgrounds are preferred, but often schools will hire anyone with a Western-looking face and a passport from an English-speaking country, regardless of their degree subject.[2] Native English teachers come from a variety of backgrounds. While some have degrees in education or English, others come from backgrounds in business, musical theatre, history or athletics, most of them with no formal training in teaching, and almost all of them non-Korean speakers. Thus, while these teachers may have the ability to properly pronounce the English language because they learned it naturally as children, many of them cannot explain grammatical or structural rules to non-native speakers. These teachers also lack a thorough understanding of Korean customs and culture, many arriving in Korea only knowing the limited information they have been taught in their secondary school educations. Very few native teachers look on their time in Korea as permanent, generally choosing to stay in Korea as English teachers only temporarily. Thus, each year, or every two years if they are lucky, a school will have to train completely new native English teachers. Schools that employ multiple foreign teachers often have a very high turnover rate, which also adds to the instability of schools and the students' English education as a whole.

Another contributing factor to the often anxiety-inducing environment in early childhood English programs is the school's curriculum. Many schools' curriculum is compiled by teachers who work for that school, sometimes native English teachers and sometimes members of the Korean teaching or administrative staff. These staff members are often not trained in curriculum development, especially those native teachers whose degrees have nothing to do with education. This leads to a large number of schools with curricula that do not follow what contemporary academic research has shown to be effective, especially with regard to increasing foreign language enjoyment (FLE) and decreasing foreign language anxiety (FLA). While some chain academies have invested in hiring professional curriculum developers in designing more effective curricula, many individually owned academies suffer from having enlisted their underqualified staff in the development of their own curriculum. Park (2014) provided an example of an English kindergarten in Bundang, whose curriculum was comprised of phonics, storytelling, and other content-based activities, such as art and science, which were taught in English. According to KEDI (2015), while the majority of schools use professionally developed materials from South Korea, some kindergartens develop their own materials (31.5%), and many (9.3%) even use textbooks designed for early childhood curricula in the United States (KEDI, 2015).

Due to the monolingualism of the majority of the native English speakers hired to teach at English kindergartens, compounded by the widely held belief that immersion teaching is the most effect kind of teaching, many English kindergartens employ English-only language policies in the classroom. As noted in Chapter 2, most studies which support a complete immersion, English-only policy in language learning are based on studies of the language acquisition processes of adults, not children. According to other studies (Fillmore, 1991; Shin, 2005), children learn more quickly with mixed instruction in L1 and L2, and generally abandon L1 by choice as soon as they are proficient enough in the L2 (Park, 2007). There are countless arguments against monolingual instruction from many experts (e.g. Auerbach, 1993; Cook, 1997; Firth & Wagner, 1997; Kachru, 1994; Park, 2007). However, many people, not just Korean educators (e.g. California Proposition 227, 1998[3]), still believe that total immersion in an L2 setting is the best way for children to learn a language; they tend to ignore the expert material that says otherwise. The hiring of monolingual English speakers also limits many English kindergarten classrooms to the use of the English-only immersion model, despite the research that shows that it may not be the most effective methodology for young children.

In terms of teaching methods, storytelling, singing, dancing, musical activities and other diverse activities are all used in teaching English (Kim & Yu, 2012). The diversity of activity type allows children to stay interested, but it limits the English taught to the communicative level, with no overt instruction on vocabulary, syntax, grammar or morphology. Furthermore, the content level and the vocabulary level are often far too difficult for young children, many of whom are having their first encounter with English in this educational environment. On top of this, the methodologies and content used in English kindergartens pose another problem in that it has no continuity in primary school education (Kim & Yu, 2012), and therefore does not become foundational for future language learning success.

Forcing Korean children to learn in an English-only environment can raise their affective filters and activate their Foreign Language Anxiety, slowing down the acquisition process initially and having negative effects on their psychosocial development (Park, 2007: 158). In a study by Saville-Troike (1984), it was shown that many of the classroom behaviour problems of ESL students were linked to the fact that, because they were deprived of any L1 input, they could not thrive in the L2 environment. The study showed that many students who acted out, or were distracted in the normal classroom, paid attention and were well-behaved when they went to their ESL classes, where they were able to have some instruction in their L1. Park (2007) showed similar results with Korean students in an American elementary school. Students who struggled in the regular classroom, were happier and much better behaved when they had some instruction in their native language whether from a fellow Korean student or from a Korean speaking ESL teaching aide. Park's study (2007) showed that not only did language acquisition improve with the addition of some L1 input, but this input also helped to alleviate some of the damage to psychosocial development that occurs when students are stripped of their L1 identity and made to operate solely in an L2 environment.

This negative attitude towards the L1 can also dramatically affect the students' Korean language development. If students are told never to speak Korean in the classroom, especially at such an important period for language acquisition, they may not be continually developing their Korean language repertoire. This can lead to language attrition and, as they are ultimately Koreans, they will need to be able to function in Korean society using the Korean language. This could make life more difficult for the children when they necessarily start their education in mainstream Korean schools. As stated earlier, the findings of Song *et al.* (2011) showed that early childhood English language learning does not necessarily disrupt first language acquisition. Yet Park's total immersion research shows that English-only policies in these early childhood English classrooms can cause negative attitudes that may stagnate L1 growth, especially in the academic registers necessary for establishing the foundational language abilities for future L1 education. Ultimately, the goal of any classroom should be to facilitate learning while simultaneously ensuring the wellbeing of the child. In the case of South Korea, early English education seems to be falling short on both of these goals. The ineffectiveness of a large portion of the English education sector is caused by under-qualified teachers, badly developed curricula and English-only policies that interfere with the students' understanding and cause anxiety, raising the students' affective filters, making language acquisition a slower and more difficult process than it need be.

4.2 State of FLA Research in South Korea

As with the state of FLA research around the world, most Korea-focused FLA research has centred on older students and adults rather than young children (Jeong, 2004; Park, 2002). Yet, a few researchers have attempted to delve into the psychological effects of the South Korean drive towards early childhood education, especially as it regards the English education system. In this brief section, we will look into the existing research on the psychological effects, both positive and negative, of the South Korean early childhood education system.

4.2.1 Psychological impact of Korean early childhood English education

4.2.1.1 Negative impacts

According to Choi (2015), seven out of ten paediatricians view the impact of early English education negatively, with 50% claiming it may not be effective enough to ensure successful language learning and could in fact have a negative impact on children's emotional development. In some cases, young children who experience early English education can show low self-esteem, lack of concentration, hyperactivity and difficulty in controlling their emotions. Also, they often find it difficult to establish a stable relationship, even with their parents, and fear studying. In particular, early foreign language education may cause stuttering and immature pronunciation in both their native and second languages.

Kim (2010) showed that young children in full-day English kindergartens are much more stressed than those who attend English academies where English is only taught for a few hours a week. In particular, those children who attended English kindergartens showed much more significant depression and social withdrawal. Wu et al. (2002) also showed that early English education could cause dissatisfaction, hate, and a loss of confidence, as well as making a child fearful and unstable. Building on these findings, Wu et al. (2005) showed that early education could cause children to become too self-conscious around others and overly dependent. In another study, Shin (2002) showed that there is a potential for problems arising in the short-term memories of young children who are forced to learn another language too early.

As shown in the work of Park (2007, 2009b), sending children abroad to study English can also have negative psychosocial effects on them. The senses of young people are overwhelmed during the period of their growing up, constantly learning and meeting different people train the cognitive, emotive and social function of the individuals that make us human. Studies have shown increased internalizing behaviour (e.g. depression, anxiety, withdrawal) in young children when their residential location is not constant; this could be extrapolated into children moving countries (i.e. foreign environment) (Rumbold et al., 2012). Therefore, when children move abroad with one or both of their parents for language education, a common practice in many East Asian countries, it is likely that the change of environment, as well as the change in language and culture might have adverse psychological impacts on the children's psychosocial wellbeing.

While these negative psychological impacts are concerning, and as shown in Chapter 3 can possibly lead to chronic conditions later in life, many parents opt to focus on the positive aspects covered in the following section, as well as the ascribing to many of the language learning myths that researchers have spent decades disproving, as they enrol their young children in various language programs.

4.2.1.2 Positive impacts

Not specific to the situation in Korea but still applicable are studies from the early days of SLA research. Stern (1967) showed that young children are easily motivated to learn new languages. Dewaele et al. (2018) asserted that FLE has a positive impact on the success of language learning in secondary-level learners. If FLE shows the same impact on YLLs, enjoyable language classrooms could be one catalyst to activating the motivation of young children to learn. Another positive aspect of learning a foreign language in early childhood, according to Cohen and Robbins (1976), is that young children do not mind making mistakes in learning languages and are therefore more willing to experiment with language.

Park and Song (2008) noted that children who learn English before they become third graders have much more confidence and less anxiety than those who have not learned English before third grade. In contrast to some of the previously cited research that noted a loss of confidence due to early childhood English language education, Park and Song (2002) showed that early English education can actually help young children's communicative ability as well as boost their self-esteem. Kim (2001) showed that those who have received early English education show much more motivation and interest in English learning throughout their education. Yi (2002) also demonstrated that early exposure to English may help children to be more confident and to like English more as they continue their education.

The above research gives some insight into the complicated decision-making process a parent must undertake when choosing whether or not to enrol their child in an early childhood English education program. Parents are confronted with conflicting research as to the positives and negatives of subjecting their child to a language at an early age. They are also subjected to the aforementioned 'English Fever' environment of the nation, which seems to pressure them to believe that without thorough English language acquisition, their child will not be successful in their future school or careers. This social pressure has driven parents to some great lengths, even above and beyond just enrolling their children in various programs. In the next section, we will examine some domestic and international news articles that shed light on the fervour of South Korean parents for English language education.

4.3 Lingual Frenectomies

In the past decade, newspaper articles have appeared in both domestic and foreign newspapers regarding the frenzy for English language education in South Korea. As portrayed in the media, certain methods of parents have captured international attention (see e.g. Demick, 2002). This is because some Korean parents have taken more unusual, or unorthodox, measures in order to ensure their children's successful English language acquisition, despite inconclusive evidence proving such procedures to yield effective results.

In the most recent OECD publication reporting international rankings of academic performance, Asian countries dominated the top 10 spots – seven out of the ten to be exact, including Japan, South Korea and China, which ranked 3rd, 9th and 10th respectively (OECD, 2017). The English effect, i.e. the perception that English is the dominating language that brings economic and education benefits to students, has dramatically influenced the curriculum in East Asia (Andrade, 2009). Curricula in the region place emphasis on English fluency with the understanding that the ability to speak English gives the child a competitive edge to compete by using English as a global lingua franca. Yet the effectiveness of these curricula varies dramatically between countries in East Asia depending on the region and the SES of the students. Often, as students are studying in order to pass a test like the TOEFL or TOEIC, communicative competence is pushed to the side in favour of the acquisition of academic language. Yet at the younger levels, emphasis on these exams is not yet prevalent, and parents focus on pronunciation as the key to fluency in these early stages.

Due to the phonological nature of Asian languages and English, the inability to enunciate /l/ and /ɹ/ sounds in words have been shown to be a common obstacle among English learners in East Asia, particularly in Japan and Korea. Some parents have taken measures in order to enhance their children's potential to be able to speak English properly by consenting to a surgical procedure called a lingual frenectomy. This procedure entails cutting the frenulum, a string of tissue that connects one's tongue to the floor of mouth, consequently elongating the tongue and supposedly increasing one's ability to pronounce English /l/ and /ɹ/ sounds more clearly (Parry, 2002).

Currently, lingual frenectomy is a treatment option for children with ankyloglossia – more commonly known as 'tongue tie' – a condition that restricts tongue mobility and subsequently hinders speech and feeding ability. It has been proven to be an effective treatment for children with this clinical condition, but there is no research evidence as of yet to suggest that a lingual frenectomy improves the second language pronunciation abilities of children who have no clinically diagnosed condition of ankyloglossia affecting their speech and feeding ability.

4.4 Applicability to a Wider Context/Target Audience

While we focus on the South Korean context in this chapter, and throughout the remainder of this book, we assert that many of the problems and proposed solutions, if not universal, can at least be applied in a wider East Asian context, in the 'expanding circle' (Kachru, 1985). Many of the problems associated with the perception of such a fervour for English are not localized to Korea, but can also be found in China, Japan, Taiwan and parts of Southeast Asia.

4.4.1 English education in Japan

Like South Korea, English education is a large part of the Japanese education system as well. According to Go and Go (2013), the Japanese government started early English education in primary school in the 1990s, as a way to internationalize the country. Alongside this move, all government documents began to be published both in Japanese and in English. Kitano (2001) showed that there was no governmental restriction or regulation on English education in Japan, unlike the government attempts to reign in English education that are seen in South Korea. However, like Korea, much of the English education is done in the private sector. Also like the situation in South Korea, the quality of English education available to children differs according to their families' SES. Children whose families can afford to pay more for education have access to more qualified teachers, better organized curricula and more exposure to English-speaking opportunities than children whose families are limited by their economic resources.

Also, similar to the situation in South Korea, many English teaching programs do not require teachers to have a teaching background or a degree related to the English language or education. These teachers also are not expected to know the Japanese language or culture. Even in Japan's most well-known teacher recruitment program, the Japan Exchange and Teaching Programme (JET), people going as Assistant Language Teachers (ALTs) not required to have Japanese competency (JET, 2019). This in turns results in many of the same problems that South Korean classrooms utilizing unqualified native-English-speaking teachers face.

4.4.2 English education in mainland China

Hu (2004) shows that English education in China is becoming increasingly important due to China's opening of their economic markets. Since 2004, the Chinese Ministry of Education has been teaching English as part of the national curriculum starting in the third grade. However, each Chinese province is given the autonomy to choose when they will begin introducing English into their local curriculum. As such, in big cities such as Shanghai, Beijing and Qingdao, they start teaching English to first graders. Hu's research shows that 63% of Chinese parents provide their children English education, and most of these children start this educational process between the ages of three and seven. Recently, online English educational industries have also begun to crop up (VIPKID, Teach Away, DaDA, QKids) allowing even more young children to have access to native speaker education within their own homes. In contrast to Japan, China regulates its English language industry closely. Even online platforms are facing new crackdowns from governmental regulations that now require teachers to be certified in Teaching English as a Foreign Language (TEFL) or Teaching English to Speakers of Other Languages (TESOL) alongside a minimum of a bachelor's degree, two years of teaching experience, and a clear background check (Xinhua, 2018). Many of these online platforms offer classes to children as young as four years old. The relative advantages and disadvantages of online English education platforms will be further discussed in Chapter 7.

4.4.3 English education in Taiwan

According to Yu Chang (2007), Taiwan opened up to English education in the public-school system even earlier than mainland China. From 2001, English has been a main subject for fifth graders. English education was implemented in the third-grade curriculum starting in 2005. Most private kindergartens teach English, and even public or state kindergartens teach English twice a week. From 2004, however, due to different social problems which arose regarding English education by foreigners, the government started to emphasize the importance of teaching the national language – Mandarin – leading to legislation that required the use of Mandarin in conjunction with English education (Klöter, 2004). Hence, the national language is encouraged to be taught prior to English, and it is illegal to teach in English only without Mandarin Chinese. From the vantage point of translanguaging education, teaching using both L1 and L2 in the classroom still facilitates successful language acquisition in a reduced anxiety environment. This will be covered in more depth in Chapter 7.

While the above examples all come from East Asian nations, many of the principles and psychosocial effects seen in all of these countries can be applied even further. With an increasingly global economy, many parents outside of East Asia are seeing the value of teaching their children a second or even third language starting at a very young age. Parents in North America are increasingly enrolling their children in Chinese and Spanish language immersion schools. Canada has offered French immersion programs for decades, and children across Europe learn second languages starting very early in their government-funded educations. Therefore, the problems expounded upon in this chapter and the ones that follow may seem familiar to people all over the world, despite their specificity to the South Korean situation. It is therefore important to extrapolate universal solutions that can be applied in any situation in which a young child is encountering education in a new language in order to provide for the psychosocial wellbeing of the child while simultaneously allowing for successful language acquisition.

4.5 Conclusion

English language instruction in South Korea has been heavily influenced by the predominance of a perception of an 'English Fever' in Korean society at large. While the government has taken some measures to curb private education and regulate the quality of English education, on the whole, there is still vast room for improvement in order to create an educational environment that reduces harmful levels of FLA and boosts FLE at all age levels, but especially among younger, more vulnerable language learners. Strategies for a more ethical language classroom pedagogy would be beneficial not only in South Korea, but also within some of the other highly English-focused nations in Kachru's 'expanding circle' that do not already emphasize FLE in their English pedagogy for YLLs. With increasing mobility across national borders, these strategies are worth implementing in classrooms across the globe.

Notes

(1) Prices in USD are as of the 12 August 2019 exchange rate.
(2) This is especially prevalent in English villages.
(3) California Proposition 227, which was passed in 1998 and not repealed until 2016, required the elimination of most bilingual classes for Limited English Proficient (LEP) students, requiring them to learn through total English Immersion as opposed to having first language support in their language learning process.

5 Sources of Increased FLA Among Young Children

This chapter looks at three main sources of increased Foreign Language Anxiety (FLA) among young children, particularly young children in Korea. In the first section, we look at myths surrounding language learning that, when believed and followed, can cause an increase in FLA and even a decrease in Foreign Language Enjoyment (FLE). In the second section we look at cultural differences between teachers and students in the classroom. In the final section, we investigate the role that parents play in language learning and how their actions might affect the levels of FLA in their children.

5.1 Myths

Various myths about language learning have been perpetuated both within and outside the field of Second Language Acquisition (SLA). In this section, we look at some of the more prevalent myths that parents and educational administrators have latched onto, informing some of their decisions regarding when and how children should start acquiring another language. Some increased rates of FLA among young children can be attributed to the belief of the following language learning myths: immersion is the only way to truly learn a language; bilingual education is dangerous and ineffective; rote learning methods are an effective model for all levels of language learning; native speakers make the best teachers; and, in acquiring a language, the younger you start, the better.

5.1.1 Immersion

Immersion language learning is often seen as the ideal model for successful language acquisition in the shortest time. Countless studies have been done showing the effectiveness of immersion schooling in the acquisition of language, particularly regarding language confidence and willingness to communicate (Baker & MacIntyre, 2000; Clément, 1980; Clément et al., 1994; Gardner et al., 1977, 1979; Genesee, 1978; Johnson & Swain, 1997; Lambert & Tucker, 1972; MacIntyre et al., 2002; Steele et al., 2017; Swain & Lapkin, 1982; Tanaka & Ellis, 2003). Yet, this model is not without its problems. While studies have shown that students enrolled in immersion language learning programs have a high chance of successful language acquisition, the measures of success often vary from school to school based on the teaching methodologies, assessment techniques and the goals of the specific immersion program (Cummins, 1998).

It is not uncommon, in an academic setting, for undue emphasis to be placed on learning the academic registers of a language to the detriment of acquiring other linguistic registers in that same language. In Genesee's (2011) discussion of Hoare's (2011) research on immersion programs in Hong Kong and Mainland China, he notes that '"schools" narrow focus on academic success' can result in programs with unofficial policies that emphasize academic achievement over linguistic competence' (Genesee, 2011: 272). Genesee goes on to discuss the struggle of immersion programs to find a balance between academic achievement and successful language learning.

Furthermore, according to Genesee (2011), parental involvement is integral for successful language acquisition in an immersion program. Whatever is learned in a classroom, whether immersion or not, must be supported and encouraged outside of the classroom as well. Students must be shown real world applications for the use of their L2, in order to facilitate more successful language learning. Language learning cannot be isolated to a classroom, even an immersion classroom.

Along with the above complications involved in immersion language learning, Genesee (2011) points out that accessibility is also often an issue. As mentioned in other parts of these texts, formal language learning that falls outside of the purvey of government-sponsored education can be prohibitively expensive for low SES families. This necessitates other methodologies of language instruction that would be more inclusive from an SES standpoint. Apart from SES concerns, students with learning disabilities are also often barred from participation in these immersive programs. Such exclusion takes place as many parents and educators believe that students who struggle with their performance in the standard academic environment would not benefit from the intensive language learning environment of an immersive classroom. This is despite research that shows they can achieve similar outcomes within immersive classrooms (Bruck, 1978, 1982; Fortune, 2011).

As concerns the main topic of this book, studies on immersion language programs have also been shown to exacerbate FLA by further raising affective filters, especially at the beginning stages of a student's immersion. An investigation by MacIntyre *et al.* (2002) showed that students in a French immersion program – who were grades 7–9 in this study – experienced anxiety across the board throughout the years of their immersion French program. While female participants displayed a decrease in anxiety in the later years, boys maintained a constant level of anxiety throughout their participation in the immersion programs (MacIntyre *et al.*, 2002). These findings are consistent with the findings reported by Dewaele *et al.* (2018) mentioned in Chapter 2 of this book. However, results of the various studies on the correlation between immersion programs and anxiety are often contradictory. Some studies have shown decreased anxiety in L2 communicative situations following participation in an immersive program (Baker & MacIntyre, 2000; Tanaka & Ellis, 2003), while others have shown increased anxiety and decreased willingness to communicate following a similar immersive experience (Kitano, 2001). Kitano (2001) speculates that this increased anxiety is caused by increased pressure to perform at an advanced level based on their own or their parents' expectations of the abilities they should have acquired during their immersion experience.

Despite the relatively high success rate of immersion language learning, the increased potential for FLA and the associated raised affective filters are negatives that parents, teachers, and educational policymakers must take into account when determining the appropriate language education programs for their children and students. As will be discussed in more depth in Chapters 7 and 8, by incorporating more FLE into the classroom, even an immersion language classroom will see linguistic benefits and positive effects on the students' psychosocial wellbeing.

5.1.2 The so-called 'dangers' of bilingual education

In recent years, the myth of the dangers of bilingualism has become increasingly dispelled as parents and educators see the value of having multiple languages in one's linguistic repertoire. In the past, many parents and teachers hesitated to embrace bilingual education due to concerns over confusing the two languages, or not being able to adequately learn the L2 because of the presence of the L1.

Much of the fear of bilingual education stems from misguided or misinterpreted advice from scholars in the early periods of linguistic research on bilingualism, most particularly from negative interpretations of linguist Werner Leopold's work in the 1950s (Grosjean, 2010; Leopold, 1939, 1952, 1970). Since that time, most linguists have spoken more of the advantages of bilingualism, creating bodies of literature refuting the myths of its disadvantages (Grosjean, 2009). However, the original damage done by early linguists remains. There are two myths that are more popular than others that we wish to debunk throughout this book, but most especially in this chapter. The first is the myth that students will learn the second language more slowly and will not learn it as well if they use both languages. The second myth is that bilingualism holds students back academically because they are unable to fully develop in either language, and therefore they cannot function at the same level as their peers.

In different studies, researchers have shown that the variance between bilingual and monolingual children's acquisition of features of language is not statistically significant (Bergman, 1976; Grosjean, 2010; Meisel, 1989; Oller & Eilers, 2002; Pearson, 1998). In a study compiled by the UK Department for Education, statistics showed that, when it comes to GCSE (General Certificate of Secondary Education) scores, a slightly higher number of students whose first language was not English (61.3%) met benchmark standards compared to those students whose first language is English (60.7%) (Stone, 2016), although this study fails to take into account possibly confounding variables like parenting styles and cultural backgrounds that might emphasize the importance of education. Various dual immersion programs in operation in Canada have also generated data disproving this notion that two languages at once are detrimental to academic development (Cummins & Swain, 1986; Genesee, 1978; Morrison, 1981). Translanguaging classrooms, where students are allowed to access all of their previous knowledge through their native language as they learn English, keeps them progressing in other subject areas while they are building up their English repertoire (Chalmers, 2019; Cummins, 2000; García, 2009; García & Li Wei, 2014; Gebauer *et al.*, 2013; Lee & Macaro, 2013; Lewis *et al.*, 2012; Smits *et al.*, 2008; Trudell, 2016; van Gelderen *et al.*, 2007).

In South Korea, in order to appear to be a school that teaches 'true English' (i.e. American English), many English nurseries/kindergartens, English villages and private academies hire monolingual native speakers, generally from North America, to come and teach classes. As these teachers are unable to speak Korean, classes must necessarily be conducted entirely in English, leading to wide-spread English-only policies in many South Korean classrooms. A major reason for the ineffectiveness of the Korean English teaching machine is their continued insistence on these English-only policies. As mentioned earlier, this myth concerning the bilingual classroom has been supported (wrongly) by many experts, and thus is widely installed in most Korean English language schools. Most of these studies, which support a complete immersion, English-only policy in language learning, are based on studies of the language acquisition processes of adults, not children. According to other studies (Fillmore, 1991; Shin, 2005), children learn more quickly with mixed instruction in L1 and L2, generally abandoning L1 by choice as soon as they are proficient enough in L2 (Park, 2007). There are countless arguments against monolingual instruction from many experts (Auerbach, 1993; Cook, 2001; Firth & Wagner, 1997; Kachru, 1994; Park, 2007). However, many still cling to the idea that monolingual immersion is the best way for children to learn a language. As mentioned in the previous chapter, Saville-Troike (1984) showed that L1 input in the L2 classroom can be invaluable in enabling many students to thrive in the language classroom as well as alleviating behavioural issues such as acting out and distraction because Limited English Proficient (LEP) students are not deprived of their main means of self-expression – i.e. their L1.

5.1.3 Rote learning

Rote learning is the pedagogical method that emphasizes memorization of terms and structures, often outside of contexts. Since the inception of language learning, students and teachers have been using rote learning methods to acquire language by memorizing vast vocabulary lists and their definitions, memorizing dialogues from textbooks and even memorizing entire passages and texts (Mayer, 2002). In East Asia, rote learning has been particularly prevalent, with a rote learning tradition dating back to the Confucian schools of the various dynastic periods of the Chinese and Korean regions, where Confucian scholars would memorize entire classical texts word for word as a great part of their education. While good for memorizing vocabulary, rote learning has been shown to be widely ineffective in engendering communicative competence.

Studies as early as 1953 have also shown ties between anxiety and effectiveness of rote learning. Montague's (1953) study showed that students with heightened anxiety learned more slowly using rote learning methods than their non-anxious counterparts. Montague's paper was examining the drive response often noted in conjunction with anxiety, i.e. that a certain amount of anxiety actually increases successful production or learning. He found that rather than producing drive in rote language learning situations, the introduction of anxiety resulted in drive reduction in the verbal tasks.

In more recent years, especially in the West, there has been a drive against rote learning methodology. Mayer (2002) emphasizes that retention and transfer are the desired outcomes in learning. While rote learning facilitates retention, it does not necessarily enable a student to transfer that knowledge to other spheres and contexts. Many educators follow Bloom's taxonomy, also formulated in the 1950s when research into the effectiveness of rote learning methods was at its height (Bloom, 1956). The taxonomy is used to determine the degree and depth of students' learning. The lowest, most shallow level of educational attainment is knowledge, followed by comprehension, application, analysis, synthesis and evaluation in ascending order. Each progressive level increases the depth of the student's learning on a topic with evaluation topping the pyramid.

Bloom's taxonomy would place rote learning on the bottom tiers of this pyramid, in which only knowledge and understanding are acquired without any application, analysis, synthesis and ultimate evaluation. In the language classroom, the goal of most students and teachers is communicative competence, which requires reaching the highest tiers of Bloom's taxonomy. It is therefore imperative to use other methods in conjunction with rote methods in order to facilitate successful language learning. Additionally, as seen through Montague's research rote learning is even less effective when students are experiencing anxiety. Thus, in order to decrease anxiety and facilitate successful language learning, a variety of methods incorporating pedagogy that encourages FLE and decreases FLA will create the best environment in which to learn languages.

5.1.4 Native speakerism

One of the main reasons South Korean parents want their children to begin learning English at such a young age is because they have heard that 'native-like' pronunciation can only be acquired prior to the end of the critical period mentioned in Chapter 3. This necessity to acquire native-like pronunciation is another part of the problem. Firstly, it is relevant to consider what precisely native English pronunciation is. As a global lingua franca, there are native speakers of English the world over who speak with varying dialects and accents of English. It is possible to take a person from India, a person from Scotland, and a person from the southern United States, for example, and find they all use different, sometimes mutually unintelligible, dialects of the same language. Even in countries where English is traditionally seen as the main spoken language, such as the United Kingdom and the United States, more diversity is becoming common. In the United States, the 2016 American Community Survey revealed that native speakers of languages other than English make up about 20% of the population. In the United Kingdom, other languages are also common; as early as the 1970s, the Inner London Education Authority found that over 100 languages were being spoken at the homes of children attending school in the city. So, what is a native speaker of English, if English can be so vastly different depending on which native speaker you are referring to? In South Korea, a native speaker is considered by the majority to be one that speaks with a standard North American accent, using American grammar, spelling and vocabulary (Ahn, 2015; Park, 2009a; Shim & Park, 2008). Certain varieties of English are assigned a status of privilege while others are discriminated against. This can cause more FLA for those students who may have learned English in a non-North American environment, such as the Philippines, when they are suddenly expected to adapt their previously acquired English to the new demands of a North American-based curriculum.

As referenced in Chapter 4, this native speaker fantasy leads parents to pay higher tuition costs to send their young children to schools who have employed teachers from North America, who more often than not are unqualified to teach English apart from having learned it themselves when they were children (Holliday, 2006; Holliday *et al.*, 2015). These teachers predominantly do not speak Korean. Many of them come to South Korea with little to no knowledge of Korean culture, customs or history, and proceed to teach English without any formal training in English grammar, syntax, phonology or morphology, not to mention pedagogy. In recent years, especially in government funded programs, a shift towards hiring bilingual teachers has been seen, but many of the successful private academies maintain their habit of hiring North American teachers to satisfy parents' native speaker fantasies.

Another problem involved with the native speaker fantasy is the simultaneous superficiality and perfectionism inherent within it. Often, the ability to speak with native-like pronunciation takes precedence over native-like command of the language and communicative competence. According to Thomson and Derwing (2014), unlike other components of L2 instruction, pronunciation is not linked to the acquisition of other core components of linguistic competence, such as syntax, morphology and vocabulary, and you can therefore have speakers with advanced English ability, but low pronunciation ability, or vice versa (Thomson & Derwing, 2014: 14). Thus, with pronunciation-led pedagogy, more important areas of English education may not directly taught or practiced. Also, the focus on one specific variety of English ignores the multitude of other varieties of English, as well as vilifying Korean-style English (Ahn, 2015). Pronunciation is necessarily localized and that does not make a particular style of pronunciation wrong, especially with regards to a global lingua Franca (Ahn, 2015).

This bias towards pronunciation-led English education is unproductive and has had many side effects (Jenkins, 2002). Though numbers have decreased in recent years due to government restrictions, native English-speaking teachers in Korea still number in the tens of thousands (Jeon, 2009). As mentioned multiple times already, many of these teachers' only teaching qualification is having received a bachelor's degree, often not even in a teaching-related field. This leads to problems of unqualified teachers who lack the training, knowledge and experience necessary to successfully teach English as a Foreign Language (EFL) (Dawe, 2014). Thus, these teachers instruct mainly pronunciation, ignoring the more important methods of building communicative competence such as 'task-based', 'interactive', 'process-oriented', 'inductive-oriented' or 'discovery-oriented' teaching methods (Savignon, 2018: 6). The lack of methodological training and consequent pronunciation focus impedes students' ultimate ability to acquire communicative competence in English.

Pervasive native-speakerist ideology has had a massive impact on English education in South Korea. In Korea, due to post-colonial American occupation, the standard American English pronunciation continues to be touted as the ideal for most people, leading to the aforementioned use of unqualified native teachers as well as the misdirected emphasis on pronunciation over actual language competency. This misdirection has led to financial waste on behalf of the South Korean government as well as individual households. Families take on financial burdens in the scramble to provide their children with the success that they mistakenly envision can only come through the ability to speak English 'like a native'. Not only are there financial effects, but this push towards native-speaker pronunciation has also led to the development of an English education system that does not encourage communicative competence. Instead, the system engenders perfectionism that can result in increased FLA in students, due to the pressure to be able to communicate using 'perfect' American pronunciation.

The terms 'native' and 'non-native' themselves are also problematic as they set up a superior vs. inferior hierarchy of competence with no possibility for advancement, as the most a language learner can hope to achieve is 'native-like' proficiency. Dewaele (2018) instead advocates for the use of L1 and LX terminology when referring to language users, which allows us to break from the 'native' and 'non-native' dichotomy. This fits alongside Cook's (1991, 1999, 2016) ideas of linguistic multi-competence, which stipulate that multilingual people are more common than monolingual 'native' speakers, making the aforementioned dichotomy of 'native' and 'non-native' and its associated hierarchy inadequate to describe reality. The dichotomy also ignores the 'unique assets of L2 users and overemphasiz[es] NS language and situations' (Cook, 2016: 186). A shift towards multi-competence ideology and the terms L1 and LX would almost make an ensuing turn towards a translanguaging pedagogy that incorporates L1 into LX language classrooms seem inevitable.

5.1.5 Age

One of the most prolific second language acquisition myths is that of age. Early studies by Penfield and Roberts (1959), combined with the spread of information concerning the critical period hypothesis, have resulted in many parents ascribing to the authors' 'younger is better' philosophy. As mentioned in Chapter 3, while there is some concrete research to support the critical period hypothesis when it comes to first language acquisition (Lenneberg, 1967; Penfield & Roberts, 1959), there is little support for a blanket application of the CPH with regards to second language acquisition.

Long's (1990) overview of all the preceding research on the maturational constraints on language development showed that decreased neural plasticity might be to blame for the decreased ability of students at higher ages to acquire a second language at native levels. He also highlighted research that showed that neural plasticity can begin to degrade in children as young as six years old, and that the average critical period length varies for different skills, e.g. the critical period for morphosyntax can be twice that of the critical period for pronunciation (David, 1985; Fathman, 1975; Long, 1990; Tahta *et al.*, 1981; Yamada *et al.*, 1980). This research supports Lenneberg's (1967) assertions that critical periods are biologically predisposed. Krashen *et al.* (1979) showed in their research that different ages of learners have a different rate of acquisition. To elucidate, adults progress through the beginning levels of morphological and syntactic acquisition at a much faster rate than children, older children acquire morphology and syntax faster than younger children and child starters outperform adult starters in the long run, though the acquisition takes longer. More recent research by Singleton and Muñoz (2011) posits that there is indeed an age difference in language learning and ultimate maturational constraints on L2 attainment; however, they note that attributing all of these constraints to a critical period is problematic. They conclude that 'human learning capacity declines gradually over the lifespan in every sphere' (Singleton & Muñoz, 2011: 419) and that CPH is insufficient for explaining the variety of L2 outcomes.

This research would support the myth that parents should start teaching their children languages at a very young age. However, these studies have generally been carried out looking at immigrant children and adults who were acquiring the second language within the context they would be using it rather than in the foreign language classroom. Pfenninger and Singleton (2016, 2017) have demonstrated in their longitudinal studies tracking early and late starting EFL learners in Switzerland that starting age has no major effect on ultimate attainment, and in fact the late starters' initial rate of acquisition was higher as their motivation was more goal-driven and future-oriented. In South Korea, the motivation and situation of language learning is different and therefore research contexts are also different. A study by Marinova-Todd *et al*. (2000) showed that age differences in language acquisition are also reflective of differences in the learning situation rather than the merely a matter of age. Muñoz and Singleton (2011) also showed that an emphasis on 'native-speaker' behaviour as the standard for measuring attainment possibly influences the perception of effects of the CPH. Therefore, the situation in Korea would require further longitudinal research to determine whether or not starting children's English language education at such early ages boosts effective acquisition in actuality, or if the same level of acquisition could be attained if the learning started at a later age. All of the various research supporting or debunking age myths is very context-specific in its variables (Stern, 1976). Therefore, it is necessary to carry out original research in each context, taking into account the overall psychosocial wellbeing of the children involved, in order to determine what is best within that educational context.

5.2 East Asian Language Anxiety, Understanding Asian Mentalities

5.2.1 Influence of culture on learning

Culture has an influence on teaching and subsequently affects learning styles. Due to local instructional styles and remnant influences of Confucianism, many students in East Asia tend to be passive learners and dependent learners; they rely on teachers providing content material and seldom ask questions in class (Biggs & Watkins, 1996; Chan, 1999). Hofstede (1980) studied the framework of culture and investigated what differentiates the different types of cultures. In the study, he established five dimensions of culture: collectivism-individualism, power-distance, masculinity-femininity, uncertainty-avoidance and long term-short term. East Asian countries typically present a high score of collectivism and high power distance, which notably differs from Western societies where they score high in individualism and low power distance. In other words, the East Asian community places an emphasis on cohesiveness among individuals rather over the self (collectivism) and their behaviour exhibits that power is distributed unevenly, indicating a hierarchy of authority (high power distance). These cultural customs are embedded in the learning styles of East Asian students. East Asian students adopt a hierarchical approach in the classroom; they only speak when asked to as this shows respect, implicit, and indirect communication and teacher-centred teaching where students expect the teacher to outline content material.

The root of this learning style can be traced back to the Confucian values, where 'strict discipline, proper behaviour and filial piety' are encouraged (Raymond & Choon, 2017: 198). Asking questions is considered to be a waste of other students' time as fellow students want to gain as much knowledge as possible (Chang & Holt, 1994). In addition, students do not consider asking questions in public as a good habit.

Although asking questions in class is discouraged, students do approach teachers after class. Biggs (1996) has noted that Chinese students, for example, are more active in one-to-one discussions. To reinforce their learning, Chinese students are reflective learners, as demonstrated by asking questions after reflection (Cortazzi & Jin, 2001). Some research has also argued that Chinese students are engaged with the class non-verbally, using unspoken agreements and contentions as a display of respect (Zhou et al., 2005).

5.2.2 Questions and FLA

Teachers commonly ask questions to their students in the classroom. Asking questions serves as a tool to gauge the interest, understanding and engagement of students. It also serves as a method of controlling students' behaviour. Common types of questions asked by teachers include closed questions (yes/no) or open and referential questions (e.g. 'what is the atomic number of oxygen?'). The different types of questions determine different responses from students; yes/no questions will not cause students to produce longer responses unless the teacher encourages students to elaborate on their answers (Yang, 2010). Different questions are therefore employed at different times, with open and referential questions appearing mainly at the beginning of a lesson

(Myhill *et al.*, 2006). Some questions also act as prompts for non-verbal communication; asking questions such as 'Who says yes? Who says no?' prompts students to raise their hands as a form of communication. In a traditional language classroom, factual questions are favoured by teachers while open questions are the least popular among teachers in a traditional language classroom (Myhill *et al.*, 2006).

Because questions are such an essential component of language learning, they are often employed in the language classroom, particularly by teachers raised or trained in the West. However, because East Asian students have been taught not to ask questions in the classroom, and most lessons are generally lecture based with very little demand for student vocal interaction, in an English educational setting, when students are unexpectedly called upon by teachers to answer a question in the target language, levels of FLA may rise as this activates the aforementioned anxiety-inducing factors, namely fear of negative evaluation (FNE) and social avoidance and distress (SAD). This again highlights the importance of cultural sensitivity in the language classroom. If teachers are aware of the increased FLA that could be caused by sudden questions, they can plan their lessons to avoid situations where a student might feel put on the spot or called out by the questions. Questions are an integral part of the language learning process as they involve exercizing critical thinking skills. We therefore do not advocate any methodology that would avoid the asking of questions in its entirety. Rather educators can find alternative environments for spontaneous question asking and answering, perhaps in small groups, or as part of a game, thereby encouraging an increase in classroom FLE rather than FLA.

5.2.3 Teachers of English to speakers of other languages (TESOL)

As mentioned earlier, the English language is sometimes perceived as the key to success, as demonstrated by the movement toward English as the medium of instruction (EMI) in education systems, especially in universities and postgraduate education. The prevalence of this perception is also demonstrated by the massive outflow of international students to institutions abroad for tertiary education. The demand for English as the dominant academic language is signified by the increased use of English in the publication of academic papers (Master, 1998). Therefore, in the academic- and career-driven East Asian culture, English is deemed as the key to advancing into the academic world, driving the transformation of the education environment in East Asia.

Due to these changes and shifts in education, foreign English teachers are in demand, with 'roughly 100,000 English teaching positions open every year' (Montose, 2016). This being the case, what should these English teachers be aware of when they go abroad to teach? Foreign English teachers have expressed in previous research that Chinese students 'hardly ever answer questions voluntarily' and there were 'too few questions and answers in class' (Wang, 2011: 80). This in turn led foreign English teachers to 'point or select a student for an answer ... the students would not tell me if they don't understand my English' (Wang, 2011: 81). Most foreign English teachers take the Socratic approach, which utilizes interaction and inquiry-based learning, the opposite of the Confucian method that much of the education in East Asia employs.

In many instances in East Asia, due to this contrast in teaching methodologies, the students simply remain silent. Silence among language learners, in which they do not practice spoken output in the Target Language (TL), has been perceived as overly prevalent in classrooms across different countries and cultures. Indeed, the proclivity toward staying silent has long been perceived as a major problem in second language teaching. Since Scollon (1985), silence has been understood as a 'malfunction' in language learners. However, students' silent behaviours may actually reflect deeper issues such as excess Foreign Language Anxiety (FLA). To avoid the potentially anxiety-provoking situation of being judged on one's foreign language competency, students may withdraw their participation by keeping quiet. In this way, FLA may be concealed from instructors, who do not understand students' internal thought processes in opting to stay silent. If students do not express their thoughts in speech, it may be hard for others to identify anxiety as the primary obstacle to their language learning and to help them to overcome it.

Students' reasons for being silent can depend on their cultural background to some extent. King (2013) examined the case of foreign language learners in Japan, who had a particular reputation for silence during classes. The investigator collected a large amount of observation data from English as a Foreign Language (EFL) classes in tertiary education in Japan. This constituted 48 hours of data observing 924 learners across nine different universities. The data was subsequently analysed with a Dynamic Systems Theory (DST) approach. The study results confirmed a strong tendency toward silence in Japanese classrooms. The prevalence of silence was in fact greater than the investigator had expected, with less than 1% of all talk being initiated by students. Additionally, over 20% of all class time showed no oral participation by either the students or their teacher. Based on this finding, the study author posited five different types of silence in the Japanese EFL classroom: *the silence of disengagement, the silence of teacher-centred methods, the silence of nonverbal activities, the silence of confusion* and *the silence of hypersensitivity to others*. It is clear that the last of these categories, *the silence of hypersensitivity to others*, is closely linked to FLA. In Japanese culture, a large emphasis is often placed on the perceptions of others in the society, a concept known as *seken* (世間) in Japanese. This can lead individuals to feel anxiety about how they are perceived by their peers. Based on this conception of Japanese culture, King (2013) argues that silence is a defensive strategy that students employ to protect themselves from potentially negative judgement by others. The study concludes that this and other factors have led to an educational culture where to not participate orally in language class is seen as normal by students and staff alike. In this way, we see how the problem of excessive silence in the second language classroom is compounded by students' FLA.

A possible limitation of King's (2013) study is that the investigator did not analyse the influence of students' gender, age and region on proclivity toward silence. Although it appears such demographic data was at least partially recorded, these factors were not factored into the discussion of results, with all the students in Japan being treated as one unit. As Japanese sociolinguists have demonstrated considerable variation in the Japanese language usage based on gender, age and regional dialect (see e.g. Didi-Ogren, 2020; Kajino, 2014; Sreetharan 2004, 2006), it is possible that behaviours like silence may also be influenced by these. An analysis that measures the effect of these factors on students' keeping silent is a potentially interesting direction for future research.

Differences in teaching and learning styles between East Asian students and their foreign teaching staff impacts students' learning progress by creating more situations in which this silent period or other manifestations of FLA may occur. Most foreign English teachers feel that students should take the opportunity of class time to practice the language. Lack of practice slows students' progress, meaning they are less likely to perform well, impacting their eventual language acquisition. This can compound with other factors that influence FLA such as perceived scholastic competence and academic achievement (Onwuegbuzie et al., 1999). For students unused to the Socratic method, raised affective filters due to being required to answer questions in a foreign language may pose as a barrier to effective communication with teachers, professors, and peers. Students who have spent their education learning grammar and vocabulary through rote learning methods will have difficulty transferring meaning from their native language to the new language. There may also be difficulty in understanding the pronunciation of native-speaking teachers (Wang, 2011). Instead of oral questions, East Asian students often prefer other discussion mediums such as reading and writing. This is because they have more time to think and prepare their discussion points. While this is the current state of language education, and increased FLA might be caused by insisting on the use of the Socratic method in English language classrooms, again, we do not condone ignoring proven language acquisition teaching methodologies in order to avoid FLA in the classroom. Teachers should approach teaching their students armed with an understanding of the students' educational and cultural backgrounds and, acknowledging the stresses that questions might induce, find ways to make learning through an inquiry-based approach enjoyable to the extent that the anxiety fades into the background. In contrast to rote learning methods, inquiry-based education requires production and critical thinking on the parts of the student. This will create a much larger network of neural linkages, thereby increasing communicative competence, which would not happen with mere reading and writing classroom experiences.

Steven and Stigler (1992) investigated the cultural differences in learning interactions between teachers and students. They looked at how different cultures perceive the role of a teacher, demonstrated by what teachers in different countries feel should take priority in their teaching. For example, teachers in China identified explaining and showing enthusiasm in the teaching as their highest priority whereas teachers in the United States expressed that sensitivity and patience are important attributes of a good teacher (Steven & Stigler, 1992). We can take from this that students' learning styles should affect teachers' teaching strategies, and because cultural educational background affects students' learning styles, it must also be taken into account when teachers design effective language teaching strategies. Thus, the language classroom should also be a place of cultural melding, as the teacher combines methodologies of both the home country and the target language in order to create a classroom environment that facilitates increased FLE as it strives to decrease FLA to the 'sweet spot' or the most appropriate level for effective language learning.

5.3 Parental Influence in Language Learning

The extent to which parents are involved in the language learning process also has an effect on the student's potential for experiencing FLA. When English is part of a student's life outside of the classroom as well, it makes the language more familiar and the student is less likely to feel the same levels of anxiety when using it as a student whose English use is limited to the classroom, as seen in the following study. However, the motivations behind parental encouragement as well as the methods of parental encouragement are also factors in the ultimate outcome of language acquisition, as well as the psychological reactions of the student to the language learning process, including likelihood of experiencing FLA.

In Korea, 'Eomma-pyo Yeongeo (English education by mom)' is popular in families with young children. 'Eomma-pyo (Mom's brand)' means that the mother, not the professional teacher, directs and teaches the child herself. In Korea, the cost of learning English through the private education sector is very high. Thus, it is considered worthwhile for the mother herself to attempt to teach her children early English using various resources. Many books about 'mother's English teaching' have been published showing that these attempts have become popular in Korean society (see e.g. Han, 2018; Hong, 2017; Kim & Ko, 2019; Nam, 2016). A cursory search for 'eomma-pyo yeongeo' on one of Korea's online bookstores Yes24 turned up over 90 different book results. In other words, most mothers are interested in teaching English at home. But for many mothers who do not really know how to teach English to their children and who may not know English themselves, this trend can become another burden, with outcomes that could possibly be detrimental to the child's long-term language acquisition.

Choi *et al.* (2019b) investigated the role of mothers in promoting young children's interest in learning English. They looked at the instruction methods of parents who taught their young children English and found that at a minimum, parents strove to provide an English education environment (i.e. reading books, video and English conversation) for their children at home. Using questionnaires, they measured the level of English interaction between mothers and their children. Mothers were asked to report on the frequency of their interaction in English with their child at home. The types of English interactions considered in this study were: (1) reading books together, (2) singing songs together, (3) doing finger-play or chanting together, (4) using internet content together and (5) communicating in English. All items were measured on a four-point Likert scale ('never' to 'frequently'). Results showed that mothers with higher integrative motivation – motivated by a desire to integrate the target language into one's life through its usage – provided more English interaction at home and provided more English private lessons to their child. On the other hand, the hypothesis that a mother's instrumental motivation – motivated by how acquisition of the language might be practical as a skill that can be used for future success – would positively affect the provision of both types of English education was rejected.

This difference can be interpreted to show that second language learners with integrative motivation participate more consistently in learning activities than those with instrumental motivation. As learners with instrumental motivation intend to learn the second language for practical purposes, such as scoring high on examinations or increased job prospects, learning activity does not occur continuously when the goal is achieved or finished, nor does it leak into other parts of the student's life as language might when acquired through an integrative approach.

On the other hand, learners with high integrative motivation who have the desire to understand certain language groups and to converse with diverse people tend to participate in second language learning more constantly. The results of this study (Choi *et al.*, 2019b) also showed that a mother's instrumental motivation did not have a significant effect on the provision of two types of English education. Such a result may be because the children investigated in this study are still very young and have not yet faced practical goals such as academic or career achievements. Meanwhile, according to the findings of this study (Choi *et al.*, 2019), mothers with higher integrative motivation tended to expose their child to English at a young age to increase their child's openness towards English. English interaction at home mediated the relationship between a mother's integrative motivation and her child's interest in learning English. In contrast, English private lessons did not mediate the relationship. English interaction at home is different from English private lessons in a sense that parents who already have intimate ties with the child are the ones providing the educational environment. In addition, interacting in English at home creates a more comfortable and natural learning environment in comparison to the artificial settings often created in classrooms (Choi *et al.*, 2019).

Through this study we see the importance of parents, particularly mothers, when it comes to the attitudes of children towards language acquisition. As parents are so influential, the way they behave towards their children can also influence levels of FLA and FLE in a particular child. While not researched in the above study, it is important that future research investigates the role that a parent's motivation plays in the levels of a child's FLA and FLE.

Apart from motivational factors, the amount of pressure to learn that parents, grandparents and even society as a whole put on children influences the psychosocial wellbeing of these students. As learning English composes part of the expected educational pursuits, this pressure extends to language learning and can influence students' chances of experiencing FLA. Most of the existing research dealing with the stress caused by parental pressure to achieve is focused on Korean adolescents. Yet these effects, which exhibit many symptoms in the adolescent years as the pressure to perform well academically is multiplied, have origins in early childhood as well (Park & Chung, 2007). In the case of Korea, Ahn and Baek (2013) show that the case is more complex than that in many other countries as the entire society is an 'academic achievement-oriented society', and its communal nature therefore tends to place even greater stress on students than one would experience in other cultures where the pressure might mainly come only from family members. Ahn and Baek's chapter is part of a volume entitled *The Psychological Well-being of East Asian Youth* (Yi, 2013). In this book, there is a section dedicated to the psychological effects of families on East Asian youths, as well as another section comprising multiple chapters on the psychological effects of education on these same youths. Stress is rampant across the youth of East Asia, and according to Ahn and Baek, 'Even though there is growing concern of the detrimental effect of academic stress on Korean youth, it is hard to deny that there still is a widespread tendency to believe that academic stress is an inevitable part of adolescent life' (Ahn & Baek,

2013: 266). This sense of inevitability is what should be addressed by policymakers in order to ensure that children's psychosocial wellbeing is better protected within the educational sector.

Baran-Łucarz (2013) proposes that perfectionism, often imposed by societal pressures, can affect the levels of FLA experienced by a student. She further surmises that just as there is a point to which anxiety is motivational in the classroom, there is a point up to which perfectionism is healthy and motivational. Past this point, however, perfectionism can be detrimental and lead to higher levels of FLA for the student (Baran-Łucarz, 2013). A study of the mental health effects of parental pressure and academic stress among Indian high school students (Deb *et al.*, 2015) showed that this anxiety-inducing parental pressure was more likely to be felt by students whose fathers had lower levels of education, thus implying that socioeconomic factors are also at play with levels of parental pressure in academics.

The above studies are but a miniscule portion of the research that has shown the significance of parental interaction in children's academics. The motivations and methods of parental pressure can lead to various outcomes both positive and negative depending on a parent's degree and methods of involvement in facilitating their child's education. With reference to language in general, this pressure can result in foreign language anxiety, among other effects on their mental health and wellbeing.

5.4 Conclusion

In this section, we have explored various factors that can exacerbate a child's FLA. While not comprehensive, the belief in various linguistic myths, ignorance of cross-cultural differences in student/teaching methodologies and mentalities and the influence of parents are some of the main factors that teachers, especially those from a different culture than that of their students, should keep in mind as they plan and execute lessons. These factors are also important to bring to the attention of policymakers who are determining education policies and English language teaching methodologies.

6 Case Study: Factors Affecting Young Children's FLA: Kindergarten vs. English Immersion Institution

In this chapter, we examine the various factors that contribute towards young children's Foreign Language Anxiety (FLA) through a case study involving children aged 3–5 years old. We conducted a comparative study – the first of its kind on this scale – which began by investigating whether there is any significant difference between the profiles of children enrolled in regular kindergartens and those enrolled in English immersion institutions. Similarly, we considered the family background of these children enrolled in each institution. We further explore whether children enrolled in one institution are more prone to FLA over children enrolled in the other. We close this chapter by assessing the most significant characteristics of the children's profiles and, correspondingly, their family's backgrounds. We discuss how these factors influence the level of FLA among the children, aiming to show how parents and teachers can help children develop a more positive attitude towards learning foreign languages.

6.1 Method

6.1.1 Participants

In order to examine the variables affecting children's FLA, questionnaires were administered to mothers and teachers of children aged 3, 4 and 5 years old enrolled in kindergartens or English immersion institutions. A total of 453 mothers and 47 English teachers participated in the study from 14 different institutions located in the cities of Seoul, Gwangju, and Busan, as well as in the Gyeonggi and Gyeongnam provinces of South Korea. Within the kindergarten setting, it was the English teachers who responded to the questionnaire, while in the case of the English immersion institutions, it was the homeroom

Table 6.1 Descriptive statistics of children

		Regular kindergarten n (%)	English immersion institution n (%)
Gender	Male	103 (47.5)	105 (44.7)
	Female	114 (52.5)	128 (54.0)
	No response	0 (0.0)	3 (1.3)
Age	3-year-old	74 (34.1)	59 (24.9)
	4-year-old	67 (30.9)	78 (32.9)
	5-year-old	76 (35.0)	98 (41.8)
	No response	0 (0.0)	1 (0.4)
Total		217 (100.0)	236 (100.0)

teachers who completed the questionnaire. The descriptive statistics of the participating children's gender and age are provided in Table 6.1 above.

6.1.2 Questionnaire content

6.1.2.1 Child variables

We collected some demographic data about the pupils. Firstly, each child's sex and age were measured through the mother's self-report questionnaire. Age was reported in months. Additionally, we enquired about Korean and English language ability, which were reported by mothers through the questionnaires. Mothers were asked to evaluate their child's listening, speaking, reading, writing, vocabulary, grammar, and pronunciation in both the English and Korean languages. All items were measured using a 5-point Likert scale, ranging from 1 = 'Very poor' to 5 = 'Excellent' as listed in Figure 6.1. The mean value of the seven subcategories was used as the final score for each language.

The temperament of each child was also assessed. Specifically, we enquired about the variables of impulsiveness and anticipatory worry. We employed Park's (2007) temperament scale, which was devised based on modified versions of the scales of previous studies (Goth *et al.*, 2003;

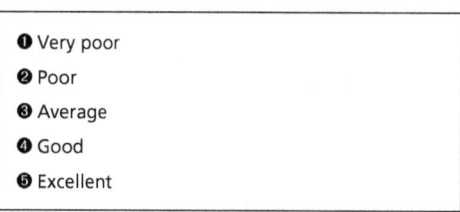

Figure 6.1 Likert scale used for evaluating English and Korean language proficiency

> ❶ Has difficulty waiting for something to end or start.
> ❷ Lacks patience.
> ❸ Easily loses interest in games or toys.
> ❹ Has difficulty sitting still compared to other children.
> ❺ Distracts easily. (Has difficulty sitting still to complete one task)

Figure 6.2 The five impulsiveness scale items

Oh & Min, 2007). Children with high scores of impulsiveness show dramatic emotional changes and tend to make hasty decisions without much thought. They are also prone to be distracted easily, having difficulty in concentration. The impulsiveness scale consists of five items (Figure 6.2), each assessed with a 4-point Likert scale.

Children with high scores for anticipatory worry tend to make pessimistic judgement about what will happen and often anticipate failures. They also have difficulty overcoming embarrassing situations. The anticipatory worry scale consists of four items listed in Figure 6.3

These items were also assessed with a 4-point Likert scale based on the mother's self-reporting. Cronbach's alpha for the temperament scale in the kindergarten questionnaire data was 0.87 for impulsiveness and 0.84 for anticipatory worry, suggesting that the reliability of the scale was satisfactory. In the English immersion institution questionnaire data, Cronbach's alpha coefficient was 0.77 for impulsiveness and 0.73 for anticipatory, also suggesting the reliability of the scale to be satisfactory.

6.1.2.2 Family variables

The educational attainment of pupils' parents was self-reported by mothers from the following selections:

(i) less than middle school;
(ii) high school;
(iii) bachelors;
(iv) masters;
(v) PhD.

> ❶ Frightens easily.
> ❷ Imagines things to be worse than they are.
> ❸ Scares easily.
> ❹ Tends to be pessimistic.

Figure 6.3 The four items of the anticipatory worry scale

Monthly household income was also self-reported as part of the parent questionnaire. Monthly household income was considered the combined incomes of all family members and was classified using the following scale:

  (i) less than $2000;
 (ii) approximately $2000;
(iii) approximately $3000;
 (iv) approximately $4000;
  (v) approximately $5000;
 (vi) approximately $6000;
(vii) approximately $7000; or
(viii) more than $8000.

Parents' English language ability was also considered. English ability was categorized into eight levels according to TEPS (Test of English Proficiency, developed by Seoul National University) standards. In addition, as the items were reverse coded during analysis, a higher score identified a higher level of parent's English language ability:

  (i) Native Level of English Proficiency
      a. Close to that of an educated native speaker. Able to perform technical tasks required in a specialized field
 (ii) Near-Native Level of English Proficiency
      a. Able to perform technical tasks required in a specialized field after short-term intensive training
(iii) Advanced Level of English Proficiency
      a. Able to perform general tasks in English after short-term intensive training
 (iv) High Intermediate Level of English Proficiency
      a. Able to perform general tasks in English after mid- to long-term intensive training
  (v) Mid-Intermediate Level of English Proficiency
      a. Able to perform some general tasks in English after mid- to long-term intensive training
 (vi) Low Intermediate Level of English Proficiency
      a. Able to perform some general tasks in English after mid- to long-term intensive training
(vii) Novice Level of English Proficiency
      a. Able to perform limited tasks in English after long-term intensive training
(viii) Near-Zero Level of English Proficiency
      a. Has very limited proficiency in English

Additionally, information about parents' residential experience in English-speaking countries was collected through mother's self-reporting.

Responses with less than a month in English-speaking countries for travelling purposes only were excluded.

6.1.2.3 Institution variables

We collected information about the teaching environment in both institutions, including the duration of English exposure per week, student-teacher ratio, teacher language use and children's language policies. All institution-related variables were reported by English teachers in both institutions. Duration of English exposure per week was determined to be the total amount of time children were exposed to English per week as calculated in minutes. For kindergartens, the duration of one English class was multiplied by the number of English classes per week, while for English immersion institutions, the duration of one English class was multiplied by the number of classes taught in English per day, then also multiplied by five for each school day per week. To determine student-teacher ratio, the number of students per one teaching staff member was investigated. For example, if two teachers taught 12 children, the student-teacher ratio was coded as 6. Through the survey questions, we measured how immersive each of the institutions is with respect to the amount of English language to which the children are exposed. We considered not only classes scheduled to teach English language specifically, but also classes that use English as the main language for teaching and communication. Specifically, teachers were asked to select from the following options their language distribution during a typical class:

(i) 100% English;
(ii) 80% English, 20% Korean;
(iii) 50% English, 50% Korean;
(iv) 80% Korean, 20% English.

Lastly, we inspected the class rules that were pertinent to children's language use during English classes. Teachers were asked to specify which class rule most closely resembled their classroom policies:

(i) mandatory English use, with students being disciplined if Korean language was used;
(ii) recommended English use, with students not disciplined if Korean language was used;
(iii) free use of Korean during classes.

6.1.2.4 Children's FLA

A modified version of scales (Choi *et al.*, 2019b) based on past literature (Brown, 2000; Horwitz *et al.*, 1986; Hwang & Choi, 2017; Kim & Kim, 2012; Na & Rhee, 2017) was used to assess the children's FLA.

In order to account for children's FLA behaviours at home and within classroom settings, mothers evaluated 4 items and teachers evaluated 5 items. These items are listed in the box below. All items were evaluated with a 4-point Likert scale. Cronbach's alpha coefficient calculated was 0.77 within the kindergarten setting, and 0.75 within the English immersion institution setting, both suggesting the reliability of the scale to be satisfactory.

Items Measured by Mother
 (i) Says 'I am bad at English' or 'I am the only one who is bad at English'.
 (ii) Pretends to be sick before English class (e.g. says 'I don't feel good today').
 (iii) Seems worried about not doing well in English class (e.g. says 'I am afraid that I won't do well in English class').
 (iv) Seems nervous that he/she may not do well in English class (e.g. says 'I feel like my heart is racing during class').

Items Measured by Teacher
 (i) Sighs frequently during class.
 (ii) Repeatedly touches a specific body part (face, hair, hand, lips, etc.) as indicating signs of nervousness.
 (iii) Avoids eye contact with the teacher when asked a question or when needed to speak in English.
 (iv) Shows a lack of confidence and says 'I can't do it' when given a task.
 (v) Frequently asks to use the restroom or says that he/she is thirsty as showing signs of nervousness.

6.1.3 Statistical analysis

We performed descriptive statistics to analyse the mean value, standard deviation, skewness and kurtosis of the variables. Statistical tests such as the t-test and chi-square tests were also conducted to observe whether variables had significant differences between the children attending the two institutions (i.e. children attending kindergartens versus those attending English immersion institutions). The data was tested for normal distribution by calculating skewness and kurtosis coefficients. The coefficients were all between 3 and 10 respectively to meet the requirement for the normal distribution (Kline, 2005). We conducted correlation analysis to investigate the relationship between the child and family variables and the child's FLA. Furthermore, multiple regression analysis was performed to determine the effects of the child and family variables on the child's FLA.

6.2 Results

6.2.1 Summary of descriptive statistics of variables

6.2.1.1 Kindergarten

Table 6.2 Descriptive statistics of children attending kindergarten

	Variables	Mean	SD	Skewness	Kurtosis
Child variables	Sex	Boys: 103 (47.5%) Girls: 114 (53.5%)			
	Age in months	63.68	10.36	–0.02	–1.21
	Korean language ability	3.50	0.77	–0.22	–0.06
	English language ability	2.16	0.80	0.16	–0.96
	Impulsiveness	2.07	0.64	0.41	–0.11
	Anticipatory worry	1.98	0.59	0.35	–0.12
Family variables	Father's educational attainment	Two- or three-year college degree or lower: 80 (36.9%) Four-year college degree or higher: 122 (56.2%) No Response: 15 (6.9%)			
	Mother's educational attainment	Two- or three-year college degree or lower: 104 (47.9%) Four-year college degree or higher: 111 (51.2%) No response: 2 (0.9%)			
	Monthly household income	5.41	2.00	–0.07	–1.27
	Father's English language ability	3.60	1.92	0.51	–0.48
	Mother's English language ability	3.07	1.64	0.76	0.03
	Father's residential experience in English-speaking country	Yes: 26 (12.0%) No: 187 (86.2%) No response: 4 (1.8%)			
	Mother's residential experience in English-speaking country	Yes: 24 (11.1%) No: 193 (88.9%)			
Institution variables	Duration of English exposure per week (minutes)	97.99	34.35	–.03	–1.62
	Ratio of children per teacher	22.39	5.03	.07	–1.25
	Language used by teachers	100% English: 0 (0.0%) 80% English, 20% Korean: 138 (63.6%) 50% English, 50% Korean: 46 (21.1%) 80% Korean, 20% English: 0 (0.0%) No response: 33 (14.2%)			
	Language policy for children	Mandatory English use: 0 (0.00%) Recommendatory English use: 152 (70.0%) Free Korean use: 32 (14.7%) No response: 33 (15.2%)			
Dependent variable	Child's FLA	1.58	0.43	0.72	0.22

6.2.1.2 English immersion institution

Table 6.3 Descriptive statistics of children attending English immersion institution

	Variables	Mean	SD	Skewness	Kurtosis
Child variables	Sex	Boys: 105 (44.5%) Girls: 128 (54.2%) No response: 3 (1.3%)			
	Age in months	65.29	10.75	−0.28	−1.05
	Korean language ability	3.72	0.65	−0.23	−0.30
	English language ability	2.98	0.85	−0.09	−0.48
	Impulsiveness	1.94	0.54	0.22	0.08
	Anticipatory worry	2.04	0.55	0.32	−0.16
Family variables	Father's educational attainment	Two- or three-year college degree or lower: 28 (11.9%) Four-year college degree or higher: 201 (85.2%) No response: 7 (2.9%)			
	Mother's educational attainment	Two- or three-year college degree or lower: 41 (17.4%) Four-year college degree or higher: 192 (81.4%) No response: 3 (1.2%)			
	Monthly household income	7.06	1.45	−1.60	2.02
	Father's English language ability	4.54	1.87	0.16	−0.87
	Mother's English language ability	3.78	1.70	0.30	−0.64
	Father's residential experience in English-speaking country	Yes: 51 (21.6%) No: 182 (77.1%) No response: 3 (1.3%)			
	Mother's residential experience in English-speaking country	Yes: 58 (24.6%) No: 176 (74.6%) No response: 2 (0.8%)			
Institution variables	Duration of English exposure per week (minutes)	784.32	233.55	.27	−.50
	Ratio of children per teacher	6.37	2.48	.24	−.63
	Language used by teachers	100% English: 91 (38.6%) 80% English, 20% Korean: 134 (56.8%) 50% English, 50% Korean: 11 (4.7%) 80% Korean, 20% English: 0 (0.0%)			
	Language policy for children	Mandatory English use: 115 (48.7%) Recommendatory English use: 117 (49.7%) Free Korean use: 4 (1.7%)			
Dependent variable	Child's FLA	1.67	0.46	0.56	−0.26

6.2.2 Comparing variables

6.2.2.1 Comparing child variables

T-tests and chi-square tests were conducted to investigate whether the children's sex, age in months, Korean language ability, English language ability, impulsiveness and anticipatory worry differ significantly

Table 6.4 Comparison of child variables between the kindergarten and English immersion institution

Variable		Number of subjects (%)/Mean ± SD		t/x²	N = 453	
		Kindergarten	English immersion institution		p	Cohen's d
Sex	Boys	103 (47.5)	105 (45.06)	0.26	0.610	
	Girls	114 (52.5)	128 (54.94)			
Age		63.68 ± 10.36	65.29 ± 10.75	−1.62	0.107	0.419
Korean language ability		3.50 ± 0.77	3.72 ± 0.65	−3.26	0.001	0.309
English language ability		2.16 ± 0.79	2.98 ± 0.85	−10.39	0.000	0.999
Impulsiveness		2.07 ± 0.64	1.94 ± 0.54	2.28	0.023	0.220
Anticipatory worry		1.98 ± 0.59	2.04 ± 0.55	−1.16	0.245	0.105

between the two groups (children attending kindergartens versus those attending English immersion institutions) (Table 6.4). The gender and age in months of the child did not show any significant difference between the two groups. However, children attending English immersion institutions, compared to those attending kindergartens, were evaluated higher for their Korean and English language ability ($t = -3.26$, $p < 0.01$; $t = -10.39$, $p < 0.001$). In addition, the children in kindergartens were rated higher for their impulsiveness than those attending English immersion institutions ($t = 2.28$, $p < 0.05$). Meanwhile, there was no significant difference in the children's anticipatory worry score between the two groups. Figure 6.4 depicts the mean scores of child variables between regular kindergartens and English immersion institutions.

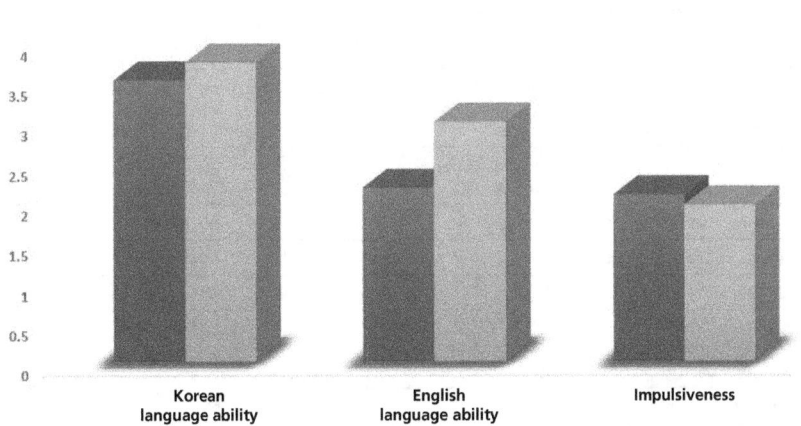

Figure 6.4 Child variables by institution

6.2.2.2 Comparing family variables

A series of t-tests and Chi-square tests were also performed to investigate whether the parents' educational attainment, monthly household income, parents' English language ability and parents' residential experience in English speaking-countries differed between the two groups (Table 6.5). All variables were shown to be significantly different between the two groups. A greater number of parents sending their children to English immersion institutions had a 4-year college degree or higher ($x^2 = 42.84$, $p < 0.001$; $x^2 = 48.38$, $p < 0.001$), earned higher monthly household income ($t = -9.78$, $p < 0.001$), reported higher English language ability ($t = -5.15$, $p < 0.001$; $t = -4.49$, $p < 0.001$) and were more likely to have residential experience in English speaking-countries ($x^2 = 7.30$, $p < 0.001$; $x^2 = 14.26$, $p < 0.001$) than parents sending their children to kindergartens. Overall, children attending English immersion institutions were from higher SES families, had parents with higher English language ability and had more experience residing in English-speaking countries than those attending kindergartens Figure 6.5 compares family variables between regular kindergartens and English immersion institutions. Figure 6.6 shows family incomes and English levels by institution, and Figure 6.7 shows family experience of residing in English-speaking countries by institution.

Table 6.5 Comparison of family variables between the kindergarten and English immersion institution

Variable		Number of subjects (%)/ Mean ± SD		t/x^2	p
		Kindergarten	English immersion Institution		
Father's educational attainment	Two- or three-year college degree or lower	80 (39.6)	28 (12.2)	42.84	0.000
	Four-year college degree or higher	122 (60.4)	201 (87.8)		
Mother's educational attainment	Two- or three-year college degree or lower	104 (48.4)	41 (17.6)	48.38	0.000
	Four-year college degree or higher	111 (51.6)	192 (82.4)		
Monthly household income		5.41 ± 2.00	7.06 ± 1.45	−9.78	0.000
Father's English language ability		3.60 ± 1.92	4.54 ± 1.87	−5.15	0.000
Mother's English language ability		3.07 ± 1.64	3.78 ± 1.70	−4.49	0.000
Father's residential experience in English-speaking country	Yes	26 (12.2)	51 (21.9)	7.30	0.007
	No	187 (87.8)	182 (78.1)		
Mother's residential experience in English-speaking country	Yes	24 (11.1)	58 (24.8)	14.26	0.000
	No	193 (88.9)	176 (75.2)		

Case Study: Factors Affecting Young Children's FLA 73

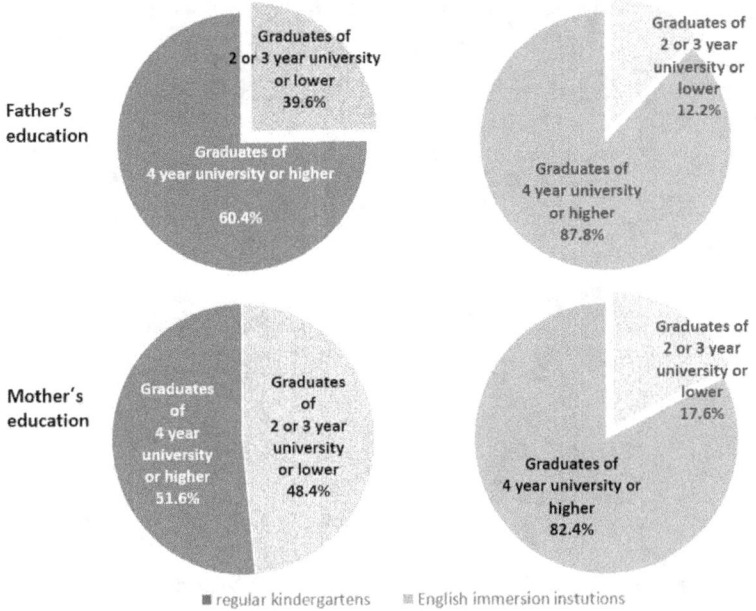

Figure 6.5 Family education level by institution

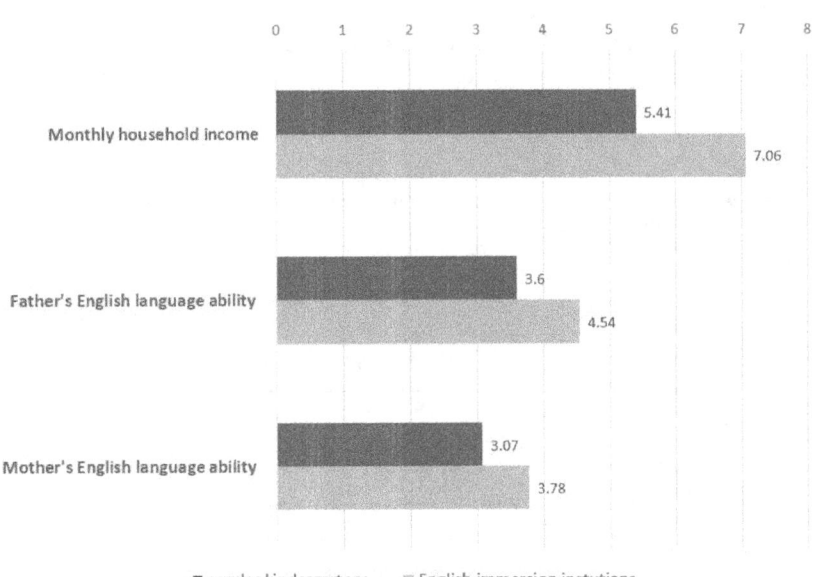

Figure 6.6 Family income and English ability by institution

74 Young Children's Foreign Language Anxiety

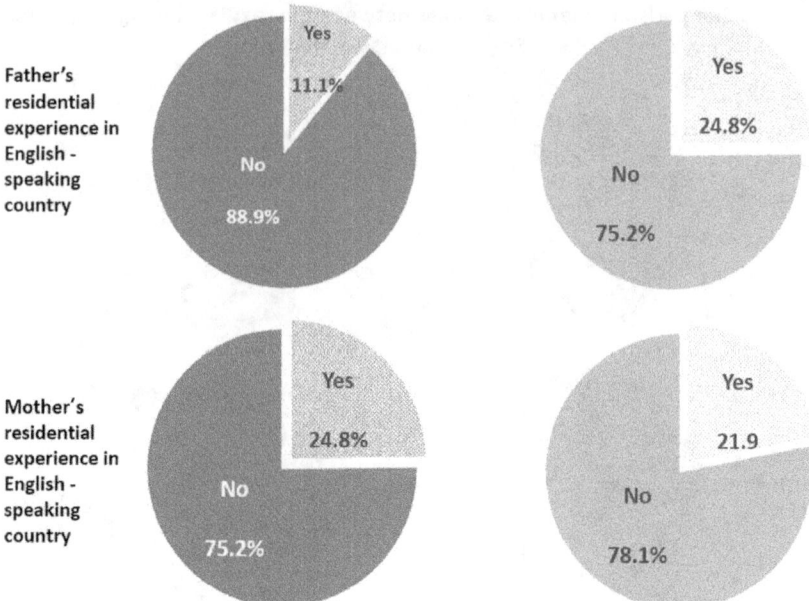

Figure 6.7 Family experience in English-speaking countries by institution

6.2.2.3 Comparing institutional variables

A series of t-tests and chi-square tests were conducted to investigate whether duration of English exposure per week, student-teacher ratio, language used by teachers, and language policy for children differed between the two groups (Table 6.6). All variables were shown to be significantly different between the two groups.

Table 6.6 Comparison of institutional variables between the kindergarten and English immersion institution

Variable		Number of subjects (%) / Mean ± SD		t/x^2	p
		Kindergarten	English immersion institution		
Duration of English exposure per week		97.99 ± 34.35	784.32 ± 233.55	−44.53	0.000
Student-teacher ratio		22.39 ± 5.03	6.37 ± 2.48	36.88	0.000
Language used by teachers	English 100%	0 (0.0)	91 (38.6)	107.76	0.000
	English 80%	138 (63.6)	134 (56.8)		
	English 50%	46 (21.1)	11 (4.7)		
Language policy for children	Mandatory English use	0 (0.0)	115 (48.7)	136.99	0.000
	Recommendatory English use	152 (70.0)	117 (49.7)		
	Free Korean use	32 (14.7)	4 (1.7)		

Table 6.7 Comparison of English education hours

Hours of English education received by children attending kindergartens and children attending English Immersion Institutions

	Hours of English Education
Kindergartens	3.42 English classes per week (28.42 mins per class)
English Immersion Institutions	4.37 English classes per week (35.89 mins per class)

First, the results showed that those children attending English immersion institutions were exposed to a higher amount of English instruction per week ($t = -44.53$, $p < 0.001$). When scrutinizing children's exposed time to English (Table 6.7), children attending kindergartens received an average of 3.42 (SD = 0.7) English classes per week and an average of 28.42 minutes (SD = 8.25) per class. The minimum value of English language exposure was 3 classes per week and 20 minutes per class, while the maximum value of English language exposure was 5 classes per week and 40 minutes per class. As for those children attending English immersion institutions, they received, on average, 4.37 classes (SD = 1.34) taught mainly in English per day and each class was an average of 35.89 minutes (SD = 4.87) in length. The minimum value of English exposure was 2 classes per day and 30 minutes per class, while the maximum value was 8 classes per day and 40 minutes per class.

The student-teacher ratio was found to be much lower in English immersion institutions than kindergartens ($t = 36.88$, $p < 0.001$). For kindergartens, the average number of children taught per teacher was 22.39 (SD = 5.03), with a minimum number of 15 students to a teacher and a maximum number of 30 students to a teacher. As for English immersion institutions, the average number of children taught per class was 6.37 (SD = 2.48), with a minimum number of 5 students to one teacher and a maximum number of 14 students to one teacher (Figure 6.8).

Regarding language used by teachers, teachers of English immersion institution used more English than those of regular kindergartens during English class ($x^2 = 107.76$, $p < 0.001$). A majority of regular kindergarten teachers (138 individuals, 63.6%) said that they used

Figure 6.8 Student-teacher ratio by institution type

80% English and 20% Korean during English classes. A further 46 individuals (21.2%) said they used 50% English and 50% Korean during class. In contrast, 91 teachers (38.6%) in English immersion institutions reported that they used 100% English in class. However, much like kindergarten teachers, a majority (134 teachers, 56.8%) said they used 80% English and 20% Korean. The remaining 11 teachers (4.7%) said they used 50% English and 50% Korean.

Also, it was found that children attending English immersion institution were recommended to use English more than those in kindergarten (x^2 = 136.99, p < 0.001). In the case of regular kindergartens, a large majority (152 teachers, 70.0%) said that, although pupils' English use was recommended, Korean use was not punished. A further 32 teachers (14.7%) said that students were free to use Korean during class. No regular kindergarten teachers reported that English was mandatory and students were disciplined for using Korean. In contrast, in the case of English immersion institutions, 115 teachers (48.7%) reported that compulsory English use was enforced. A slightly greater number (117 teachers, 49.6%) said that English use was recommended but students were not disciplined for using Korean. Only 4 teachers (1.7%) responded that students were free to use Korean during class. These results indicate that, overall, regular kindergartens were more permissive toward Korean language use when compared to English immersion institutions. Figures 6.9 and 6.10 represent the amount of language that teachers use during English class and the class policies for children's language use during English class.

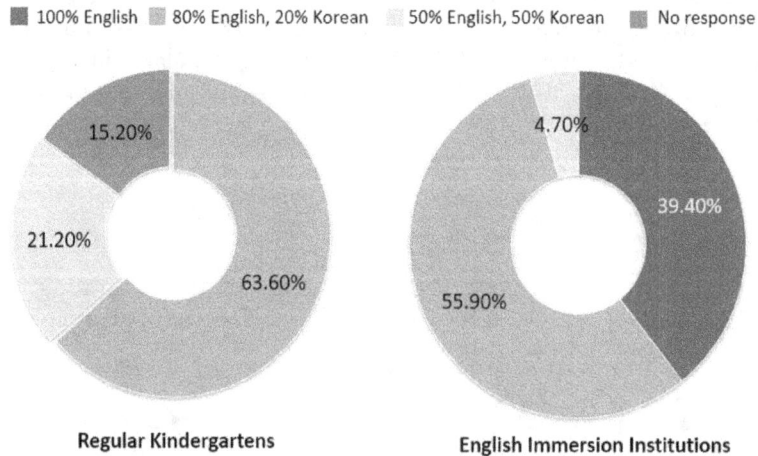

Figure 6.9 Language use by institution type

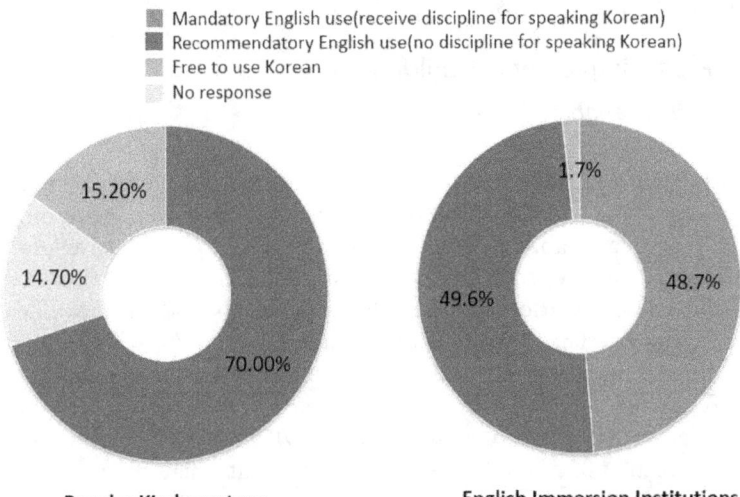

Figure 6.10 Language rule by institution type

6.2.2.4 Comparing children's FLA

The difference in the children's FLA score based on the type of institutions attended, namely, English immersion institutions versus regular kindergartens, was also investigated. The average score of the children's FLA differed based on the type of institution the children attended ($t = -2.16$, $p = 0.031$). The average English language anxiety score for children enrolled in kindergartens and English immersion institutions was 1.58 ($SD = 0.43$) and 1.67 ($SD = 0.46$) respectively (Figure 6.11). That is, levels of English language anxiety in children

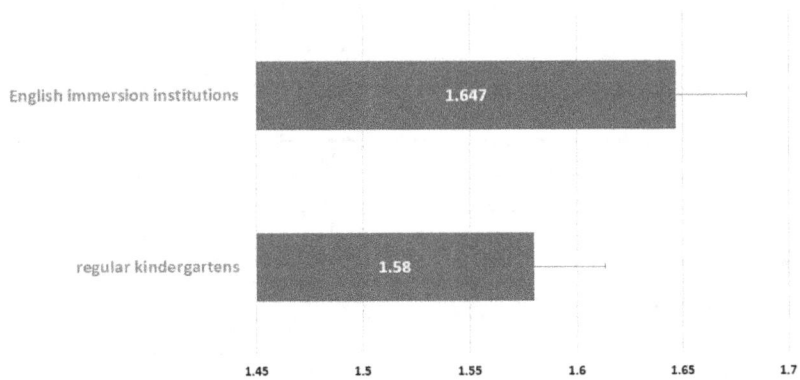

Figure 6.11 FLA by institution type

6.2.3 Predicting factors of children's FLA

6.2.3.1 Child variables

(1) Regular kindergarten

Multiple regression analysis was conducted on children attending regular kindergartens in order to investigate whether sex, age in months, Korean language ability, English language ability, impulsiveness and anticipatory worry significantly predicted their FLA. Prior to the analysis, the correlation between the error terms and multicollinearity were examined. The Durbin-Watson statistic was 1.70, which was close to 2, indicating that there was no correlation between the error terms. The Tolerance and Variance Inflation Factor (VIF) was also considered. The tolerance computed was between 0.707 and 0.947 and the VIF was between 1.056 and 1.414, indicating that there were no major multicollinearity issues.

According to the multiple regression analysis, children's sex, age in months, Korean language ability, English language ability and anticipatory worry were not significant predictors of children's English language anxiety (Table 6.8). Meanwhile, the children's impulsiveness ($\beta = 0.16$, $p < 0.05$) significantly predicted the children's FLA. The result implies that children with a higher level of impulsiveness were more likely to experience a higher level of anxiety in English learning in the kindergarten context.

(2) English immersion institutions

Similarly, multiple regression analysis was conducted on children attending English immersion institutions in order to investigate whether sex, age in months, Korean language ability, English language ability, impulsiveness and anticipatory worry significantly predicted their FLA. Again, prior to the analysis, the correlation between the error terms and

Table 6.8 The predictors (child variables) of children's FLA (kindergarten)

Variables	B	SE	β	p
Intercept	1.62	0.28		0.000
Gender	−0.03	0.06	−0.03	0.690
Age in months	0.00	0.00	0.01	0.897
Korean language ability	−0.06	0.05	−0.11	0.194
English language ability	−0.08	0.04	−0.14	0.060
Impulsiveness	0.11	0.05	0.16	0.038
Anticipatory worry	0.08	0.06	0.10	0.169
$R^2 = 0.120$, F = 4.215, $p = 0.001$				

Table 6.9 The predictors (child variables) of children's FLA (English immersion institution)

Variables	B	SE	β	p
Intercept	1.28	0.29		0.000
Gender	0.02	0.06	0.02	0.704
Age in months	0.01	0.00	0.24	0.000
Korean language ability	−0.09	0.05	−0.14	0.043
English language ability	−0.13	0.04	−0.25	0.000
Impulsiveness	0.14	0.05	0.17	0.009
Anticipatory worry	0.06	0.05	0.08	0.216
$R^2 = 0.194$, F = 8.394, p = 0.000				

multicollinearity were examined. The Durbin-Watson statistic in this case was 1.62, which was close to 2, once again, indicating that there was no correlation between the error terms. The Tolerance and Variance Inflation Factor (VIF) was between 0.835 and 0.966, and 1.035 and 1.198, indicating no major multicollinearity issues.

Table 6.9 shows the results of the multiple regression analysis. The children's sex and anticipatory worry did not significantly predict the children's English language anxiety. Meanwhile, children's age in months ($\beta = 0.24$, $p < 0.001$), Korean language ability ($\beta = -0.14$, $p < 0.05$), English language ability ($\beta = -0.25$, $p < 0.001$), and impulsiveness ($\beta = 0.17$, $p < 0.01$) significantly predicted the children's FLA. The result implies that if children's age in months and impulsiveness are higher, and their Korean and English language ability is lower in comparison with that of their peers, the children's anxiety in English learning increases.

6.2.3.2 Family variables
(1) Regular kindergartens

Multiple regression analysis was conducted on children attending kindergartens to investigate whether the parents' educational attainment, monthly household income, parents' English language ability, and parents' residential experience in English-speaking countries significantly predicted their children's FLA. Prior to the analysis, the correlation between the error terms and multicollinearity were examined. The Durbin-Watson statistic was 1.84, which was close to 2, indicating that there was no correlation between the error terms. The tolerance and Variance Inflation Factor (VIF) was between 0.478 and 0.829, and 1.207 and 2.094, indicating no multicollinearity issue. The results (Table 6.10) showed that the parents' educational attainment, monthly household income, parents' English language ability, and parents' residential experience in English-speaking countries do not significantly predict the FLA of children attending kindergartens.

Table 6.10 The predictors (family variables) of children's FLA (kindergarten)

Variables	B	SE	β	p
Intercept	1.31	0.28		0.000
Father's educational attainment	−0.07	0.09	−0.09	0.388
Mother's educational attainment	−0.01	0.08	−0.02	0.870
Monthly household income	0.03	0.02	0.14	0.103
Father's English language ability	0.02	0.02	0.08	0.449
Mother's English language ability	−0.00	0.03	−0.02	0.882
Father's residential experience in English-speaking country	−0.07	0.11	−0.06	0.505
Mother's residential experience in English speaking country	0.15	0.12	0.11	0.209
$R^2 = 0.033$, F = 0.844, p = 0.552				

(2) English immersion institutions

Similarly, multiple regression analysis was also conducted on children attending English immersion institutions to investigate whether the parents' educational attainment, monthly household income, parents' English language ability and parents' residential experience in English-speaking countries significantly predicted their children's FLA. Again, prior to the analysis, the correlation between the error terms and multicollinearity were examined. The Durbin-Watson statistic was 1.84, which was close to 2, indicating that there was no correlation between the error terms. The tolerance and Variance Inflation Factor (VIF) was between 0.478 and 0.829, and 1.207 and 2.094, indicating no multicollinearity issue. The results (Table 6.11) showed that the parents' educational attainment, monthly household income, parents' English language ability and parents' residential

Table 6.11 The predictors (child variables) of children's FLA (English immersion institution)

Variables	B	SE	β	p
Intercept	1.31	0.28		0.000
Father's education level	−0.07	0.09	−0.09	0.388
Mother's education level	−0.01	0.08	−0.02	0.870
Family monthly income	0.03	0.02	0.14	0.103
Father's English language ability	0.02	0.02	0.08	0.449
Mother's English language ability	−0.00	0.03	−0.02	0.882
Father's residential experience in English language speaking country	−0.08	0.11	−0.06	0.505
Mother's residential experience in English language speaking country	0.15	0.12	0.11	0.209
$R^2 = 0.033$, F = 0.844, p = 0.552				

experience in English-speaking countries do not significantly predict the FLA of children attending the English immersion institution.

6.2.3.3 Institution variables

(1) Regular kindergarten

Multiple regression analysis was conducted on children attending kindergartens to investigate whether duration of English exposure per week, student-teacher ratio, language used by teachers and language policy of children affected children's FLA. The correlation between the error terms and multicollinearity issue were examined. The Durbin-Watson statistic was 1.96, which was close to 2, confirming that there was no correlation between the error terms. The tolerance and Variance Inflation Factor (VIF) was between 0.156 and 0.392, and 2.553 and 6.394, indicating no multicollinearity issue.

The results (Table 6.12) showed that duration of English exposure per week and language policy of children ($\beta = 0.56$, $p < 0.01$) significantly predicted children's FLA. In other words, the longer the duration of exposure to English classes per week, the higher the FLA of children learning English. Also, children in classrooms where speaking English during class is recommended showed higher levels of FLA than those who could freely use Korean during English class ($\beta = -0.24$, $p < 0.05$).

(2) English immersion institution

Multiple regression analysis was conducted on children attending English immersion institutions to investigate whether duration of English exposure per week, student-teacher ratio, language used by teachers and language policy of children affected children's FLA. The correlation between the error terms and multicollinearity issue were also examined. The Durbin-Watson statistic was 1.73, which was close to 2, confirming that there was no correlation between the error terms. The tolerance and Variance Inflation Factor (VIF) was between 0.674 and 0.901 and 1.110 and 1.458, indicating no multicollinearity issue.

The results (Table 6.13) showed that duration of English exposure per week, student-teacher ratio, language used by teachers, and language policy did not significantly predict children's FLA.

Table 6.12 The predictors (institution variables) of children's FLA (kindergarten)

Variables	B	SE	β	p
Intercept	1.59	0.33		0.000
Duration of English exposure per week	0.01	0.00	0.56	0.002
Student-teacher ratio	0.01	0.01	0.11	0.374
Language used by teachers	−0.16	0.17	−0.17	0.342
Language policy of children	−0.25	0.12	−0.24	0.038
$R^2 = 0.157$, $F = 7.741$, $p = 0.000$				

Table 6.13 The predictors (institution variables) of children's FLA (English immersion institution)

Variables	B	SE	β	p
Intercept	2.03	0.24		0.000
Duration of English exposure per week	0.00	0.00	−0.14	0.068
Student-teacher ratio	0.01	0.01	0.08	0.288
Language used by teachers	−0.07	0.06	−0.08	0.236
Language policy of children	−0.09	0.07	−0.10	0.201

$R^2 = 0.040$, $F = 2.312$, $p = 0.059$

6.3 Discussion

We examined whether the child variables (sex, age in months, Korean language ability, English language ability, impulsiveness, anticipatory worry), family variables (parents' educational attainment, monthly household income, parents' English language ability, parents' residential experience in English-speaking countries) and institutional variables (duration of English exposure per week, student-teacher ratio, language used by teachers, language policy of children) differ significantly between children attending kindergartens and those attending English immersion institutions. We also investigated whether each variable has a significant effect on the children's FLA.

We first explored whether child variables (sex, age in months, Korean language ability, English language ability, impulsiveness, anticipatory worry) differed significantly between the two groups (children attending kindergartens versus those attending English immersion institutions), and found that Korean and English language abilities of children attending English immersion institutions were evaluated to be higher compared to those in kindergartens. Meanwhile, children attending kindergartens were rated higher for their impulsiveness than those attending English immersion institutions. Among child variables, there was no significant difference in the children's sex, age in month and anticipatory worry.

We next examined whether family variables (parent's educational attainment, monthly household income, parents' English language ability, parents' residential experience in English-speaking country) differed significantly between the two groups. We found that there were significant differences in all variables; parents sending their children to English immersion institutions had higher educational attainment, monthly household income, English language ability and more experience of living in English-speaking countries than parents sending their children to kindergartens. It was clearly shown that parents with higher SES tended to choose English immersion institutions over kindergartens.

We also investigated whether institutional variables (duration of English education per week, student-teacher ratio, language used by teachers, language policy for children) differed between the two groups. Children attending English immersion institution were exposed to a higher amount of English instruction and classrooms had lower student-teacher ratios compared to children in regular kindergartens. In addition, teachers at English immersion institutions used more English on average during English classes, while regular kindergartens were more permissive toward children's Korean language use than English immersion institution.

Importantly, we found that there was a significant difference in the levels of FLA between children attending regular kindergartens and those attending English immersion institutions. That is, children in English immersion institutions felt a higher level of FLA than those attending kindergartens. English immersion institutions carried out most interactions in English and children from immersion institutions were encouraged to use English more than Korean compared to children at regular kindergartens. Some institutions even disciplined young learners when they used Korean. This environment may have raised FLA among children who use Korean as their first language outside of the institution. These results made us to look more closely at factors that would have affected their FLA.

First, we examined the effects of child variables on children's FLA. For both kindergartens and English immersion institutions, heightened levels of impulsiveness in children correlated to increased levels of FLA. Impulsiveness can be a disadvantageous temperament in language learning; impulsive children tend to have more difficulties in learning situations because they find it more difficult to control their behaviours (Eisenberg *et al.*, 2009). Impulsive children also have a lower level of language comprehension because they are less likely to focus on the sentences they are hearing (Andreou & Trott, 2013). It can therefore be interpreted that for these children the characteristic of impulsiveness has contributed to increasing their FLA.

However, unlike regular kindergarten students, the FLA of children attending English immersion institutions was also influenced by their age in months, Korean language ability and English language ability. It was observed that children with older age and lower levels of Korean and English language ability tended to have higher FLA. Sheo *et al.* (2019) also showed that the higher the children's age in months, the higher the FLA would be. As children grow up, their cognitive ability develops, and they can evaluate themselves more objectively. Thus, it is presumed that as children grow up, their anxiety towards English learning increases as well (Sheo *et al.*, 2019). Such tendencies were more prominent in English immersion institutions than general kindergartens. Children's Korean and English language abilities were further seen to significantly predict their FLA in the case of English immersion institutions. It is assumed that this is because the level of English language ability expected and demanded from English immersion institutions is much higher than that of general kindergartens. As shown in this study, English immersion institutions often encourage both teachers and children to use English more frequently as the main language for communication and instruction compared to kindergartens.

When the family variables of children were investigated in relation to children's FLA, the results showed that parents' educational attainment, monthly household income, parents' English language ability and parents' residential experience in English-speaking countries do not predict the children's FLA in both kindergartens and English immersion institutions. These results are in stark contrast with a preceding study (Butler, 2014) that reported parents' socioeconomic status could be a crucial variable in learning English as a foreign language. The rationale behind this conclusion was that it requires extensive amounts of resources and money to teach English in an EFL environment that does not use English language daily. We posit that the discrepancy between our study and the one done previously can be explained by the fact that the focus of this study is not on the achievement of English learning but rather on FLA. We further refer to the work done by Sheo et al. (2019), which supports our conclusion by showing that the parents' socioeconomic status did not significantly affect children's FLA. Rather, it was the parents' beliefs about early childhood English education that had significant effects – the more the mother perceived early childhood English education positively, the lower the level of children's FLA. Children of mothers who thought that English education is helpful for cognitive development also tended to show higher FLA (Sheo et al., 2019). Many previous studies (Hwang & Choi, 2017; Choi et al., 2019b) also found that the mother's belief in English education is a significant variable that affects the children's attitude toward learning English. This study investigated the characteristics of the individual and family variables of children attending kindergartens and children attending English immersion institutions. We further examined which variables significantly affected the children's FLA. The variables that were shown to significantly predict children's FLA in regular kindergartens were impulsiveness, duration of English exposure per week, and classroom language policies. The significant predictors of children's FLA in English immersion institutions were impulsiveness, age in months, Korean language ability and English language ability. It is noteworthy that impulsiveness was a predictor of children's FLA in both groups. It is expected that this research can provide the basic data necessary to support children and help them develop a more positive attitude towards learning foreign languages.

Lastly, when institution variables were examined, children attending regular kindergartens felt more FLA as the duration of exposure of English class per week increased. However, such findings should be carefully interpreted and not be compared directly because the duration of exposure of English class per week differed in level between the two types of institutions. In other words, based on our results, it would be difficult to conclude that the long duration of exposure to English per week explains the FLA of children attending English immersion institutions in any way. Also, children whose classroom policies recommended speaking English during English class showed higher levels of FLA compared to those who could freely use Korean during English class in the case of regular kindergartens. In regular kindergartens, despite the lower amount of time children were exposed to English, being in an environment where they could not use their first language appears to have increased their FLA.

In the case of English immersion institutions, institutional variables did not have a significant effect on children's FLA. Based on the results of this study, we can conclude that the levels of FLA in children attending English immersion institutions can be affected by the children's individual characteristics such as impulsiveness, age in months, English ability and Korean ability rather than by family variables or institutional variables.

Though thoroughly vetted and carefully administered, this study still encountered limitations due to its methodology and the subject of its research being young children. In any questionnaire-based study, there will inherently be a self-reporting bias which may affect the results to some degree. However, as preliminary results that lay a foundation for more expansive future research, the study discussed in this chapter is very valuable in showing empirically the effect that parental, and particularly maternal, attitudes about English language and education can have on a child's level of FLA. By carefully comparing the developmental trajectories of children between those attending regular kindergartens and those attending English immersion institutions, we also showed that language-learning context can also affect children's levels of FLA.

7 Effects of Innovative Language Learning on Foreign Language Anxiety and Foreign Language Enjoyment

The perception of an 'English Fever', as discussed in Chapter 4, has produced a culture in South Korea where repetitive memorization of grammar is favoured, rapid improvements in proficiency are demanded and there is an emphasis on passing tests. Young learners encounter strict, rigid teaching methods that are often based on total immersion and 'One Language at a Time (OLAT)', or an 'English-only' policy. Such methods have been heavily criticized by many scholars (Auerbach, 1993; Cook, 1999; Park, 2007). In this book, we have reported various ways in which young children suffer as a result of these methods. Indeed, the zeal for English education has become so extreme that each day, on average, around 100 young Korean students go abroad for their education (Park, 2012). As established in previous chapters, this 'English Fever' culture has produced very high levels of Foreign Language Anxiety (FLA) among young learners. In fact, in the South Korean educational sector, English education stands out as one of the most worrying social phenomena that young Koreans encounter.

Such repetitive and stressful teaching methods may additionally reduce students' Foreign Language Enjoyment (FLE). If we are to reduce FLA and also increase the level of FLE, it is important to consider alternative models of language teaching. While young children are capable of acquiring a second language effectively, methods matter: their attention will be better held if they find an activity fun. In this chapter, we present alternative pedagogical methods that may have the effect of reducing FLA and/or increasing FLE. We first provide a discussion of the effects of FLA and FLE. We then introduce technological language teaching methods and the idea of Task-based Language Teaching (TBLT) with examples from previous studies. From there, we will present a case study by Park *et al.* (2019) about young Korean children's

EFL vocabulary learning through cooking, in which the authors implemented TBLT with Korean kindergarten pupils in the form of a cooking exercise. This case study demonstrates how young learners of English can enjoy learning while also improving their performance. Through our discussion, we hope to raise awareness of the problems with current English teaching methods used in South Korea and other Asian countries which are thought to be experiencing an 'English Fever'.

7.1 Effects of FLA and FLE

Building on past research regarding FLE and FLA, Boudreau *et al.* (2018) took an idiodynamic approach to examining the rapidly changing relationship between enjoyment and anxiety in second language communication on a moment-to-moment timescale. The paper foregrounds beliefs of anxiety as the strongest predictor of success or failure for second language students (MacIntyre, 1999) and how positive emotions, specifically enjoyment, work to 'broaden people's momentary thought action repertoires and build their enduring personal resources' (Fredrickson, 2004: 1369). Subsequently, the research advocates the exploration of a dynamic conceptualization of emotion processes in the context of language learning. The mixed methods approach of the investigation produced dense, individual-level data that could be interpreted with a focus on differences across a group of people or changes within an individual over time.

The results showed that the changing relationship of enjoyment and anxiety impacts the speaker's experience in the context of second language communication in meaningful ways. The trajectory of the two emotions may be convergent, divergent or operating wholly independently of one another unpredictably, therefore reinforcing notions on the effects that the ratio of enjoyment to anxiety has on a foreign language learner and speaker. Limitations to this study exist, such as the artificiality of the setting that was also mentioned in some of the participants' interviews, discrepancies in how the rating software was used by each participant and that the sample consisted solely of native English speakers who speak French as their second language. As noted in the essay, different language learning motivations, including learning a heritage language, may result in a different emotional response during learning and communication tasks – a thought that is to be investigated to a certain degree in this study. While foreign language learning elicits both enjoyment and anxiety, as the literature on the subject has shown, there remains a need for further investigation pertaining to the role of classroom enjoyment in language learning and identifying other sources of FLA in different languages. Research into FLE and FLCA is wide and diverse as shown in Chapters 2 and 3 of this book. However, the existing research, while vibrant, typically focuses on older students in secondary schools or adult education, and while studies of the East Asian context have started coming forth in recent years much more work remains to be done in this region. This chapter, particularly through the case study at the end, hopes to fill some gaps in the research regarding the effectiveness of FLE in the motivation of YLLs' language learning specifically in the Korean context, thus expanding research on FLA and FLE in the East Asian context as well as research involving early childhood education.

7.2 Technological Methods

Young children are increasingly spending 'screen time' with handheld computing devices. At the same time, the number of technological language learning solutions aimed at children has also been rapidly increasing. Nowadays, innovative English education is available through the internet, e.g. blogs, podcasts, digital storytelling, wikis, video calling, Social Networking Services (SNS), QR code scanning and so on (Drury, 2013). Viewing English material through YouTube is a particularly popular language learning method as well (Nunez, 2015). Sundqvist (2009) analysed the effectiveness of extramural English (EE) activities, those that involve engaging with English outside of the classroom including through technology. The study was carried out with secondary school students and showed that more time spent on EE activities correlated positively with levels of oral proficiency and vocabulary. While this study was carried out with older students and not YLLs, it does point at the effectiveness of technological methods when it comes to language learning.

The number of educational smartphone applications (apps) aimed at children has also greatly increased (Dumais, 2016). As children are already so familiar with apps and already use them for play, there is potential for applications to teach foreign languages with high enjoyment and minimal anxiety. An advantage of apps is that they are also able to provide children with instant feedback for active learning. Some recent studies have shown choosing a good educational application and using it properly under parental intervention is known to help children learn languages (Dumais, 2016). For example, the potential for apps to improve early literacy skills and increase school readiness for low-income children has been suggested through empirical study (NYU Steinhardt, 2015). Also, in the context of children's EFL study, the results of Pemba *et al.* (2016) indicate that app usage may improve English accent acquisition among Chinese five-to-six-year-olds. This study compared different methods of instruction by allocating children to one of two groups: one that utilized a pronunciation app with video of native English speakers' speech, and a control group that followed a traditional curriculum taught by non-native speakers of English. The children's pronunciation was subsequently scored by English native speakers.

The researchers found that the children who used the tablet-based app showed a strong and significant improvement over the control group. Such studies demonstrate how apps have the potential to make language learning more effective and enjoyable for children. Accordingly, various language education apps for young children utilizing augmented reality or the Internet of Things (IoT) are currently being developed in Korea (Jeong *et al.*, 2019; Seo *et al.*, 2015).

Similarly, Artificially Intelligent (AI) speakers are also becoming popular in young children's English education in South Korea. It has been suggested that AI speakers can reduce learners' anxiety about English and improve their motivation to learn (Jeon, 2020). AI language software can also provide learning tailored to each student's needs and connect students through digital media (Woolf *et al.*, 2013). Current research suggests elementary school students are more open to AI teachers than teens (Park & Shin, 2017). School shutdowns due to the Covid-19 pandemic forced numerous teachers and students to embrace this kind of technology in the classroom to continue teaching and learning remotely, and much of it may be here to stay now that students and teachers have more experience in its utilization (Lee, 2020).

When it comes to using technology and media for language learning however, Sundqvist and Olin-Scheller (2013) caution that problems can arise when the language encountered through technology and media is not reiterated or incorporated in the language classroom. In their study, Sundqvist and Olin-Scheller (2013) showed that as teachers struggled to close the gap between intramural and extramural English, students' motivation suffered. Thus it is important that if teachers and parents encourage the use of technology and media to acquire English outside of the classroom, measures should then be taken to incorporate the language acquired through EE activities into the classroom itself in order to build bridges between the different registers encountered by the students.

7.2.1 Language learning with iPads

Young children's interaction with Artificial Intelligence (AI) is increasing, and there is evidence to suggest that this development can be used to boost early literacy and language development. Emerging research also points towards positive gains when technology is used cross-linguistically, suggesting that technology may be used to decrease FLA and increase FLE in bi- or multilingual children (Kim *et al.*, 2019).

It is not uncommon nowadays to see young children interacting with tablets or iPads – usually one belonging to a parent or sibling. In their research into the use of iPads as literacy aids in early education, Beschorner and Hutchison (2013) highlight this technology's touchable interface, mobility, and availability of apps which allow children to explore, discover, make choices and complete other tasks associated with early literacy development. In particular, they argue that the digital environments provided by an iPad cover all the 'roots of literacy', namely: reading, writing, listening and speaking. These communicative processes can all be achieved through interaction with an iPad, and the specific functions of this device allow for easy repetition of audio content, and intuitive movement through written works. However, Beschorner and Hutchison (2013) also emphasize that the media with which children interact should be developmentally appropriate.

In a similar study, although one which focuses more on cross-linguistic uses of tablet technology in early education, Sandvik et al. (2012: 206) argue that iPads should be used as a 'scaffold for language learning', highlighting the need to situate effective use of iPads as tools for literacy within broader learning processes. In particular, they note that integrating iPad use with daily activities, and the addition of simultaneous communication with a teacher, both boost the benefits of use. Whilst studies of computer use demonstrate a lack of 'exploratory talk' among students, Sandvik et al. (2012) found that iPad use fostered extensive interaction among children. They note in particular the importance of socio-dramatic play for the development of discursive skills, and that second-language learners traditionally participate less in such activities, suggesting apps which focus on interactive storytelling as a possible remedy for this. In general, children make greater vocabulary gains when using iPads.

When it comes to early literacy, many of these vocabulary gains are tied to other forms of learning based on logic, memory and situation recognition. For example, a young child recognizing their favourite app on an iPad is likely to involve recognition of colour and shape, as well as memory of the icon's location on the screen, rather than indicating specific recognition of the programme's name. This kind of multifaceted recognition helps to build vocabulary at an early age, however, it may limit use in vocabulary acquisition for older children. If a child is accustomed to using technology, they may be able to navigate an iPad or application in a foreign language based on knowledge of the technology's user interface without needing to rely on (and therefore improve) a target language. Therefore, for older children, more in-depth and intentional interaction in the target language will be required in order to contribute to language learning.

A particular benefit of using iPads in language learning is the potential for combatting FLA, often noted to be a significant barrier to the development of literacy skills in second language learners. The use of technology offers multiple alternative means of improving language skills – such as the use of a chatbot – which avoid the need to communicate directly with others. As discussed above, the iPad in particular offers a highly portable means of engaging with all key literacy skills. Nevertheless, attention needs to be paid to ensure that an overreliance on technological 'scaffolding' does not leave language learners lacking in the emotive abilities which also play a crucial role in successful communication. iPads and other technologies show clear benefits to language acquisition, in addition to opportunities to displace foreign language anxiety. However, it seems that the best results are achieved when these technologies are used in interaction with other people and in daily activities and play the role of training wheels.

7.3 Task-based Language Teaching (TBLT)

Another prevalent teaching method, which may or may not be combined with technological techniques, is Task-based Language Teaching (TBLT). TBLT is a method that can produce high levels of language learning enjoyment as well as effectiveness (Seedhouse, 2017). It is a well-established approach that emerged in the early 1980s, prompting learners to achieve a goal or complete a task (Skehan, 1998, 2003). It emphasizes communication and the practical use of language, thus moving away from the repetitive grammar-translation method. According to Bygate *et al.* (2001, cited in Ellis, 2003: 5), a task is 'an activity which requires learners to use language, with emphasis on meaning, to attain an objective'. Much like real-world tasks such as asking for directions, TBLT aims to develop students' language by providing a task which requires the use of specific vocabulary and syntactic structures to complete. Tasks are compound collaborative learning activities which give rise to real language use while engaging learners in a variety of cognitive processes. The activities stimulate the practice of oral and written skills as well as language production and reception. Some of the main principles of TBLT are as follows: meaning is primary (language use rather than form); there is a communication problem to solve; classroom tasks relate directly to real world activities; and the assessment is done in terms of outcomes. Not only does Ellis (2003: 320) insist that 'there is a clear psycholinguistic rationale (and substantial empirical support) for choosing "task" as the basis for language pedagogy', but Skehan (1998) suggests that tasks can provide learners with an opportunity to get involved in activities, which in turn sharpen their grasp of the language. Tasks thus serve as powerful mediators of language learning, with the usefulness of TBLL in foreign language learning by adult learners having been shown through various studies (Ellis, 2003; Kiernan & Aizawa, 2004; Seedhouse, 2017).

7.3.1 Task-based language teaching (TBLT) and cooking

Within the category of TBLT, our case study in this chapter focuses on the specific task of cooking and its use in language pedagogy. Cooking is a commonly adopted theme for TBLT studies as it has been shown to make learning effective but also enjoyable (Seedhouse, 2017). In fact, cooking's benefits to adult learners who are learning European languages has been widely attested. With regard to foreign vocabulary learning, Pallotti *et al.* (2017) presented two empirical studies: one in which 50 adult participants engaged in a cooking activity to assess 16 English vocabulary items, and the other where 36 were involved in the same task to learn 10 Italian vocabulary items. Both studies demonstrated statistically significant improvements in the acquisition of vocabulary items. In addition to this, Park and Seedhouse (2017) explored the effect of touching real objects on vocabulary acquisition by comparing the learning outcomes from a real-world learning environment with classroom environments in a quasi-experimental design. Working with 48 international participants, the investigators demonstrated a significant difference in Korean vocabulary learning. The study contributed to building up one more dimension of the psycholinguistic factors of vocabulary learning in the field of applied linguistics by showing that engaging in physical activities makes a difference.

On the other hand, while there have been many studies on adults, there is a lack of equivalent research which demonstrates the pedagogical impact of cooking in the case of young learners. The needs of young children are potentially different for adults as playful learning is particularly essential. According to Hirsh-Pasck *et al.* (2009), in preparing for entrance into formal schooling, young children need both unstructured free time and playful learning under the gentle guidance of adults. Such playful learning may support better academic and social outcomes as well as strategies for lifelong learning. Potential reasons are that play boosts the motivation (Hyson, 2010) and creativity (Zosh *et al.*, 2016) of young children. Additionally, implicit learning can be more appropriate than explicit learning in many contexts: children learn languages, even second languages, implicitly, whereas adults rely on explicit strategies (DeKeyser, 2003; Ellis, 2009).

As young children learn best when they are experiencing the world practically through play, cooking is a popular activity adopted in young children's learning in general. Children are able to explore the cooking materials using all five senses. They can additionally learn physical and chemical scientific concepts through mixing, cutting, and kneading, as well as other basic concepts like size, shape, colour, taste, touch and smell (Dahl, 1998). Cooking is an interesting activity that can make a very effective and authentic experience in a curriculum that integrates all areas of language, mathematics, science, art, nutrition, and creativity, as well as enjoyment of food (Dahl, 1998; Jill, 1995). For young children, the multi-sensory learning experience that cooking provides can boost their eagerness and enthusiasm in foreign language learning, particularly encouraging their interactive, spontaneous participation during the session (Griva & Sivropoulou, 2009).

Despite a range of theoretical claims on the effects of cooking for vocabulary learning, there has been little empirical research examining the link between a real-world activity and its pedagogical influence. The majority of vocabulary studies on children's L2 vocabulary learning in context have focused on learning with texts presented in a single modality. In recent years, many studies have explored the effects of presenting information using multiple modalities such as text, audio and visual materials on L2 vocabulary learning (Al-Seghayer, 2001; Duquette & Painchaud, 1996; Mousavi et al., 1995). The results showed positive effects in retention of words learned from multimodality. However, researchers have paid insufficient attention to one more dimension for young learners' vocabulary learning – the kinaesthetic mode.

Additionally, a simulated cooking exercise was assessed in Guía et al. (2016) from the perspective of its effect on 5–10-year-olds' EFL learning in Spain. The study combined cooking TBLT with technology, specifically examining IoT and wearable computers. The results indicated the activity was beneficial to children's foreign language learning. In particular, the use of the technologies freed instructors from having to keep records of the tasks performed by each student during the class session. Instead, the instructors could focus their efforts on creating a friendly environment and encouraging participation, helping students to feel comfortable engaging in chat and becoming better prepared for social interaction in a foreign language (Guía et al., 2016). However, a limitation of the study is that the cooking activity was fully simulated using props and technology, limiting the extent to which students could use all five senses in their learning as in real cooking. As a result, it is not a good indicator of the effect of genuine cooking exercises with real ingredients.

In summary, previous studies are limited in that they have primarily applied a cooking-based approach to adult learners in European contexts for vocabulary learning, not young learners. Taking these limitations into consideration and hoping to advance research in this area, we conducted a case study on how a cooking activity engaging all five senses assists young Korean EFL learners' vocabulary learning, which is presented in the following section. We follow the definition of 'task' by Bygate et al. (2001). Our focus is on vocabulary acquisition. Using both quantitative and qualitative methods, we demonstrate that tasks such as cooking produces not only better performance, but also creates a positive, enjoyable learning environment for young children.

7.4 Case Study: Young Korean Children's L2 Vocabulary Learning Through Cooking

In this study, we present cooking as an innovative language learning method for young EFL learners to help them learn L2 English without FLA. We explored the role of cooking as a task in Korean young children's English vocabulary learning.

7.4.1 Methodology

7.4.1.1 Research design

This study employed a mixed-methods approach that can bridge the gap between different ways of seeing, interpreting and knowing (Greene, 2007). Combining both quantitative (QUAN) and qualitative (QUAL) approaches has been known to offer 'a powerful third paradigm choice that often provide[s] the most informative, complete, balanced, and useful research result' (Johnson et al., 2007: 129). Of the various mixed-method research models, we chose Creswell and Plano-Clark's (2011) *Explanatory Design*. This design starts with QUAN data, followed by QUAL data for detailed exploration of the findings. In this study, test results demonstrated the extent to which young students from two different groups could learn through a cooking activity, while interviews explain why learning differences occur. That is, QUAN analysis offers 'learning outcomes' whereas QUAL data shows 'learning processes' for the different outcomes.

7.4.1.2 The experiment

This study has three features: a pre-test-post-test design; a treatment group with control group; and random assignment of study participants (Shapley et al., 2010). The classical experimental study involves comparing the impact of an intervention with what would have happened if there had been no intervention. What is essential for the validity of an experiment is the randomization of participants. The experiment 'engenders considerable confidence in the robustness and trustworthiness of causal findings' (Bryman, 2012: 50). In other words, an experimental research design assures internal validity. This design was therefore fitting.

To explore the hypothesis of this study, participants were recruited and randomly assigned to one of two groups: the treatment group and the control group. To minimize confounding variables, the chosen participants were all the same age and attending the same school.

The treatment group carried out a cooking task using tangible objects, and the control group conducted the same cooking task simply with photos of the objects. To be explicit, the difference was that the former group experienced real-world cooking, whereas the latter one simulated the activity. This study aimed to examine if a meaningful task using all five senses is more effective than an ordinary task involving fewer senses with regard to vocabulary acquisition. The intervention was thus whether young learners used all five senses (in particular, touch and taste) or fewer senses (sight) in performing the task of cooking. Two groups alike went through pre-, immediate post- and delayed post-testing two weeks later. To implement the experiment, we adopted Nation and Webb's (2011) experimental design for vocabulary learning, which starts with the administration of a pre-test to all study participants followed by the treatment and control groups undergoing treatment one or treatment two. This is followed by administering the same immediate post-test to all participants – both treatment and control – and then the same delayed post-test a short period of time later.

7.4.1.3 Participants

Participants were all from the same kindergarten in Kimpo, Gyeonggi Province in South Korea. The kindergarten is located in a relatively rural area and English is not the main focus of education. This stands in contrast to the focus of many kindergartens in Seoul, particularly in wealthy areas like Gangnam. The children had an almost ab-initio level English background. For this study, 66 young learners were chosen and then randomly divided into two groups with 33 people each, on the assumption that 30 could be targeted in the event a few students did not turn up. As participants were young learners whose physical and intellectual development vary month by month, this was a potentially confounding variable. Thus, we will introduce the specific age demographics for each group. The overall average age of all participants was 66.92 months ($SD = 2.90$). The average age of the Objects Group (OG) students was 66.48 months ($SD = 2.65$), while the age of their Photo Group (PG) counterparts was 67.36 ($SD = 3.12$), showing no significant difference in age.

The number of children unable to complete the experiment was higher than our initial predictions. This was due to a high drop-out rate and young students' lack of concentration resulting in incomplete task implementation. A total of 50 students took part in two groups (25 per group) with 21 males (42%) and 29 females (58%) (Table 7.1).

7.4.1.4 Target word selection

We selected 10 concrete nouns as the target words. We chose nouns because they are the easiest word class to learn. Concrete nouns were selected because they are 'learnt more easily than abstract ones, and because the concrete noun items are learnt more quickly and effectively if objects are nonverbally referred and used as stimuli' (Ellis & Beaton, 1993, cited in Seedhouse, 2017: 210). Bearing in mind the number of syllables in the target words, three words were difficult ones ('cranberry', 'cashew nut' and 'persimmon'), four were of medium-level difficulty

Table 7.1 Participants by group

	Objects group	Photo groups	Total
Male	12 (48%)	9 (36%)	21 (42%)
Female	13 (52%)	16 (64%)	29 (58%)
Total	25	25	50

('bowl', 'raisin', 'strawberry' and 'plate') and three were easy words ('banana', 'honey' and 'yoghurt'). English loanwords are prevalent in contemporary spoken Korean and young children may be more familiar with English words than Sino-Korean words (Kiaer, 2014). For example, the word 'banana' does not have a native Korean counterpart, so we expected everyone may know this word. As the dish young students made was fruit salad, one of the children's favourites, 10 target vocabulary items included the name of ingredients and the equipment necessary to make it.

7.4.1.5 Task and test procedures

The basic task and test procedures followed Park and Seedhouse's (2017) model below (Figure 7.1), with a slight amendment. In classroom A, a teacher used real materials to physically demonstrate how to make the dish. On the other hand, in classroom B, she only employed photos simulating how she would make it. In this way, the teacher guided the two groups in carrying out the cooking task according to a three-phase framework of TBLT. The teacher was an American student majoring in Korean in Korea University. She was fluent both in Korean and English. She introduced herself in Korean in order to help children to feel relaxed. All of the instructions in the class were delivered both in English and in Korean, firstly in English then in Korean, in both groups.

In the *pre-task*, the teacher asked students to collect each item, such as 'cashew nut' and 'honey', one by one. Students were required *during-task* to manipulate what they had collected. The control group learners took the same step, simulating the dish-making activity with photos. A teacher offered instructions such as 'put cashew nuts into a bowl'. During both stages, the teacher offered verbal repetition of the word when requested, but not more than twice for the same word.

The post-task involved eating the dish as well as sharing their ideas about which food item was the most delicious. The two photos in Figure 7.2 show the contrast between the two classrooms.

Figure 7.1 Test and task procedures

Figure 7.2 Different learning experiences in the during-task step of mixing ingredients – Photo Group (PG) vs. Object Group (OG)

As the written form of a word constitutes part of vocabulary knowledge, the teacher used visual materials throughout the lesson in both classrooms, in the form of PowerPoint (PPT) slides on a screen, on which the written form of each target word was shown. There were 46 slides, which showed young learners individual items of the target word as well as images of the process of making the dish (Figure 7.3). The same slides were projected in both groups to avoid any confounding variables.

To gauge students' vocabulary knowledge, there were three tests: pre-test, immediate post-test and delayed post-test. The pre-test was an oral production test. Each individual was shown ten real objects and then asked to produce them in English one by one, during which a research assistant held an audio recorder by hand to record their performance. No receptive test was administered in the pre-test, as

Figure 7.3 Using PowerPoint (PPT) in the class

learners' random matching may compromise the actual vocabulary learning. The two post-tests consisted of a receptive and productive test. The productive test was intentionally always administered before the receptive test. This was because if learners first take the receptive test in which written words of the target vocabulary are provided, this may expose learners to the target word once more, potentially contributing to the increase in vocabulary scores. The receptive test involved matching written names of target words with the correct photos on a test sheet within 2 minutes. They were instructed to keep what they did not know blank. This was because otherwise they would take a guess which may compromise the assessment of their actual knowledge. The productive test was the same as in the pre-test. Two weeks later, delayed post-tests involved both receptive and productive tests.

In the receptive tests, each correct answer counted for one point with wrong answers counting for zero. Totals for each condition were then calculated. However, a different method was needed in the verbal production tests to quantify the ability in L1-L2 and L2-L1 production as students might be able to show low levels of learning. Therefore, this study adapted the Lexical Production Scoring Protocol-Spoken (LPSP-Spoken) that Barcroft (2002) suggests as a way to quantify the scores. As learners acquire new words in bits and pieces, the measure that is sensitive to partial word learning is appropriate (Barcroft, 2002). The framework includes a five-way scale: 0, 0.25, 0.5, 0.75 and 1, depending on how a learner performs in production tests. It was based on this scoring scheme that this study could mark learner's partial knowledge of lexical items. The grade range is as below (Table 7.2).

In order to gather data on learning process of the two groups, we conducted a focus group interview. The interview approach is valuable because it 'offers the opportunity of allowing people to probe each other's reasons for holding a certain view' (Bryman, 2012: 503). This focus group allowed learners to present their views on their own learning experiences. Six students from each group (12 in total) were randomly selected to participate in the focus group interviews. The focus group interviews were conducted following the immediate post-test administered after the cooking session. The interview questions are as follows:

(i) Do you like cooking?
(ii) If so, why?
(iii) What were any difficulties you had while you were cooking?

Table 7.2 Marking range

	Minimum	Maximum
Productive test	0	10
Receptive test	0	10

(iv) Between making the dish using real objects and cooking using just photos of objects, which would you prefer?
(v) In this case, why do you think that option is more fun?
(vi) Did the cooking activity help you learn English words? If so, how did it help you?
(vii) Do you think you learned anything other than English words?
(viii) Why do you think so?

The interviews were conducted in Korean and translated into English. Children's interviews were recorded and transcribed by two graduate students. We also interviewed the teacher who led the two classrooms. The interviews were then analysed using a qualitative content analysis approach.

7.4.2 Results

7.4.2.1 Learning outcomes

This section presents statistical evidence to determine whether the treatment group shows greater gains in vocabulary learning than the control group. This quantitative evidence demonstrates students' learning as a product of cooking as a TBLT activity.

This study employed two statistical approaches for analysis based on Pallant (2013). First, as the study saw a change in vocabulary scores over the three time periods (pre, immediate and delayed), it used the 'One-Way Repeated Measures ANOVA', which is a technique to determine whether there is a significant difference in the data in different columns. The data met the requirements for a repeated measures ANOVA. The normal distribution test was performed using Mauchly's Test of Sphericity and the data was not significantly different from the normal distribution. However, this tool cannot explain the difference of the mean scores between two groups or two intervals for comparison; therefore, a t-test was used. The next table presents the results of a one-way repeated measures ANOVA on pre- (prior to the intervention), immediate (following the intervention), and delayed- (two-week follow-up) tests. Table 7.3 displays data for productive tests and Table 7.4 displays data for receptive tests.

Two groups experienced a gradual rise in vocabulary scores, with a little decline in the Photos Group between Immediate- and Delayed-test. There was a significant effect for time, $F(2, 24) = 62.59$, $p = 0.000$, $\eta^2 = 0.69$, multivariate partial eta squared = 0.69, which indicates a

Table 7.3 Mean differences (standard deviation) for productive tests through ANOVA

Group	Pre-test	Immediate test	Delayed test
Objects Group	1.53 (1.44)	3.20 (1.50)	3.30 (1.90)
Photos Group	1.09 (1.11)	2.25 (.93)	2.10 (.92)

Table 7.4 Mean differences (standard deviation) for receptive tests through ANOVA

Group	Pre-test	Immediate test	Delayed test
Objects Group	1.53 (1.44)	3.08 (2.97)	3.64 (3.37)
Photos Group	1.09 (1.11)	1.68 (1.68)	1.60 (1.56)

large effect size. Moreover, there were also significant interaction effects between Time and Group ($p < 0.05$).

Tables 7.3 and 7.4 show similar results for the receptive and productive tests. Both groups saw an increase in vocabulary acquisition over time, with a little drop in the Photos Group between Immediate- and Delayed-test. There was also a significant effect for time, $F(2, 24) = 10.68$, $p = 0.000$, $\eta^2 = 0.18$, multivariate partial eta squared $= 0.18$, which shows a large effect size. Furthermore, there were also significant interaction effects between Time and Group ($p < 0.05$). These significant changes are seen in Figure 7.4.

There were significant differences in vocabulary points over three periods for both productive and receptive tests. The following table (Table 7.5) demonstrates the difference between the mean scores of each group.

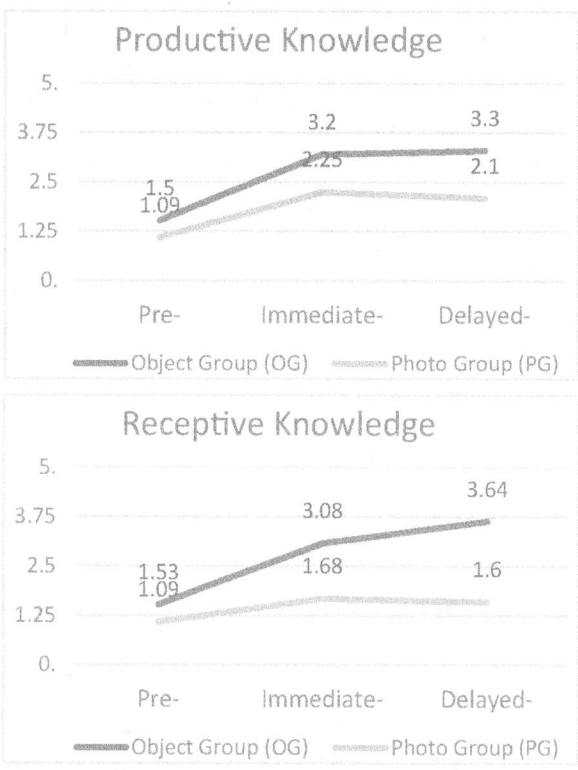

Figure 7.4 Productive and receptive test results

Table 7.5 T-test and mean scores of vocabulary knowledge

Group	Tests	OG (n = 25)	PG (n = 25)	T	p
Productive Knowledge	Pre	1.53 (1.44)	1.09 (1.11)	1.21	0.232
	Immediate post	3.20 (1.50)	2.25 (.93)	2.69*	0.010
	Delayed post	3.30 (1.90)	2.10 (.92)	2.84**	0.007
Receptive Knowledge	Immediate post	3.08 (2.97)	1.68 (1.68)	2.05*	0.047
	Delayed post	3.64 (3.37)	1.60 (1.56)	2.75**	0.009

*$p < 0.05$, **$p < 0.01$, ***$p < 0.001$

The table above shows the overall vocabulary gains over time between two groups. Although there was a slight difference between two groups (1.53 and 1.09) in vocabulary knowledge in the pre-test, the difference was not statistically significant. This shows that both PG and OG groups did not have any background in English. Overall vocabulary gains over time are clearly shown in Table 7.4. In both productive and receptive knowledge, the OG showed a greater increase in vocabulary acquisition than the PG.

The mean differences between the pre-test and post-test should demonstrate change over time to prove that the OG benefitted from using real objects for vocabulary learning. Thus, we compared whether there is a statistically significant gap between immediate post-test with pre-test and delayed-post-test with pre-test. The results are shown in Table 7.6 below.

In Tables 7.6 and 7.7, we can see that the two groups saw increases in vocabulary gains in the productive tests and these were statistically significant. The mean differences were, however, higher in the OG than the PG: for immediate test, OG (MD(Means in difference) = 1.67, $t = -7.81$,

Table 7.6 Mean differences between pre- and immediate post-test of productive skills

Group	M(SD)		T	p	Cohens' d
	Pre	Immediate post			
Object group	1.53 (1.44)	3.20 (1.50)	−7.81***	0.000	1.47
Photo group	1.09 (1.11)	2.25 (.93)	−5.53***	0.000	1.02

Table 7.7 Mean differences between pre-test and delayed post-test of productive skills

Group	M(SD)		T	p	Cohens' d
	Pre	Delayed post			
Object group	1.53 (1.44)	3.30 (1.90)	−7.77***	0.000	1.69
Photo group	1.09 (1.11)	2.10 (.92)	−4.91***	0.000	1.02

Table 7.8 Mean differences between pre-test and immediate post-test of receptive skills

Group	M(SD)		t	p	Cohens' d
	Pre	Delayed post			
Object Group	1.53 (1.44)	3.08 (2.97)	−3.105**	0.005	0.66
Photo Group	1.09 (1.11)	1.68 (1.68)	−1.477	0.153	0.41

$p < 0.001$, $d = 1.47$) and PG ($MD = 1.16$, $t = -5.53$, $p < 0.001$, $d = 1.02$); for delayed test OG ($MD = 1.77$, $t = -7.77$, $p < 0.001$, $d = 1.69$) and PG ($MD = 1.01$, $t = -4.91$, $p < 0.001$, $d = 1.02$). Similar results were seen for receptive tests as in Tables 7.8 and 7.9 above. While both groups registered a rise in learners' vocabulary gains, only the OG showed statistically significant levels: immediate test ($MD = 1.55$, $t = -3.11$, $p < 0.01$); delayed test ($MD = 2.11$, $t = -3.68$, $p < 0.01$).

The mean differences in vocabulary scores were higher for the OG than the PG for both the post-test and delayed-post-test, and in both receptive and productive areas. The differences were statistically significant in all cases. Interestingly, in both productive and receptive tests, the OG experienced a gradual increase in their gains over time from 3.20 to 3.30 and 3.08 to 3.64, whereas the PG registered a decline from 2.25 to 2.10, and 1.68 to 1.60.

These results clearly demonstrate that when carrying out a cooking activity, manipulating real objects is more effective for vocabulary acquisition than simply looking at photos. Young learners were able to learn English vocabulary items at a significantly higher level for both spoken and written media, and in both the immediate-post-test and delayed-post-test. Furthermore, even with regards to long-term gains, students using real objects scored more than their counterparts.

The overall scores were higher in productive tests than in receptive tests. This is probably because of the nature of the lecture and tests. Students could be exposed to the phonological sounds of target words during a teacher's demonstration, which might help them take oral productive tests. On the other hand, in receptive tests where an ability to read the words and match them with photos was required, a teacher rarely offered help to the students. What was really interesting was the score differences of stark contrast in all tests, even delayed post-tests, between the two groups, which we discuss in the following section.

Table 7.9 Mean differences between pre-test and delayed post-test of receptive skills

Group	M(SD)		t	p	Cohens' d
	Pre	Delayed post			
Object Group	1.53 (1.44)	3.64 (3.37)	−3.675**	0.001	0.81
Photo Group	1.09 (1.11)	1.60 (1.56)	−1.786	0.087	0.38

7.4.2.2. Learning processes

The difference in the scores of the two groups can be understood by exploring the learning processes involved through analysis of the focus group interview transcripts. This section presents 12 randomly selected learners' views (six from each group) about their own learning experiences. The interview was conducted in Korean and translated into English. Interviewee's answers were short but very clear. The first question was about whether or not they like cooking when they are at home with family members, and why or why not. All the children liked cooking itself, as shown in the illustrative quotes in Table 7.10.

Clearly, every young learner enjoyed the activity of cooking and there were various reasons for this. They enjoyed eating and tasting the dish, doing the activity itself and spending time with their parents. This shows their experience is related to physical senses. When performing activities, in particular cooking, all five senses are activated in relation to their learning and memory input (Trubek & Belliveau, 2009). Furthermore, young learners were fond of 'doing' the activity itself in learning a foreign language (Doughty & Long, 2003). Young learners were motivated by doing the activities and this increased their FLE. This led us to wonder if 'learning by doing' had helped them to gain vocabulary knowledge. When asked if they had learned English by cooking, the two groups gave their opinions as shown in Table 7.11 (many students expressed similar opinions, which are represented by the responses of the few students below).

Table 7.10 Answers to 'Do you like cooking? If so, are there any reasons?'

Object Group (OG)	Photo Group (PG)
Yes. (Jae, Han, Ju, Cha, Tae, Seo)	Yes. (Da, Jun, Min, Eun, Hye, Son)
It's just fun. (Jun)	I like just making the dish. (Min)
It's fun helping my mum cook. (Jae)	It was fun eating the dish. (Da)
It was great fun to bake bread together with my mum. (Cha)	Because [after making it] I can eat it and it's delicious. I can cook it again myself. (Eun)

Table 7.11 Answers to 'Does a cooking activity help you learn English words? If so, how did it help you?'

Object Group (OG)	Photo Group (PG)
Strawberry (Han)	I learned 'strawberry'... that's it. (Son)
Cranberry (Jae)	I love learning English through cooking and singing. (Son)
Bowl (Han)	
I learned how to cook. (Jae, Ju, Cha)	
I learned English and how to cook. (Han, Tae)	
I also love learning English through singing. (Chae)	

Table 7.12 Answers to 'Which activity would you prefer to do: cooking with the real objects or photos of food? In either case, why do you think it is more fun?'

Objects Group (OG)	Photo Group (PG)
Real (Han)	Not real (Eun)
Fun eating the dish. (Ju)	It was a fake! (Da)
Delicious (Han)	Boring (Min, Eun)
Smell of yogurt and strawberry (Ju)	Not being able to eat (Min)
I could feel the taste. (Han)	No fun because there is no food. (Jun)
Strawberry and plain yogurt changed its colour from white to pink when mixed. (Jae)	Angry because I couldn't eat. (Da, Eun)

Students in both groups had learned English vocabulary items as demonstrated by the statistics discussed above, but to a different extent. Students from OG could make more sounds of the target words than PG learners, according to the interview scripts. Interestingly, the learners in both groups saw 'cooking' and 'singing' as a motivating vehicle by which they can learn English. Just as Paterson and Willis (2008) found that music can provide an excellent way for children to learn and memorize words and phrases, young learners were found to be more engaged in learning English by 'doing' – carrying out real world activities. In a similar way, 'cooking' opened a space in which kids are exposed to spoken and written English with a clear purpose. We can see specifically how children think about their own experience in the quotes listed in Table 7.12.

OG students found their learning activity more real, enjoyable and hands-on, valuing the use of all five senses. On the other hand, PG learners found the activity unrealistic and boring due to not being able to eat food. Two students even became angry because they had no end product. Thus, whether the activity children had performed was 'real' or 'unreal' determined their attitudes toward the two difference experiences. We thought this might result in very different levels of motivation for students in the two cases, leading to different levels of learning processes. Throughout the interviews, we noticed something distinctive which might account for the difference in their learning outcomes. It is illustrated in their comments in Table 7.13.

The real activity of cooking with final product was so impressive that children wanted to do the same task again when they got home.

Table 7.13 Answers to 'Was the dish you made any good? What did you like? (OG)' 'What did you like? (PG)'

Object Group (OG)	Photo Group (PG)
I'd like to make it again at home tonight. (Han, Jae)	Strawberry, banana and cranberry (Da)
	Banana (Hae)
I remember the recipe. (Jae, Han, Cha, Ju) first strawberry, (Han, Ju-in chorus) then banana, (Ju) and persimmon and raisin (Han)	Banana and strawberry (Da)

Asked how they could do it again, they said that they would try to remember the procedures of making the dish. This helped them not only think about the recipe, but practice and repeat the target vocabulary one by one. Repetition has a tremendously powerful consequences for the learning process (Kurhila & Kotilainen, 2017). It is in this moment of reflection that they were internalizing and learning the linguistic information. On the other hand, there was no sign of this process in the case of the PG. They were able to recall a few vocabulary items, but no more meaningful action for language learning was shown.

The children in this study reported that cooking with real ingredients was more enjoyable and this increased their motivation for doing the language learning activity, thereby ultimately making the activity more effective. The heightened levels of FLE associated with carrying out the cooking activity with real ingredients contributed to students' vocabulary learning. In contrast, simple observation of photos was seen as boring and unreal, which resulted in relatively less successful outcomes. This is not to say that students did not have a sense of motivation in their experience, but rather suggests that multi-sensory materials increase levels of FLA and can effect a higher level of learning compared to the other case. Highly motivated learners achieve greater success in language learning than those who are not (Gu & Johnson, 1996; Sanaoui, 1995). It is for these reasons that the two groups achieved different learning outcomes. This study shows that innovative language learning encourages more FLE, which can facilitate more successful learning.

The reasons for different learning outcomes and processes also emerged from interviews of a teacher, who led the two classrooms. She pointed out clear differences in terms of motivation as shown below:

Q: *What was your teaching experience like?*

A: *it was really neat to be able to do an experience like this to see the difference between kids learning when they actually do the experiment as opposed to just learning vocabulary by flashcards or pictures.*

Q: *Did you feel any difference between the two groups?*

A: *Yeah the first group was just the picture group, and I think they were kind of disappointed and less active in the experiment because it wasn't actually food and just pictures so it didn't mean as much to them, I think. And then the second group was more active and wanted to participate more I think because it was actually food and they knew they'd be able to eat it later ... just because they know they can eat the food because they have it and if they're only doing it with pictures, it's fun, but it doesn't give as much motivation. I think also because kids like to be able to do things by themselves and if it's actually real then they can touch it and feel it, and it's more sensory.*

The teacher found that while the PG students could have fun, it was to a lesser degree due to having only photos and no end product. In contrast, OG learners showed more active participation because of the presence of real objects and foods they could touch. The multi-sensory activity gave them an unrivalled level of motivation, thus enhancing vocabulary learning. This supports the findings of a previous study (Trubek & Belliveau, 2009). However, it turned out the teacher was wary of the feasibility of the task itself, as shown in the comments below:

Q: Do you think this is feasible to use in institutions to teach?

A: I think they definitely could, maybe not as an everyday thing, that would be pretty hard because it takes a lot of time, money, resources, and other things, but I think every once in a while it's definitely a good idea.

When asked in terms of pedagogic practicality in a classroom, she said that available resources and commitments might make it hard for the task to be implemented. Given the current educational situation for Korean EFL young learners in terms of likely barriers, it is true that it is hard to implement real world tasks. Nevertheless, our study indicates that a cooking activity might increase students' motivation and thus is to be recommended. The findings suggest that real world tasks serve as a vehicle through which EFL young learners improve language skills in an enjoyable manner.

7.4.3 Discussion

This case study aims to combine cooking with language learning to create an effective language learning environment for young children. The so-called 'English Fever' in South Korea has been the main cause of foreign language learning anxiety in young Korean EFL learners (Park, 2007). In order to create a fun and enjoyable language learning environment for young learners, in this chapter we adopted cooking in Task-Based Language Teaching (TBLT). The results support the claims of TBLT in that language learning combined with real-life connection is much more effective than language learning without any real-life connection or task (Seedhouse, 2017). Focus group interviews show how children who have participated in the real cooking activity enjoyed the lesson, whereas children who only learned vocabulary through manipulating non-real objects like photos soon lost their interest.

In South Korea, for EFL vocabulary learning, the repetition-based method without any real-world connection is extremely popular and widespread. Although this approach may be efficient in the short term, the vocabulary learned without any real-world connection may soon be lost in due course. Similarly, Peterson and Mulligan (2012) report a surprising negative repetition effect, in which participants who studied a list of cue-target pairs twice recalled fewer targets than a group who studied the pairs only once. TBLT-based vocabulary learning may look more costly and less effective compared to simple repetition-based vocabulary learning. Contrary to this belief, our study shows that real-life connection and actual activity are powerful tools for vocabulary learning. These findings have both pedagogical and practical implications. Educators might be able to come up with other tasks and activities for children (e.g. traditional games) and adapt them for the classroom as pedagogical resources. We can see many examples of schools putting into practice programs where, for example, students are sent on field trips to places like museums. We believe that this trend is related to the physical component of such learning experiences and the associated educational benefits. Given the sheer enjoyment of experiencing a real-world activity, the curriculum can be developed in a way that has a great deal to offer to language learners. This study demonstrates that TBLT is effective for young learners studying English. They are able to acquire language in a fun, naturalistic context, and their linguistic knowledge lasted longer than it did with a repetition-based method. With this in mind, it is important that teaching strategies for innovative language learning be developed, shared, and implemented in classrooms of YLLs, encouraging FLE in order to increase language learning motivation and ultimate language attainment and retention.

7.5 Conclusion

Due to the perception of an 'English Fever', young EFL learners in South Korea not only lose motivation to learn a language but also develop Foreign Language Anxiety (FLA) and related psychological, physical and social problems. Some of the key causes of the problems are a highly pressurized environment and a demand for high performance. This chapter showed an innovative way of learning: language learning through cooking. We demonstrated that using cooking as a task in TBLT can help young EFL learners not only enjoy language learning but also help them to perform better. Despite theoretical claims that using all five senses would naturally contribute positively to young learners' foreign language learning, there have not been many studies to support such claims. In this sense, this chapter builds upon previous literature by conducting empirical research showing that physical, real-life tasks significantly make a difference in young EFL learners' vocabulary learning, and also affects their level of their motivation. This increased motivation is at least partially a product of the FLE that is encouraged in the hands-on task-based learning activity. Considering a rising interest in cooking in many countries, we believe that the approach can be widely used.

A limitation of the case study is participants were too young for us to elicit strong opinions in interviews. It is therefore recommended that older groups of young learners be included in future research in order to examine their perspectives and attitudes in more detail towards learning through real-life tasks. Dewaele and MacIntyre (2014) showed that specific activities that empowered students and utilized the students' linguistic creativity such as debates or video making elicited more FLE and less FLCA. While Dewaele and MacIntyre's (2014) study was carried out with secondary school students, it shows a precedent that more productivity driven, task-based learning helps to create a more enjoyable and motivated classroom. The study in this chapter shows similar findings for YLLs. Further research like this with YLLs, particularly through analyses of participants' detailed comments on such learning methods, would reveal more clearly the potential of this real-world task-based approach.

8 Towards a More Ethical Learning Environment

Thus far in this book we have presented generalized information about FLA and anxiety in young children as well as FLE as a classroom counterpart. We have provided insight into the specific context of FLA in South Korean early childhood English education by laying out research including case studies. We have also offered methodological suggestions for alleviating FLA in the classroom. The purpose of this chapter is to build on all of this previous information and lay out in an orderly manner our recommendations for creating an ethical English classroom for YLLs, focusing on the recognition, alleviation and prevention of FLA, as well as the encouraging of FLE. First, we summarize signs that parents and teachers can look for in order to identify FLA in its early stages and prevent it from becoming a chronic issue. We then look at the literature on methods for alleviating anxiety in classroom settings and adapt these methods to fit the early childhood English classroom. In the third part of this chapter, we reaffirm translanguaging as an ideal method for encouraging additive bilingualism in an ethical language classroom. Finally, we emphasize the importance of increased awareness among parents, educators and policymakers concerning FLA, its effects and methods for its alleviation.

8.1 Warning Signs and Detection of Children's Anxiety

The best way to prevent long-term effects of anxiety on children's brains is by detecting it early. In order to do so parents and educators should be trained in recognizing signs of anxiety in their children and students. Being aware of these signals that indicate anxiety in children enables earlier diagnosis and consequently early receipt of the corresponding treatment. As described in Section 2.2.2, the increased emotional signals from the amygdala interacting with other parts of the brain interferes with a lot of the child's ability to cognitively function. Some more serious signs include:

- difficulty in concentrating;
- insomnia; increased incidence of having nightmares;
- loss of appetite;

- seeming easily irritated;
- display of negative emotions (e.g. crying, outbursts of anger).

However, prior to displaying these signs of anxiety in progress, teachers can be on the lookout for signs that might indicate the beginnings of foreign language anxiety, and as we continually reiterate, early detection is key. In 1989, The National Council of Teachers of Mathematics suggested that teachers look for the following signs in students. If these signs are absent, then the students might be experiencing at least a mild form of anxiety (we have changed the wording slightly to fit the foreign language classroom):

Signs of a minimally or non-anxious student (Furner & Berman, 2003: 170)

- The student can **confidently** use the language they know to communicate ideas.
- The student is **flexible** in their approach to language use, trying a variety of methods and verbal arrangements to convey meaning.
- The student **perseveres** in relaying ideas in the target language, does not easily give up.
- The student seems **interested, curious** and **inventive** in the language learning process.
- The student can **self-reflect** on and **self-monitor** their own production while using the target language (including self-correction).
- The student can '**focus on the value** of and appreciation for [English] in relation to its real-life application, and use as a tool for learning'

Teachers should be aware of these signs of a non-anxious student and plan their lessons in such a way that they will be able to note whether or not their students are displaying these signs as they operate within the classroom environment.

While these anxious and depressive symptoms are strong indicators of anxiety in children (Nhsinform.scot., 2019), they are based mostly on visual observation by or interactions with a parent or teacher. There are also other tools available to identify whether the child is likely or unlikely to have anxiety. One screening tool used by the Anxiety and Depression Association of America suggests asking parents/carers to answer questions like 'does your child worry excessively about a number of events or activities?'. A certain score on this survey will prompt the parent/carer to book a doctor's appointment and seek help (Adaa.org., 2019).

Wearable technology has also become available to detect anxiety and alert the wearer. Much of this technology is intended for long-term wear for those on with autism spectrum disorder (ASD). Airij *et al.* (2016) created a wearable device to detect stress in autistic children. The device is able to pick up on physical warnings of anxiety before they manifest in external behaviours. The device is also non-invasive and appropriate for sensitive children. Airij *et al.*'s (2016) device consists of two sensors, a pulse sensor to measure heartrate and a galvanic skin response (GSR) sensor that reads changes in sweat gland activity. While the prototype for this anxiety detecting this device required more equipment than a simple watch would. As technology allows for smaller and smaller wearable devices, hopefully one day this will become practical for children with ASD as well as in classrooms where students might continually encounter high-anxiety inducing situations. These devices could also be practical during the trial phase of various curricula to measure the anxiety levels that particular language exercises induce in students.

Some anxiety-related research has used the measurement of cortisol levels to determine the anxiety levels of children, rather than surveys, observation or self-reporting measures. Researchers have used this technique extensively to test the anxiety levels of children in daycare settings and first day of school situations (Gutteling *et al.*, 2005; Sims *et al.*, 2005, 2006; van der Merwe *et al.*, 2011; Vermeer & van IJzendoorn, 2006; Vliegenthart *et al.*, 2016) – it appears to have been a popular technique in the Netherlands in the early 2000s. One positive of using cortisol measurement is that it does not require any form of self-reporting or survey among a population that is not yet fully literate. However, measuring cortisol levels does also present some problems. If a student presents with a higher level of cortisol, it could be for a variety of factors. Usually the sample is taken from saliva, which, while not extremely invasive, would still require some level of imposition on the subject, which could raise cortisol levels. Heightened cortisol levels could come from anxiety caused by home life or social interactions between students in the classroom. While it is helpful to know that a student has a heightened cortisol level, the cause might not necessarily be the one for which the researcher is testing. Also, from a practical standpoint, testing cortisol levels is not very helpful for teachers or parents in detecting anxiety.

As technology is still in the process of developing to meet the needs of anxious children, and cortisol testing is highly impractical to implement on a consistent basis, we therefore recommend that parents, teachers and those who care for children be trained in noticing the signs of both an anxious student and a non-anxious student. We particularly recommend that teachers working in language classrooms, or in classrooms with a large number of non-native English speakers, be trained in recognizing these signs so that they can be part of the early detection system.

8.2 Practical Solutions for Alleviating Anxiety

Anxiety has become a common psychiatric disorder that is often experienced by youth, with prevalence especially peaking during adolescence (Hartley & Casey, 2013). While risk factors are multi-faceted, with links to environmental, psychological and biological factors (Schmidt et al., 2005), in FLA, it is hypothesized that the trigger for such an experience in children is situation specific, induced by fear of negative evaluation and negative communication apprehension, which might impair one's ability to function in a foreign language (Sparks & Ganschow, 2007). A variety of treatment methods have been well established to treat anxiety through medical intervention. Yet there are also interventions that can be taken on the part of the teacher or parent in order to reduce school-related anxiety so that it does not worsen to the extent that medical intervention is necessary.

8.2.1 Classroom solutions

Researchers have located ways to alleviate certain other kinds of anxiety. As math anxiety and general test taking anxiety have been more widely studied, a variety of techniques have been suggested for the improvement of students' mental wellbeing in those fields. As many of the causes and symptoms of math anxiety, test anxiety and foreign language anxiety overlap, we feel that consideration should be given to the implementation of these alleviation techniques in the FLA field as well. Most anxiety-related studies agree that the first step towards alleviating anxiety is early detection (see e.g. Bhatia & Goyal, 2018; Rockhill et al., 2010). Therefore, as expressed elsewhere in this book, it is important for educators and parents to be familiar with the signs that initially signal the onset of anxiety. Early identification can aid in preventing anxiety from becoming a chronic issue.

Once classroom anxiety is identified, however, what do we do to reduce it and avoid it worsening? In their study of math anxiety, Maloney and Beilock (2012: 405) showed that one way to alleviate the effects of anxiety on output in a testing situation was the 'regulation and control of negative emotions'. Maloney and Beilock suggested that, in order to encourage the control of negative emotions, students be allowed 15 minutes prior to a task to write about their emotions freely. In an early childhood language classroom, often this would not be possible, but a similar exercise with emotion cards or through conversation with a teacher or peer could help both the child and teacher to understand the emotional state with which the child is approaching the language learning task. Negativity can also be alleviated through re-framing techniques that cast the negative aspects of the situation in a positive light. Maloney and Beilock (2012: 405) observed that 'telling students that physiological responses often associated with anxious reactions (e. g. sweaty palms, rapid heartbeat) are beneficial for thinking and reasoning can improve test performance in stressful situations'. They also suggested reframing the testing situation to seem like a challenge as opposed to a threat. This supports our earlier assertions on the importance of emphasizing FLE in the language classroom. FLE will cause students to mentally reframe the work that is asked of them and help them to form more positive emotions concerning these tasks, which will then aid them in their successful completion despite any underlying anxiety.

Furner and Berman (2003) compiled much of the existing research on math anxiety up to that point and gave a concise summary of what they viewed as the best methods for the prevention and reduction of math-related anxiety. In the following chart, I include their final list of suggestions on the left and how they could work in an early childhood language classroom on the right:

Furner and Berman's (2003) suggestions, taken from The National Council of Teachers of Mathematics (NCTM)	Application in an early childhood foreign language classroom
Accommodating for different learning styles.	Flexible lesson plans that allow for students of all learning types to learn in the way that best works for them (e.g. visual, aural, kinaesthetic, verbal, logical, social, solitary).
Creating a variety of testing environments	Similar to the first suggestion, teachers can create a variety of ways to assess the students' language acquisition. They should not all ascribe to what is typically thought of as a test, and the students do not even need to know that they are being assessed.
Designing positive experiences in math classes	Focus on including experiences that will create positive attitudes and emotions towards both the target and home language within the classroom setting in order to ensure FLE.
Refraining from tying self-esteem to success with math	Especially at such a young age, do not scare the children into learning English by making them think it is the only conduit through which they can have a successful career/life in the future.

(*Continued*)

Emphasizing that everyone makes mistakes in mathematics	As mentioned in earlier chapters, perfectionism can lead to higher instances of FLA, therefore encouraging an environment in which mistakes are accepted and learned from rather than denigrated is important to creating a positive, low-anxiety learning environment.
Making math relevant	In Chapter 7, we discussed Task Based Language Teaching (TBLT), which enables students to learn and use the target language in order to be able to actually complete an activity or task. This is one way to emphasize the relevance of the language. Interactions with materials and speakers of English can also aid in showing the relevance of learning English. However, these encounters must be planned well in order to make sure a sudden encounter with a native speaker does not induce more anxiety.
Letting students have some input into their own evaluations	This suggestion can be directly applied to early childhood language learning classrooms. Teachers and parents can have conversations with children about what they find difficult about the topics they are learning. This in conjunction with formal and informal assessments should be adequate in providing educators with the information they need to determine how students are progressing and where they need more help.
Allowing for different social approaches to learning mathematics	Similar to the first point, varying approaches and the ways in which the target language is used in interactions with classmates, teachers, family members and the outside world will facilitate more positivity and comfort in using the target language.
Emphasizing the importance of original, quality thinking rather than rote manipulation of formulas	Chapter 5 discussed the perils of rote learning with regard to increased potentials for FLA. Rote learning techniques reject the higher levels of Bloom's taxonomy, ultimately creating anxious students who lack communicative competence. Teachers must therefore use more communicative teaching methods and reduce the number of rote learning methods used in early childhood language classrooms.

(*Continued*)

Characterizing math as a human endeavour	This point is probably more easily achievable with language learning, as languages are inherently linked to people and cultures. However, emphasizing the communicative usefulness of learning English for actual social interactions with other English-speaking people is important in the classroom. This will help in making English learning more of a 'human endeavour' than merely a set of grammatical rules to learn and apply to a long list of typed vocabulary words.

In accordance with our discussions in the first section of this book, most studies on math and test anxiety cite increased positivity towards the topic or task as one of the best methods for alleviating anxiety. This coincides with MacIntyre and Mercer (2014) and MacIntyre et al.'s (2016) work, as well as Dewaele and MacIntyre (2014) and Dewaele et al.'s (2019) emphasis on positive psychology.

8.2.2 Native English teachers in Korea

As mentioned before, many schools in South Korea employ native English-speaking teachers. A recent study shows that the fervour for learning English from 'native speakers' is largely due to the view that the pronunciation of a native speaker is superior, making them the ideal model of correct English pronunciation (Ahn, 2020). Ahn's study showed that 'people in general admire "native" speaker-like English and associate this concept as part of an improved English pedagogy, with "native" speaker-like English often seen as being American "native" speaker English' (Ahn, 2020). Thus, private English teaching institutions and some public schools as well, opt to hire these native-speaking teachers to satisfy parents that the students will be learning 'correct' pronunciation. When these teachers from various English-speaking countries go to South Korea to teach English, they are often untrained in early-childhood education, and therefore unfamiliar with techniques for recognizing and reducing anxiety in their classrooms. Many teachers are also often ignorant of various cultural incongruencies between Korean culture and their own cultures. As discussed in Section 4.2, various tendencies of foreign teachers in Korean, such as asking questions and group discussions, are in contrast with the teaching styles to which students are accustomed. This lack of cultural awareness on both sides can lead to increased FLA on the part of the students. As the adult in the room, it is incumbent upon the foreign teacher to learn about these cultural differences in order to soften the impact of various methodologies on the South Korean students.

Many schools already have teacher training programs in place to help new teachers adapt to schools and their various English curricula. Schools and administrators could adapt these existing training programs to incorporate training on FLA and FLE. By educating teachers on the signs of FLA and emphasizing the importance of FLE for the successful language acquisition, perhaps much could be done in creating a comfortable and ethical learning environment for young language learners. Schools who do not have a training program in place, must implement one, especially for native English-speaking teachers who are unfamiliar with local culture and customs.

Governments can also play an important role in ensuring the safety and efficacy of early childhood classrooms by implementing more stringent qualification measures for teachers, to ensure that teachers are familiar with standard teaching pedagogy and various classroom language teaching methodologies. As of the publication of this book, the requirements for being issued a South Korean E2 Visa – the visa specifically for native English-speaking teachers – were the following: be a native English speaker from an approved country, have a bachelor's degree, have no criminal convictions, have no outstanding health issues, hold TEFL/TESOL Certification if you are going to be working in a public school. While these measures have been getting stricter over time to ensure that no teachers can fake their qualifications or have a criminal record, the measures regarding actual teaching qualifications have only changed to require TEFL/TESOL certification for positions in public schools. Many individual private language schools have implemented their own requirements that teachers be TESOL/TEFL/CELTA certified, but as of yet, no government requirements regarding prior training as a teacher have been implemented for private institutions – where a large portion of early childhood English education takes place. In order to facilitate safer and more successful language learning, TEFL/TESOL requirements should be implemented not only for teachers going into public schools, but for native teachers going into all educational institutions. Teachers who are already trained to teach will hopefully be better informed regarding classroom anxiety and better equipped to adapt to the needs of anxious students. They will therefore need less additional training on the topic as they begin teaching in a new classroom environment.

Teachers who are already TEFL/TESOL trained might still be underqualified to teach English to YLLs. Most TEFL/TESOL certification programs are geared towards teaching methods for adult students. Therefore, those who have these certifications might not have encountered the information on and methodologies in early childhood education. These same teacher training programs, as well as on-site trainings at the individual school level, need to address this lack of training in early childhood education as well as include material on recognizing FLA, and methods for its alleviation. Many training programs focus on building teachers' knowledge of the English language and the different methods for teaching it, yet they lack material that recognizes the presence of mental health strain on students and its possible effects. While we do not advocate that all teachers become trained mental health professionals, we do appreciate the role that teachers have first responders of sorts to the mental health challenges of their students. In order to be able to recognize and address these challenges in the proper way, teachers require adequate training.

8.2.3 Therapeutic/medical interventions

Sometimes, a student's anxiety cannot be alleviated through personal, parental or teacher intervention, and must therefore be addressed by a mental health professional. There are various interventions that a mental health professional can use to relieve a child's anxiety, or to accept the anxiety and be able to function better when anxious. In this book we will list a few of the more common therapeutic interventions that parents and teachers might also find helpful when trying to understand how best to help their children/students. These methods should be fully understood before being implemented and we therefore recommend consulting with a mental health professional as well as reading up on these methods before implementing them. The methods that are most commonly used with children experiencing anxiety are Cognitive Behavioural Therapy (CBT), Mindfulness and Growth Mindset.

Cognitive behavioural therapies aim to reduce emotional reactivity. CBT is one of the methods that has been around the longest and therefore is the form of therapy with the strongest base of evidence. CBT helps children to become cognitively aware of the influence that thoughts have on behaviours. The child learns to understand that they are doing what they are doing because of the feelings that they have, and then learns to process their emotions. With anxiety, CBT identifies the cause of the anxiety and seeks to desensitize that fear in a way that is tailored to the individual. This therapy addresses the neurobiological process of recognizing and reacting to the fear, resulting in that particular behaviour that signals anxiety. Such behaviour includes depressive and externalizing symptoms like being easily irritable, feeling restless, and having difficulty in concentrating; and internalizing behaviours like being on edge, self-soothing mechanisms like internal counting, stonewalling (silent period), or self-defeating thoughts (e.g. 'I am so stupid') (Burghy *et al.*, 2012). CBT focuses on the interconnected triangle of thoughts, actions, and feelings (see Figure 8.1). While CBT is not usually addressed in teacher training programs, we assert that it should be, particularly as part of the training we recommended previously in this chapter. CBT is a tried and true method.

Another effective method that can be learned and implemented by both parents and teachers is Mindfulness. This method encourages

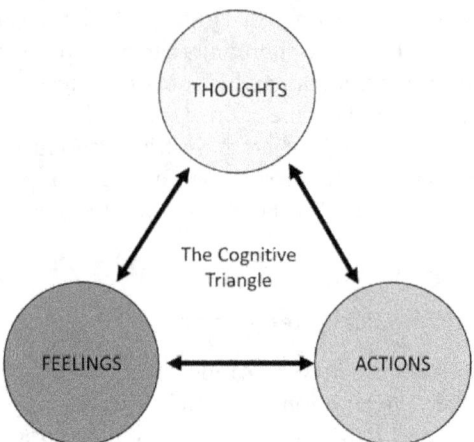

Figure 8.1 The cognitive triangle of interactions that are the focus of cognitive behavioural therapy

awareness and acceptance of where the thoughts, actions, and feelings are coming from. Once the child recognizes and accepts the source of these thoughts/actions/feelings, they then have more control and can work to reframe things in a more positive and productive light. Sometimes situations are just bad, and students have to work to recognize this, then address how to react to it in a better way. From a neurobiological standpoint, mindfulness allows the child to slow things down enough that they are aware of what they are saying and doing. The child can then choose their reaction, rather than just acting emotionally.

The third method, Growth Mindset, is especially prescient for teachers and parents of children suffering from FLA. In her 2008 book *Mindset: The New Psychology of Success*, Dweck introduces her dichotomy of growth mindset vs. fixed mindset. A fixed mindset is focused on the 'now', whereas a growth mindset is focused on 'yet'. When imbuing a classroom full of students with growth mindset a teacher must focus on the mentality of 'not yet' as opposed to failure. Praising a student for intelligence or talent makes students more vulnerable when they do inevitably make a mistake. However, in encouraging a growth mindset, the teacher will praise hard work, strategy and progress. This in turn creates resilience and determination when mistakes are encountered, equipping students to be able to process errors, learn from them and correct them in the future. This mindset of 'not yet' can help all students to work hard to progress. 'When educators create grown mindset, environments steeped in "yet", equality can happen' regardless of supposed socioeconomic boundaries (Stanford Alumni, 2014). Growth mindset transforms the meaning of effort and difficulty, rather than meaning a student is 'dumb', when applied, growth mindset helps students to look forward with the mentality that they have a chance to become smarter. In the early childhood language classroom, teachers can help students with a fixed mindset to change it and focus on their hard work and progress rather than on what they feel that they cannot do. Rather than allowing students to say 'I can't do this, it's too hard', a growth mindset allows them to say 'I can't speak this language, yet', thereby acknowledging the difficulty and struggle of learning a language, but still pointing them in the direction of progress.

While the above three methods can be learned and implemented by educators, another therapeutic option can also prove useful. As a child's success in education depends heavily on their home situation and the support and interest of the parents, the family unit as a whole is an essential supporter in a child's language learning journey. As discussed in Chapters 4, 5 and 6, in the South Korean case specifically, the attitude of the mother towards the English learning process has a demonstrable effect on the child's attitude and levels of anxiety. Thus, there can be recourse to family therapy that can encourage increased parental support and understanding within the family dynamic. This can also help to train parents in the previously mentioned methods, which would naturally help the parents to pull back the amount of pressure placed on their child. Family therapy can also help the family work together to address the child's anxiety in a systemic way. If the methods of alleviation are being applied systemically then they will work better towards successful, low-anxiety language acquisition.

There are some pharmacological treatments such as administering Selective Serotonin Reuptake Inhibitors (SSRIs) that have been shown to be effective in relieving anxiety, especially in conjunction with CBT; however, these can take 2–4 weeks to take effect and unpleasant side effects may be experienced. They should only be tried under the advice and strict guidance of a medical professional after the above methods have been tried and there is still little to no improvement in the child's levels of anxiety.

We recognize the value of the above therapeutic methods. Many of them have been tried and tested for years and have been shown through multiple studies to work with students of various ages. Teacher training in all countries should strive to implement training in the above methods and any future therapeutic methods that prove successful in order to give teachers a larger repertoire of tools they can call upon to help relieve their students' anxiety within the classroom and encourage more enjoyment in the classroom and ultimately more academic progress.

8.3 Creating a Welcoming Environment

As FLA is a situation-specific type of anxiety, building rapport, utilizing distractions (e.g. videos), memory reconstruction, interventions that enhance sense of control and environmental change (i.e. changing the features that elicit the negative emotion of the patient) can help in alleviating the level of anxiety experienced by students. Keeping the student informed regarding what is happening in their environment may address their worries and simultaneously prepare them for what they are about to experience (Newton *et al.*, 2012). General pedagogical practice includes previewing the class at the beginning, or providing a class guide of some sort, either spoken or on the board, before the class begins. Ensuring that all new language teachers, especially native English-speaking teachers who may not have previous training in early childhood education, are trained in implementing the foundational aspects of their classroom – including previewing each day, building rapport with the students, educational distracting techniques and other interventions – will help to ensure a classroom more supportive of students' progress and psychosocial wellbeing.

While building a rapport with one's students starts from the very moment they meet in the classroom, even after this initial meeting, teachers can continue to build or improve rapport with their students. In these latter instances, adapting teachers' teaching methods may be beneficial to building rapport with the students. For instance, teachers can try moving away from traditional assessment and error correction methods (i.e. creating a classroom environment focused on testing or creating a competitive drive among the students) towards a supportive learning environment where errors are not seen as an indication of failure, thereby shaping the classroom into a friendly and safe space where children are welcomed to freely express themselves without fear of remonstration (Pichette, 2009).

8.3.1 Translanguaging classrooms

As mentioned in Chapter 5, one environment-focused teaching method specific to the foreign language classroom is translanguaging. Over the past decade, translanguaging has been garnering much attention from educators hoping to create language learning environments that encourage language enjoyment, downplay situations that might increase FLA, and aid in additive second language acquisition. A translanguaging classroom is the alternative to English-only classroom teaching models, and we put it forward as an ideal practice for alleviating FLA among young language learners.

In a translanguaging English classroom, rather than having an L1 vs. English distinction, both languages are used productively as students use their L1 repertoire to help build up their English semiotic repertoire. As discussed in detail in Chapter 5, much of the fear of bilingual education stems from misguided or misinterpreted advice from scholars in the early periods of linguistic research on bilingualism. Parents and some educators' belief that students will learn the second language more slowly and will not learn it as well if they use both languages, and that bilingualism holds students back academically because they are unable to fully develop in either language and therefore they cannot function at the same level as their peers need to be widely debunked. In various studies, researchers have shown that the variance between bilingual and monolingual children's acquisition of features of language are is not statistically significant (see e.g. Bergman, 1976; Grosjean, 2010; Meisel, 1989; Oller & Eilers, 2002; Pearson, 1998). In a study compiled by the UK Department for Education, statistics showed that when it comes to GCSE scores, a slightly higher number of students whose first language was not English (61.3%) met benchmark standards compared to those students whose first language is English (60.7%). Various dual immersion programs in operation in Canada have also generated data disproving this notion that two languages at once is detrimental to academic development (see Section 5.1.2). Translanguaging classrooms, where students are allowed to access all of their previous knowledge through their native language as they learn English, keeps them progressing in other subject areas while they are building up their English repertoire.

Translanguaging allows students to access all their semiotic resources in order for them to be able to exchange fuller and richer communication with their conversational counterparts. If they are forced to speak one language alone, their abilities of expression would be restrained. In their article clarifying the concept of translanguaging, Otheguy *et al.* (2015) assert that in a language learning classroom, i.e. a classroom specifically for the acquisition of the language components explicit to a specific cultural, political or social group, translanguaging must be limited in order to assess the acquisition of specific language components. However, in a situation where a student's ability to express themselves is being tested rather than some specific lexical or grammatical component in the other language, it is important to give students the chance to use 'all the learners' linguistic and semiotic resources' (Otheguy *et al.*, 2015: 305). In other words, in a classroom, a student should be allowed to use all of the words and structures available to them in their linguistic arsenal in order to best express themselves. In the current educational methodology, multilingual students and language learners are expected to limit their expressions to a much lower percentage of their whole linguistic repertoire. This barring of access to existing knowledge can work to increase a student's FLA, which could dramatically decrease the success of their language acquisition.

A 2007 educational guidance booklet from the UK government addresses 'Continuing the development of first language'. The UK government openly recommends the use of the first language 'as a tool for learning'. The booklet goes on to describe how to best make the new students feel welcome in their new school, stating that 'using bilingual staff and other children who share the child's home language not only simplifies communication with children who are new to English, it also conveys the message that the language and culture the child brings to the school are actively valued' (DCSF, 2007: 15). This recognition of the value of translanguaging in allowing students to learn better and to feel more comfortable, thereby lowering affective filters and FLA, especially during the early stages when a student is transitioning into a language classroom, is a valuable step in the educational process. It is the characteristic of translanguaging in the classroom helping to decrease affective filters, thereby lowering FLA, that we wish to highlight as the facet that makes it an ideal practice for implementation in early childhood English classrooms in South Korea and beyond. If students are allowed to translanguage with their teacher and their peers in the language learning classroom, motivation increases. As affective filters are lowered, FLA decreases, and students gain confidence as they realize how much of their linguistic repertoire they have already developed.

Translanguaging in the classroom is one method that teachers can do to create a welcoming classroom environment. UNICEF (the United Nations Children's Fund) has declared that there are three dimensions to educating children that must be taken into account when ensuring that human rights are respected in educational settings: the right of access to education, the right to quality education, and the right to respect within the learning environment. UNICEF writes that in order for this right to be realized, 'education must be provided in a way that is consistent with human rights, including equal respect for every child, opportunities for meaningful participation, freedom from all forms of violence and respect for language, culture and religion' (UNESCO/UNICEF, 2007: 4). We assert that this can be achieved through a translanguaging approach in the language classroom. Translanguaging respects the difference in linguistic repertoire between individual students and allows all students in the language classroom to have the opportunity to participate meaningfully.

8.3.2 Pedagogical methods for a comfortable, enjoyable classroom

In Chapter 7, we also outlined the benefits of other methodologies such as Task-Based Language Learning (TBLL) and the use of various technologies in the classroom as methods for encouraging FLE in the language classroom. We believe that combined with a translanguaging approach, these methodologies will contribute positively to the creation of a welcoming and enjoyable environment in the early childhood language classroom. These approaches are particularly suited for younger language learners as they often encourage the use of technology, which many children enjoy. They also employ a variety of approaches, making them suitable for students with a variety of learning styles. Many traditional pedagogical methods ignore kinaesthetic learning, but TBLL harnesses this style and allows students to learn in a different, enjoyable way.

Like TBLL, smartphone applications and AI can be used to increase the amount of enjoyment that students experience in the language classroom. Many children already like to play on smartphones and tablets, teachers might as well take advantage of this to encourage more successful and more comfortable language learning. Apps and the use of AI can help encourage children to experiment with their language without the worry of negative assessment by a teacher or a peer, thereby isolating the enjoyment factor of language learning, free from much of the FLA that some students might experience through direct interaction with teachers and peers.

Translanguaging, TBLL, and the use of technology can help create a language learning environment for young language learners that is healthy, encourages FLE and attempts to alleviate factors that might cause increases in FLA. We consider attempts to create these kinds of classroom environments to be more ethical learning environments that attempt to align with UNICEF and UNESCO's vision for a more human rights-based education for all children.

8.4 The Importance of Awareness

While it is good to think about ways that we can improve young children's language learning environments, recommendation and implementation are not the same thing. It is important that a variety of people who influence the language education of young children be made aware of all of these available methods for the improvement of young children's educational experiences, including but not limited to government agents over education, school administrations, teachers, and parents.

Those in charge of a child's institutional education should be made aware of the effectiveness of translanguaging in classrooms, as well as the dangers of FLA, especially on the long-term psychosocial wellbeing of children. Teachers, especially under-qualified native English-speaking teachers, need to go through a training process specifically targeted at awareness of different FLE-encouraging pedagogical practices, as well as how best to teach English to young children of a different cultural background. As outlined at the beginning of this chapter, it is also important for them to be aware of the different signs of anxious and non-anxious students. If teachers are trained and aware, it can help, to some degree, to alleviate the effects of FLA.

However, we would like to emphasize in this book, that one of the most important roles that affects the wellbeing of the child, is the role of the parent. As shown in Chapter 6, parental attitude towards the target language (English) was a major determining factor that affected the young children's FLA. Even more important than socioeconomic status, the study in Chapter 6 showed that a mother's attitude can affect a child's level of FLA. It is therefore important that parents be aware of the effect that they can have both on their child's experience with FLA, as well as on the success of their child's English language acquisition journey by not falling prey to the myths of second language acquisition and consistently placing their children in healthy language learning environments. As parents, teachers and policymakers are increasingly conscientious about the decisions they make regarding the environments in which children will learn English, they will be able to create more intrinsically motivated students, which will ultimately lead to more successful and maintainable language learning.

As belief in a 'critical period' for language learning is widespread, regardless of the research that other language learning variables trump age (Muñoz & Singleton, 2011; Pfenninger & Singleton, 2016, 2017), particularly as regards phonological acquisition, young children will continue to receive language education in early childhood. The suggestions put forward in this chapter are targeted towards creating a safe language learning environment that will activate the children's minds rather than their anxiety. We reiterate that every child is different, and healthy language acquisition will look different for every child; however, we believe that these methods and practices will help to establish a foundation on which parents and educators can work to build safe and successful learning experiences for each child.

Conclusion

Our purpose in writing this book was to present an overview of Foreign Language Anxiety, its causes, its effects and its potential solutions in an organized manner, alongside original research, classroom trials and case studies. It is our hope that by compiling all of this information and adding newly emerging research to the existing body of literature, this book will be beneficial to parents, teachers and policymakers in creating foreign language learning environments in which young language learners can thrive and be successful in both their language acquisition and in maintaining good mental health. Furthermore, through this book, we have contributed to the body of literature on FLA in the East Asian context, specifically the South Korean context. In the existing literature, although recently there has been some work done in Chinese and Japanese contexts (Hoare, 2011; Jiang & Dewaele, 2020; Li, 2019; Li & Xu, 2019; Li et al., 2018; MacWhinnie & Mitchell, 2017; Noguchi, 2019; Yan & Dewaele, 2018, 2020; Yashima, 2002), most research has been focused on European contexts, or adult learners of English living in predominately English-speaking countries. While the literature has diversified in terms of researching anxiety among Japanese, and more recently, Chinese learners, we have found there is still a deficit in the South Korean context. By giving more insight into the Korean context and showing its applicability to similar situations in other Asian countries and beyond, we hope to further expand the geographic areas and cultural contexts that are currently being investigated with regards to the effects of FLA on young language learners.

In the second chapter of this book, we showed the extensive body of research that exists on Foreign Language Anxiety, as well as the burgeoning field of research on foreign language enjoyment. We laid out in detail the long-term effects that prolonged anxiety can have on children. Experiencing consistent anxiety during childhood can predispose children to more serious mental health conditions later in life (Denham, 2003; Gadye, 2018; Pollak et al., 2000; Post et al., 1998; Salisch, 2001). It is therefore imperative to work at reducing FLA to the point that it can be helpful in driving the language acquisition process rather than raising affective filters to the degree where language acquisition becomes impossible, and the stage is set for long-term negative repercussions.

The first few chapters of the book looked at various metrics for measuring FLA, most of which are designed for adult language learners, who are already literate in at least their L1. Early childhood FLA has not had the same attention, and as we have shown, the same metrics cannot be used with children, who have not yet learned to read. We therefore proposed and tested new metrics as a first step for filling this gap. We also note that self-reporting metrics, no matter their design, are inherently flawed and have therefore outlined various alternative methods using new technology to measure anxiety in children. As of yet, use of these testing methods is economically or methodologically prohibitive in most cases as they require the purchasing of expensive materials or of repeated invasive saliva-based testing. However, as technology continues to improve, and as more and more people become accustomed to wearing smart watches with built-in heart monitors, some of which have even started reading and estimating blood oxygenation, this technology could be utilized to track the anxiety of children in classrooms, making it easier for research to be carried out, and less ethically worrisome for data to be collected amongst this vulnerable population of language learners.

While the long-lasting psychological implications of FLA are of course its worst potential effect, another detriment of FLA is that it makes language learning less effective when experienced at heightened levels, effectively wasting the child's opportunity to learn. We propose that many common teaching methodologies in South Korea and beyond – e.g. rote learning and memorization techniques, the direct translation approach, English-only immersion – are actually introducing more potential for FLA into the early childhood English classroom, which in turn decreases the effectiveness of the language acquisition process in many cases. While not significantly correlated with any reduction in FLA, teaching methods emphasizing foreign language enjoyment (FLE) have been shown to facilitate more successful language learning (Dewaele *et al.*, 2018). In this book, we looked at TBLT specifically as it relates to cooking and showed that actually physically doing tasks in the classroom led to more enjoyment in the language learning process. Building from this preliminary positive response in an early childhood English classroom, the same studies could be carried out with other task-based approaches to learning, including the pre- and post-tests to determine the students' levels of language acquisition, thereby demonstrating more definitively that task-based fun enjoyed in the early childhood classroom can positively affect the language acquisition of the students involved, as the ideal classroom is both enjoyable and educationally effective.

The preliminary positive results regarding TBLT shown through the case study of young Korean children learning though cooking highlight the importance of re-thinking how we motivate and teach young children in the language classroom. When students are making connections and actually performing tasks, as opposed to pretending to perform tasks, their enjoyment is heightened, and their motivations increase. Schools, teachers and curriculum designers should take this into account as they determine the most effective ways to make their classrooms successful.

Throughout this book, we have also advocated for the adoption of translanguaging practices in the language classroom. By allowing both L1 and L2 to operate in the classroom, a portion of the FLA experienced by the young children can be prevented. Park (2007) showed that when students are in a classroom where they are unable to use their L1 to communicate, but also lack the L2 ability to express themselves, they often experience heightened levels of FLA that raise affective filters, cause behavioural issues, and overall impede the learning process. By giving students access to their L1 repertoire, on which they can fall back when their L2 abilities prove inadequate, there will be a reduction of FLA, resulting in lowered affective filters, increased motivation, and more effective language learning, as shown in Park's (2007) research through the introduction of a Korean-speaking classroom aide to help a Korean-speaking student in an English immersion classroom. A translanguaging approach to teaching also ensures the maintenance of a student's L1 and avoids immersion classroom tactics that tend to villainize their L1 and valorise the L2, tactics which can lead to the unfortunate early internalization of socially dictated language hierarchies.

In this book, we have also shown the important roles that both parents and teachers play in the language acquisition process of YLLs. The case study in Chapter 6 highlighted the importance of parents' educational beliefs in predicting a children's levels of FLA. The study supported Sheo *et al.*'s (2019) research that showed parents' positive perceptions of English education affecting children's attitudes towards learning English. Therefore, parents should attempt to engender positive associations of the target language in their children and support them in building integrative motivation for learning the language rather than instrumental motivation. This study also showed that, particularly in regular kindergartens, students' FLA levels increased as the duration of exposure to English increased, and the more strictly English-only policies were enforced during that time. Thus, particularly in regular kindergarten institutions where English is a just a class period a few times during the week, teachers should be aware of the effects of their classroom policies on students' levels of FLA. Again, this can be alleviated somewhat by adopting a translanguaging ethos in the classroom. Continued access to the L1 implies that the English-only policies are much looser and can alleviate some of the FLA that might result from trepidation over being cut off from their L1 during English lessons.

We also discussed the roles of foreign teachers in Chapter 4 and the ways in which they might contribute to the FLA of students through ignorance of local culture, inability to communicate with the child using the child's L1, and utilizing North American politeness strategies, which tend to calculate relationships much closer than Korean politeness strategies do, resulting in discomfort and anxiety (Holtgraves & Yang, 1990; Song, 2014). This is all compounded by high turnover rates among foreign teachers, which forces the children to be constantly adjusting to new teaching dynamics and personalities. Having foreign teaching staff is seen as lending credibility to Korean English schools, as many parents ascribe to the myth of the 'native' speaker, idealizing the North American accent in particular. As discussed earlier, there are many social implications to this tendency because foreign teachers, especially in the beginning, can cause students undue anxiety due to their aforementioned lack of knowledge about local culture, language and customs. Not only foreign teachers, but also Korean teachers can affect the levels of anxiety in their students depending on the teaching methods they use in the classroom. As shown throughout this text, more task-based and translanguaging approaches that aim to engender more FLE, all while the teacher remains constantly aware of and looks for the signs and symptoms of FLA, will help the teachers to control – at least to some extent – the teacher-induced FLA in the language classroom.

Finally, a Korean – and general East Asian – social factor discussed throughout this work has been the concept of 'English Fever'. Though this concept is not limited to the East Asian sphere, there are certain negative repercussions from this social phenomenon that have reverberated throughout this part of the world. Generally defined, the concept of English Fever is the parental push for English education, based on their subscription to the belief in the primacy of English as global lingua franca. The acquisition of English will consequently enable one's child to access global markets and opportunities. However, this fever must be viewed critically for what it is: a consequence of the post-colonial era and neoliberal imperialism. Cho's (2015) article on the topic explores 'linguistic insecurity' and perfectionism as consequences of heightened competitiveness between Korean students to achieve 'unrealistically high "native-like" expectations of their English' (Cho, 2015: 687). Cho (2015) critiques the way that the competitive pursuit of 'perfect English' has been 'uncontested, reinforced, and naturalized through neoliberal ideologies in Korean society and how it feeds into linguistic insecurity' (Cho, 2015: 693). In modern Korean society, English is often looked at as a commodity rather than a self-improving skill, leading to predominantly instrumental motivation on the part of the learners. As Cho (2015) demonstrates through an analysis of returnees from studying abroad in English-speaking countries and those who acquired their English on Korean soil, the pursuit of English in the 'English Fever' economy of Korea is a 'no-win situation, in which whatever linguistic competence achieved is constantly discounted and devalued' (Cho, 2015: 708). Therefore, it is not only at the level of YLLs that FLA is problematic, but throughout the entire system in which the impossible myth of 'native-speaker' perfectionism is interwoven. This myth is being engendered in younger and younger children, as shown in the fourth chapter of this book, and is resulting in the increased popularity of *jogi yuhak*, or early study abroad, in which one parent moves abroad with the child to facilitate English language acquisition, while the other parent stays behind in Korea to fund the endeavour. In YLL classrooms in Korea, a translanguaging approach is easily facilitated as many teachers are bilingual and children have constant access to their native language outside of the classroom. However, in the early study abroad classroom in English-speaking countries, translanguaging becomes much more complicated and often relies on a friendly classmate who might also have a Korean background (Park, 2007). It is therefore important not only to address the methodology and practice of early childhood English education in South Korea and beyond, but also to take a closer look at the factors instigating 'English Fever' and analyse their wide-reaching and critical effects. Effects which are becoming deeply rooted in societies in East Asia and the world over.

Implications for Practice

Despite the need for deep societal reflection on the causes and effects of 'English Fever' and the pursuant perfectionist tendencies, there are some pragmatic approaches that can be taken on the school and family levels to alleviate the immediate causes and effects of FLA among South Korea's increasing numbers of YLLs. The main issues that need to be addressed are teacher training, classroom pedagogy, teaching methodology, and English language curricula.

As demonstrated by the limited current body of research on YLLs in East Asia, the specific student struggles that are causing elevated levels of FLA need further documentation. However, based on the investigations carried out for this book, we can recommend the implementation of explicit teacher training for those who are teaching YLLs, particularly those teachers teaching in a nation/culture with which they are unfamiliar. As noted in Chapter 4, in South Korean kindergartens, particularly immersion kindergartens, often a teacher's national and ethnic background is considered to be one the most important selection criteria, alongside a baseline education level of a bachelor's degree, leading to a highly problematic selection process that favours young, white, North American teachers. This leads to teachers, who are new to the Korean language and culture and often teaching in general, being thrown into classrooms mere days after arriving in the country. In some cases, they are expected to teach with very little training in teaching methodology, but more generally they are equipped with little to no knowledge and understanding of which North American customs and mannerisms might be anxiety-inducing to their students. We would therefore propose studies to be undertaken in order to determine which cross-cultural misunderstandings elicit the most negative responses in the classroom, and that a training program for all E2 visa holders – the visa specifically for English teachers of non-Korean descent – be designed for new arrivals to complete prior to their first days of working in Korea.

Training programs could include information on spotting signs of FLA, as outlined in Chapter 8, as well as other culturally specific factors related to education, such as question asking, and other pedagogical approaches that students find anxiety inducing as discovered through the proposed classrooms studies. Training programs for all teachers in early childhood classrooms should also include sessions on the importance of mindfulness, growth mindset and other therapeutic approaches for alleviation of FLA, so that students who are anxious can be de-escalated in the classroom before being labelled as a behavioural problem. Furthermore, this training should make teachers aware of the growing body of research that demonstrates the effectiveness of FLE in the language classroom. Enjoyment in the classroom has been shown across a large body of research (see Chapter 2) to create environments for more effective language learning. While the current research does not show any significant mitigating effects of FLE on FLA (Dewaele & MacIntyre, 2016; Dewaele et al., 2018), classroom enjoyment may at least help to create an environment where perhaps the negative effects of FLA might be alleviated to some degree. This requires further studies to better understand the relationship between anxiety and enjoyment. To conclude, teacher training needs to be expanded to include briefings on FLA, its symptoms and techniques for how to alleviate it among learners.

However, the impetus for implementing a training program falls to administering educational bodies, whether at the government or individual private institution level. No matter the type of educational institution, the training program designers need to be familiar with and integrate the body of research on FLA, its causes and remedies, as well as prevalent cross-cultural misunderstandings between newly arrived non-Korean English L1 teaching staff and their young students. If the state level educational bodies take charge of this for state-run public kindergartens, this supplementary teacher training can be standardized, as well as added to teacher qualification exams in the case of staff with Korean teaching certifications. As government regulation of private kindergartens is less consistent, different approaches will be necessary, but it is our hope that this book, particularly the suggestions in Chapter 8, can serve as a reference for general guidelines as to what might be included in such a training. As in the state-run institutions, however, we hope that training programs for all educational facilities (public and private) will be created by qualified teacher training specialists. This same approach needs to be taken with regard to YLL English language curricula, which can be altered to include more TBLT approaches as well as a greater emphasis on FLE.

While training modules can be useful, further research needs to be carried out to continue to determine the most ethical and effective combinations of teaching practices that will ensure educational success while maintaining children's psychosocial wellbeing. The two major case studies in this book offered preliminary insights into an area needs to be expanded into a large body of research. In Chapter 6, we saw that children in English immersion kindergartens tended to experience higher levels of FLA compared to their regular kindergarten counterparts. The results also showed that impulsive children have lower levels of language comprehension, which can then result in heightened levels of FLA. One important result from this study showed that stricter English-only policies in kindergartens resulted in higher levels of FLA. Thus, in deciding on classroom policy, it is important that these English-only policies be reconsidered, especially in light of all the research on the effectiveness of translanguaging classrooms (Chalmers, 2019; Cummins, 2000; García, 2009; García & Li Wei, 2014; Gebauer *et al.*, 2013; Lee & Macaro, 2013; Lewis *et al.*, 2012; Smits *et al.*, 2008; Trudell, 2016; van Gelderen *et al.*, 2007). The study also showed that more than socioeconomics, parental attitude towards English learning was a predictor in the amount of FLA experienced by YLLs. The effects of parental attitude should also be made more widely known, particularly as the popularity of 'Mom's English' educating methods are becoming more and more widespread. In summation, the study from Chapter 6 demonstrated the importance of further researching anxiety-inducing factors in immersion kindergartens, re-evaluating English-only classroom policies, and emphasizing to parents the importance of their own attitudes in their child's language learning process.

In Chapter 7, Task-based Language Teaching was investigated using a cooking exercise in kindergarten classrooms. The results of this study showed that students maintained interest in classroom activities longer and had heightened motivation when they were performing hands-on tasks with tangible outcomes. This then led to more successful learning outcomes. These results have pedagogical implications. In this preliminary study, it appears that incorporating physical components in classroom lessons, alongside providing real-world experiences and connections, can raise levels of FLE and thereby increase motivation and educational attainment. Therefore, in lesson planning and curriculum development for YLLs these activities with physical components should be incorporated where possible. The results of the investigation in Chapter 7 offered an example of an innovative and practical way to approach teaching and learning: learning language through cooking. Further research into other methods of TBLT will help to provide a wider range of effective approaches to how young EFL learners can enjoy language learning while also improving their performance. Though, it is important to remember that such findings are not necessarily limited to

EFL learners; the implications are transferrable to language learning in a much broader sense.

Chapter 7's TBLT case study results showed that students who had participated in the hands-on activity and produced a completed edible result at the end of the lesson had better results in the delayed post-test as well, implying that the increased motivation in the classroom provided longer lasting results than the trial group who merely used pictures of the food to complete the task. This has certain implications for long-term language learning efficiency. Increasing FLE in the language classroom may facilitate the marriage of interest and language, leading to more long-term maintenance of material learned in the classroom. What the students learn when enjoyment is more of an intentional factor may last longer and become embodied knowledge, which is the ultimate goal of integratively motivated language learners.

Ultimately, teacher training, curriculum improvement and shifts in pedagogical methodologies can only do so much. Changes in educational policy, assessment, and testing systems will also need to shift to ensure a more psychologically healthy learning environment for students throughout all levels of their education. This will require engagement at all levels of society to make English acquisition more than just a TOEIC/TOEFL test score or a line on a resume, both of which are not indicative of a person's actual communicative competence. Incorporating practical language use into the classroom and designing testing models around true communicative competence will hopefully create more motivated and psychologically healthy language learners.

Reflections for Further Research

Though the main focus of this book has been on the situation of young learners in South Korea, there are many other places where young children's language acquisition processes are similarly anxiety-inducing. This book could be particularly valuable in other East Asian countries where there is a heightened zeal for English education due to a perceived 'English Fever' coupled with neo-Confucian values on learning, as well as other places around the world where English scores are considered to be one of the more important factors in social mobility. However, the research can also be relevant for language teachers in any part of the world. The fundamentals of FLA and FLE, as examined in this book, are not limited to East Asia; the importance of striking the right balance between the two remains critical in a variety of learning situations. Therefore, the research results and pedagogical suggestions within these chapters can be applied around the world as a means of safeguarding young children's education. Today's global population is exceedingly mobile, which is something to consider in how we treat children, particularly as the majority of them had no choice in their move. Anxiety can cause enough problems in young children without their educational environment adding more, particularly as early negative experiences can have a lasting impact on later life (Denham, 2003; Gadye, 2018; Pollak et al., 2000; Post et al., 1998; Salisch, 2001). If FLA occurs in the young children in South Korea that were investigated in this book's studies with Korean students who were surrounded by their home language outside of the classroom, imagine how much more complex the situation might be for children who are transplanted into a new society where they lack the familiarity of their home language in the world outside of the classroom as well. As a result, these children may feel more insecure and threatened. In this situation of heightened anxiety, how can these children be expected to try to learn another language in a psychosocially healthy way? We propose that a safe language learning classroom environment where FLE is the focus and translanguaging encouraged, can become a refuge for these children.

Building on the preliminary results in this book, we hope that researchers will look further into situations like this. Once it is possible to reliably gauge the levels of FLA experienced by YLLs learning their L2 in a new country, not surrounded by their L1, we can then move forward to designing methods for FLA alleviation and the introduction of situation-specific FLE pedagogical models. One of the desired outcomes of this book was to highlight the gaps in the existing research that need to be filled in our quest to provide the best language learning environment possible for young children. To begin with, we challenged and dispelled a number of myths – including the so-called 'dangers' of bilingual education and rote learning – surrounding the sources of increased FLA among young children in Chapter 5. With regards to an East Asian context, we further noted the importance of understanding the wider mentalities that have an effect on how teaching and learning are carried out. Addressing such aspects of FLA is important in order to then ascertain areas which need further development. Future work needs to be done to determine the proper relationship between FLA and translanguaging pedagogy through expansive classroom trials. We acknowledge that this is quite difficult as the research would involve working with children, who are a very vulnerable and often unpredictable population. In the studies for this book, we noted that small behavioural issues – e.g. speaking out of turn, lack of focus, difficulty sitting still – occasionally occurred while carrying out the studies. Some children are also shy around strangers which can affect both their behaviour and responses as well as their anxiety levels during a given activity. Thus, researchers must make great efforts to avoid inadvertently creating anxious environments in their quest to find solutions for classroom anxiety. These mitigating efforts will of course vary based on the specific students and classroom contexts of each study.

The research on the existence and causes of FLA in young language learners is underdeveloped and needs a much more in-depth investigation. The study conducted for Chapter 6 of this book, which is the largest study of its kind undertaken in South Korea thus far, found promising results that mothers' attitudes towards language learning are influential in predicting the amount of FLA a young child will experience, while socioeconomic factors did not show any significant influence on a child's levels of FLA. This line of research is ripe for a much larger transnational study that aims to investigate the roles of factors like language policies, parental attitudes, and socioeconomics in predicting FLA levels in young children. By carrying out similar studies in other national and cultural environments the role of parental attitudes in general could be further examined and confirmed as more than just a Korean cultural phenomenon.

To conclude, we would like to highlight some particular areas that we feel are most ripe for further research. First, we need more expansive classroom studies that look at expanded student and teacher variables to determine further sources of early childhood FLA. These studies could look at more specific classroom pedagogical practices to determine which types of classroom activities and teaching methods result in the best balance between effective language acquisition and low levels of FLA. Also, a deeper investigation into the interplay between FLA and the variables discussed in Chapter 6 that is carried out in other nations with similar education systems may provide interesting transnational results.

To facilitate the above research, however, we need to carry out more anxiety studies – both FLA and general classroom/testing anxiety – with young children in order to fine tune the existing metrics for determining levels of FLA, or to discover even better and more accurate testing models. Metrics also need to be adapted for measuring FLE in YLLs. As technology continues to develop, perhaps wearable technology will become more accurate and practical for the purpose of carrying out this kind of experiment, thereby negating the need for self-reporting metrics, which are unreliable in the best of cases, and unpredictable with children.

Once metrics are improved and confirmed through rigorous testing and the various factors that contribute most to FLA in YLLs are isolated, a proceeding research path should be the creation of translanguaging curricula and the provision of functionally bilingual teachers to facilitate learning to determine empirically if this methodology will reduce FLA. If this hypothesis proves correct, it will show that translanguaging creates a low FLA environment as children have recourse to their L1 when they are not equipped to communicate in their L2.

FLA also needs to be investigated in various educational settings. For the majority of this book, when we have been talking about classrooms, we have been referring to 'off-line' classrooms. However, the increase in the number of online classrooms in recent years, which jumped exponentially in 2020 due to the onset of the global SARS-CoV-2 (Covid-19) pandemic, leads to a need to consider the role of FLA in these spaces. Virtual classrooms come with a completely different dynamic and consequently different variables that can determine whether a student will experience anxiety – e.g. the presence of a parent in the room during class time, the number of previous lessons taken online, experience with the online platform, the number of distractors in the students' immediate vicinity. Future studies need to look at the most effective ways that online teachers can boost FLE, as well facilitate educators in knowing and softening variables that might lead to heightened levels of FLA while teaching remotely.

Recent advances in artificial intelligence and student interactions with new language learning technology have shown promising results in successful language learning and a reduction in anxiety levels (Jeon, 2020). Fear of negative evaluation is not nearly as strong when students are facing an AI through their screen as it would be with a real person. As technological fluency becomes ever more important at earlier and earlier ages, the introduction of AI technology into the language classroom is inevitable. It is therefore incumbent upon researchers and educators to implement it in classrooms in the safest and most effective ways for the children, using appropriate metrics to observe students' psychological reactions as new methodologies are introduced. Thus, we recommend that studies be undertaken to measure the varying levels of anxiety experienced by students in classroom conversations facilitated by a teacher, an online teacher, and an AI – controlling for other variables of course – that would allow researchers to determine both the levels of FLA experienced in each situation as well as their success in language acquisition.

While this book has focused predominantly on the East Asian educational model, FLA is a universal challenge in language classrooms, and FLE could be a universal boon in classroom effectivity. Thus, wider knowledge of this research and expanding the scope of the research to include younger children will be essential in building healthy and effective learning environments. We hope that if nothing else, this book is effective in raising awareness of the causes and effects of FLA and challenging the language learning myths that have perpetuated anxiety-inducing learning environments for decades. While the focus was a South Korean context, knowing and dispelling these myths will help to improve language learning classrooms everywhere, for everyone, regardless of nationality, language background or age. Parents, teachers, and policymakers need to focus on creating classrooms where the focus is FLE and not high test scores or unrealistic goals for attainment of perfect, native-speaker-esque English. As this book has explored, managing both FLA and FLE within the classroom setting is crucial to moving towards a more ethical and effective language learning environment. These 'ethical' classrooms can be achieved through proper information given to parents, FLA-specific training for language teachers, and a flexible language classroom in which translanguaging is encouraged and FLE the focus.

Appendix A: Anxiety Metrics

All metrics are the intellectual property of those cited:

The Revised Children's Manifest Anxiety Scale (RCMAS) – Reynolds and Richmond (1978)

'What I think and Feel': Read each question carefully. Put a circle around the word YES if you think it is true about you. Put a circle around the word NO if you think it is not true about you

1. I have trouble making up my mind.	Yes / No
2. I get nervous when things do not go the right way for me.	Yes / No
3. Others seem to do things easier than I can.	Yes / No
4. I like everyone I know.	Yes / No
5. Often I have trouble getting my breath.	Yes / No
6. I worry a lot of the time.	Yes / No
7. I am afraid of a lot of things.	Yes / No
8. I am always kind.	Yes / No
9. I get mad easily.	Yes / No
10. I worry about what my parents will say to me.	Yes / No
11. I feel that others do not like the way I do things.	Yes / No
12. I always have good manners.	Yes / No
13. It is hard for me to get to sleep at night.	Yes / No
14. I worry about what other people think about me.	Yes / No
15. I feel alone even when there are people with me.	Yes / No
16. I am always good.	Yes / No
17. Often I feel sick in the stomach.	Yes / No
18. My feelings get hurt easily.	Yes / No
19. My hands feel sweaty.	Yes / No

20.	I am always nice to everyone.	Yes / No
21.	I am tired a lot.	Yes / No
22.	I worry about what is going to happen.	Yes / No
23.	Other children are happier than I am.	Yes / No
24.	I tell the truth every single time.	Yes / No
25.	I have bad dreams.	Yes / No
26.	My feelings get hurt easily when I am fussed at.	Yes / No
27.	I feel someone will tell me I do things the wrong way.	Yes / No
28.	I never get angry.	Yes / No
29.	I wake up scared some of the time.	Yes / No
30.	I worry when I go to bed at night.	Yes / No
31.	It is hard for me to keep my mind on my schoolwork.	Yes / No
32.	I never say things that I shouldn't.	Yes / No
33.	I wriggle in my seat a lot.	Yes / No
34.	I am nervous.	Yes / No
35.	A lot of people are against me.	Yes / No
36.	I never lie.	Yes / No
37.	I often worry about something bad happening to me.	Yes / No

Social Anxiety Scale for Children (SASC)- La Greca et al. (1988)

Item	Type
1. I worry about doing something new in front of other kids.	FNE*
2. I worry about being teased.	FNE
3. I feel shy around kids I don't know.	SAD**
4. I'm quiet when I'm with a group of kids.	SAD
5. I worry about what other kids think of me.	FNE
6. I feel that kids are making fun of me.	FNE
7. I get nervous when I talk to new kids.	SAD
8. I worry about what other children say about me.	FNE
9. I only talk to kids that I know really well.	SAD
10. I am afraid that other kids will not like me.	FNE

*Fear of Negative Evaluation
**Social Avoidance and Distress

Children's Test Taking Anxiety Scale (CTAS) – Wren and Benson (2004)

Item	Type
1. I wonder if I will pass.***	Thoughts
2. My heart beats fast.	AR*
3. I look around the room.	OTB**
4. I feel nervous.	AR
5. I think I am going to get a bad grade.	Thoughts
6. It is hard for me to remember the answers.	Thoughts
7. I play with my pencil.	OTB
8. My face feels hot.***	AR
9. I worry about failing.	Thoughts
10. My belly feels funny.	AR
11. I worry about doing something wrong.	Thoughts
12. I check the time.	OTB
13. I think about what my grade will be.	Thoughts
14. I find it hard to sit still.***	OTB
15. I wonder if my answers are right.***	Thoughts
16. I think that I should have studied more.	Thoughts
17. My head hurts.	AR
18. I look at other people.	OTB
19. I think most of my answers are wrong.	Thoughts
20. I feel warm.	AR
21. I worry about how hard the test is.	Thoughts
22. I try to finish up fast.	OTB
23. My hand shakes.	AR
24. I think about what will happen if I fail.	Thoughts
25. I have to go to the bathroom.***	AR
26. I tap my feet.	OTB
27. I think about how poorly I am doing.	Thoughts
28. I feel scared.	AR
29. I worry about what my parents will say.	Thoughts
30. I stare.	OTB

*AR: Autonomic Reactions
**OTB: Off-Task Behaviours
***Items that were deleted following testing

Child Math Anxiety Questionnaire (CMAQ) – Ramirez *et al.* (2013)

Item
1. How do you feel when taking a big test in your math class?
2. How would you feel if you were given this problem? *'There are 13 ducks in the water. There are 6 ducks in the grass. How many ducks are there in all?'*
3. How would you feel if you were given this problem? *'You scored 15 points. Your friend scored 8 points. How many more points did you score than your friend?'*
4. How do you feel when getting you math book and seeing all the numbers in it?
5. How do you feel when you have to solve 27 + 15?
6. How do you feel when figuring out if you have enough money to buy a candy bar and a soft drink?
7. How do you feel when you have to solve 34 – 17?
8. How do you feel when you get called on by the teacher to explain a math problem on the board

(Students selected how they feel using this sliding scale)

Appendix B: Kindergarten vs. Immersion English Parent Surveys

Survey Questionnaire for Parents[1]

Personal information

1. How old are you?
   Father:
   Mother:
2. What's your occupation?
   Father:
   Mother:
3. What is your monthly income?
4. When is your child's date of birth?
5. What is your child's gender?
6. Does your child have any siblings?

1. How is your English?
   Father:
   Mother

Please tick the right box.

a) advanced level (can communicate with the English speakers freely) ☐
b) approximate to the advanced level (with some extra intensive study, can communicate with the English speakers freely) ☐
c) high level (after a short-period intensive study, can conduct tasks in English without problems) ☐

---

[1] Translated from the original Korean

d) upper high level (after a mid-long period intensive study, can conduct tasks in English without problems) ☐
e) intermediate level (maybe able to do the task in English after medium-long-period study) ☐
f) lower intermediate level (maybe able to communicate in English after long-period study) ☐
g) low level (maybe able to communicate in English after long-period study, yet will mostly struggle and find it hard) ☐
i) rock bottom level (can't communicate in English at all) ☐

2. A question for the father – have you ever lived in an English-speaking country? How long did you stay?
3. A question for the mother – have you ever lived in an English-speaking country? How long did you stay?

Mother's Questionnaire:
Please tick the box, showing your thought and behaviours.

a) Strongly disagree ☐ b) Disagree somewhat ☐
c) Agree somewhat ☐ d) Strongly agree ☐

1. I have a great interest in English education. ☐
2. I myself feel the necessity of learning English. ☐
3. I want to learn English for my own sake. ☐
4. I think it is important for me to learn English in order for me to teach my child English. ☐
5. I believe that my child's English will be improved when they learn together with me. ☐
6. I think it is important to teach English in nursery schools. ☐
7. I think my child must study English. ☐
8. I think it is desirable to learn English before primary school. ☐
9. English learning must be compulsory in primary school. ☐
10. Teaching English for young child in nursery schools causes an economic burden. ☐
11. English education causes too much burden on a young child. ☐
12. Learning English before primary school is inefficient. ☐
13. For a young child, learning both Korean and English is burdensome. ☐
14. Learning English before primary school will make it harder for young children to establish their identity as Korean. ☐
15. To learn English before primary school will be destructive in learning Korean. ☐

16. If a child is unable to learn English well at a young age, they may be daunted by it later. ☐
17. I think my child is too young to learn English. ☐
18. I think studying English as early as possible is more efficient. ☐
19. It is good to study English every day. ☐
20. I believe that a child who studies English early will have a better command of English later. ☐
21. I believe that children tend to develop native-speaker-like pronunciation the more they are exposed to English at an earlier age. ☐
22. I think it is more important for my child to be able to speak English than Korean. ☐
23. I want my child to have the right balance between speaking Korean and English. ☐
24. I believe that bilingual children have better mental abilities than monolingual children. ☐
25. I believe that studying English improves my child's intelligence. ☐
26. I believe that studying English improves my child's problem-solving abilities. ☐
27. I believe that it is beneficial for my child to study all subjects in English. ☐
28. I believe that studying English improves my child's overall academic achievement. ☐
29. I think studying English provides a better opportunity for my child to be able to communicate with more people worldwide. ☐
30. I believe that studying English makes my child become social and good at making friends. ☐
31. I believe that good English command will help my child to become more confident. ☐
32. I believe that studying English improves my child's emotional development. ☐
33. I think if you are good at English, you will earn more money. ☐
34. I believe that good English command can make one more competitive in the global market. ☐
35. I believe that good English command will give one a better chance to have a good job. ☐
36. I believe that studying English will enable my child to understand other cultures better. ☐

Mother's goals for the child's English education
Please circle as many as are relevant
1. Increased interest in English
2. Good pronunciation
3. Vocabulary development
4. Understanding other cultures
5. Decreased anxiety when speaking with foreigners
6. Developing communicative ability
7. Improving basic skills needed at school
8. Improving basic skills for future success in the society

Please circle how your child thinks and behaves normally.
1. My child finds it difficult to wait until the end of a task.
2. My child is very impatient.
3. My child becomes easily bored even with the toy or games that he likes.
4. My child becomes more easily distracted than other children.
5. My child cannot stay calm.
6. My child easily startles.
7. My child imagines always the worst scenario.
8. My child become easily pessimistic and negative.
9. My child becomes easily frightened.
10. My child is calm even in a new environment.
11. My child tends to overcome stress quickly and easily.
12. My child likes meeting new people.
13. My child feels fearful and nervous when going into a new place.
14. My child is shy.
15. My child is afraid of standing in front of others and sing or dance.
16. It takes long time for my child to become comfortable with strangers.
17. My child becomes easily nervous in a new, strange environment.
18. My child becomes easily nervous when he/she knows others are watching them.
19. My child does not want us to leave them alone in a new, strange environment.
20. My child easily gives up when the instruction for a new toy is hard.
21. My child is determined to finish the work after they start.
22. My child plays with one toy for a long time.
23. My child likes to solve a difficult puzzle patiently.
24. My child is trying hard to do all things well.
25. My child is sort of a perfectionist and tries hard until they finish the work.
26. My child does not stop working until they finish it.

27. My child tries hard until they are good at it.
28. My child is passionate to learn and practice what they learn.

Please circle how your child reacted last 6 months
1. My child often said 'I am not good at English'. 'I am the only one who is not good at English'.
2. My child pretends to be unwell before studying English.
3. My child looks forward to English lessons.
4. My child wishes they could study English more.
5. My child is worried that they will perform badly in their English lesson.
6. Before studying English, my child complains about their physical condition (e.g. saying I have a tummy ache).
7. My child asks questions about English.
8. My child says they like English very much.
9. My child says they hate English.
10. My child does not resist when we play using English-learning materials at home.
11. My child is eager to play with parents while using English-learning materials at home.
12. My child does not like to interact with us in English or do any English-related activities (e.g. when we try, they block their ears).
13. My child says that they do not want to go to English lessons.
14. My child enjoys singing and playing in English.
15. My child says that they want to speak better English.
16. My child has a great interest in English.
17. My child doesn't want to participate in English lessons.
18. My child is nervous about their performance during English lessons.
19. My child uses what they learn during English lessons.
20. Before English class, my child feels nervous and keeps asking 'Am I doing English today?'
21. My child shows great curiosity for new words.
22. My child finds English class fun.

Mother's evaluation of the child's English.
Please rate your child's English proficiency (1-5) 1 is poor 5 is excellent.

Listening ☐	Speaking ☐
Reading ☐	Writing ☐
Vocabulary ☐	Grammar ☐
Pronunciation ☐	

Please read this and answer the question or circle your view on English learning at nursery.

1. When did you child start English learning in the nursery?
   Please write down the age of your child (in months).
2. How much do you pay monthly for the special English tuition in the nursery?
3. Are you satisfied with the special English tuition in the nursery?
   a) Not satisfied at all
   b) Somewhat unsatisfied
   c) Somewhat satisfied
   d) Very satisfied
4. Recently, the ministry of Education banned English tuition at nursery schools in order to protect children from the stress of English education. What is your view?
   a) agree
   b) disagree
   c) no idea

4-1. what would you do if English learning is not achieved in the nursery?
   a) I won't teach my child English
   b) I will try to find alternative way (e.g. visiting tutor, private academy)
   c) other thoughts

4-2. if you have chosen to find an alternative way of teaching English, how much can you spend for your child's English education?

Read the following and circle your view on English education in the nursery

   a) it's not a problem for us at all
   b) it's not a too bad problem
   c) a little problem
   d) big problem

1. It causes too much financial burden.
2. It causes too much academic burden for young children.
3. The children will not be able to use what they learn so the learning outcomes are only effective in the short-term.
4. My child does not make an expected progress.
5. My child does not show great interest on English learning.

6. My child developed some resistance/reluctance to speaking English.
7. My child does not show an improved understanding of other cultures.
8. My child does not show an improved friendly attitude towards foreigners.
9. My child experiences confusion in speaking Korean due to English learning.

Please circle the material you use when you teach English at home. Also indicate how many minutes/hours you use them in a week. Please indicate whether the child uses it alone or with another sibling or parents.

1. Books
2. Picture card
3. TV
4. CD or MP3
5. DVD player
6. Computer (desktop or notebook)
7. Smartphone or tablet
8. AI speaker

Please indicate how private English education is conducted outside English nursery.

1. Through a babysitter who can speak English (e.g. Philippine nationality)
2. Through a visiting tutor
3. Through visiting an institute or study programme
4. Through special activities where English is the instruction language (e.g. Ballet in English)
5. Through a telephone teacher
6. Through an online 1:1 teacher

The following question is about English camp. Please answer.

1. English camp in Korea

    Have you been there? How many times? How old was your child? How many hours was your child there per a week? How long did they participate in the camp?

    Were you (mother) satisfied?

2. Overseas English camp

    Have you been there? How many times? How old was your child? How many hours was your child there per a week? How long did they participate in the camp?

    Were you (mother) satisfied?

Which form of English learning program do you use most frequently?

1. Through a babysitter who can speak English (e.g. Philippine nationality)
2. Through a visiting tutor
3. Through visiting an institute or study programme
4. Through special activities where English is the instruction language (e.g. Ballet in English)
5. Through a telephone teacher
6. Through an online 1:1 teacher

What is your (mother) view on the method you chose in the above question?

1. It causes too much financial burden.
2. It causes too much academic burden for young children.
3. The children will not be able to use what they learn so the learning outcomes are only effective in the short-term.
4. My child does not make an expected progress.
5. My child does not show great interest on English learning.
6. My child developed some resistance/reluctance to speaking English.
7. My child does not show an improved understanding of other cultures.
8. My child does not show an improved friendly attitude towards foreigners.
9. My child experiences confusion in speaking Korean due to English learning.

What is your (mother) view on the method you chose at home – in terms of its educational, entertainment values, as well as your overall use satisfaction?

1. books
2. picture card
3. TV
4. CD or MP3
5. DVD player
6. Computer (desktop or notebook)
7. Smartphone or tablet
8. AI speaker

How do you interact with your child in English and how many minutes/hours do you interact daily? When did you start interacting with your child in English? Was the child's sibling or your partner present too?

1. Reading English books together
2. Listening to English nursery songs and sing together

3. Playing games in English
4. Watching English videos together
5. Using internet content together

Are you (mother) satisfied by the method you chose?

a) Not satisfied at all
b) Somewhat unsatisfied
c) Somewhat satisfied
d) Very satisfied

References

Adaa.org (2019) Screening for an anxiety disorder: Children. Anxiety and Depression Association of America, ADAA. See https://adaa.org/living-with-anxiety/ask-and-learn/screenings/screening-anxiety-disorder-children.

Ahn, H. (2015) Awareness of and attitudes to Asian Englishes: A study of English teachers in South Korea. *Asian Englishes* 17 (2), 132–151. https://doi.org/10.1080/13488678.2015.1036602.

Ahn, H. (2020) South Korean perceptions of 'native' speaker of English in social and news media via big data analytics. *Journal of English as Lingua Franca* 9 (1), 33–56.

Ahn, S.Y. and Baek, H.J. (2013) Academic achievement-oriented society and its relationship to the psychological well-being of Korean adolescents. In C.-C. Yi (ed.) *The Psychological Well-being of East Asian Youth* (pp. 265–279). Dordrecht: Springer.

Aida, Y. (1994) Examination of Horwitz, Horwitz, and Cope's construct of foreign language anxiety: The case of students of Japanese. *The Modern Language Journal* 78 (2), 155–168.

Airij, A.G., Bakhteri, R. and Khalil-Hani, M. (2016) Smart wearable stress monitoring device for autistic children. *Jurnal Teknologi* 78 (7–5), 75–81.

Al-Seghayer, K. (2001) The effect of multimedia annotation modes on L2 vocabulary acquisition: A comparative study. *Language Learning & Technology* 5 (1), 202–232.

Andrade, M. (2009) The effects of English language proficiency on adjustment to university life. *International Multilingual Research Journal* 3 (1), 16–34. https://doi.org/10.1080/19313150802668249.

Andreou, G. and Trott, K. (2013) Verbal frequency in adults diagnosed with attention-deficit hyperactivity disorder (ADHD) in childhood. *ADHD Attention-Deficit and Hyperactivity Disorder* 5 (4), 343–351. https://doi.org/10.1007/s12402-013-0112-z.

Arnsten, A. (2009) Stress signalling pathways that impair prefrontal cortex structure and function. *Nature Reviews Neuroscience* 10 (6), 410–422. https://doi.org/10.1038/nrn2648.

Ashcraft, M.H. (2002) Math anxiety: Personal, educational, and cognitive consequences. *Current Directions in Psychological Science* 11 (5), 181–185. https://doi.org/10.1111/1467-8721.00196.

Ashcraft, M.H. and Kirk, E.P. (2001) The relationships among working memory, math anxiety, and performance. *Journal of Experimental Psychology: General* 130 (2), 224–237. http://dx.doi.org/10.1037/0096-3445.130.2.224.

Auerbach, E.R. (1993) Re-examining English only in the ESL classroom. *TESOL Quarterly* 27 (1), 9–32. https://doi.org/10.2307/3586949.

Baddley, A. (2003) Working memory and language: An overview. *Journal of Communication Disorders* 36 (3), 189–208. https://doi.org/10.1016/S0021-9924(03)00019-4.

Bae, S.H. (2013) The pursuit of multilingualism in transnational educational migration: strategies of linguistic investment among Korean jogi yuhak families in Singapore. *Language and Education* 27 (5), 415–431.

Bae, M.S. and Seo, H. (2011) Current condition and perspectives of directors and teachers toward early English education for infants: Focusing on Busan Area. *The Journal of the Korea Contents Association* 11 (6), 510–521. DOI: 10.5392/JKCA.2011.11.6.510.

Baker, L. and Cantwell, D.P. (1982) Developmental, social, and behavioral characteristics of speech and language disordered children. *Child Psychiatry and Human Development* 12 (4), 195–206. https://doi.org/10.1007/BF01812585.

Baker, L. and Cantwell, D.P. (1987a) Comparison of well, emotionally disordered, and behaviorally disordered children with linguistic problems. *Journal of the American Academy of Child & Adolescent Psychiatry* 26 (2), 193–196. https://doi.org/10.1097/00004583-198703000-00012.

Baker, L. and Cantwell, D.P. (1987b) A prospective psychiatric follow-up of children with speech/language disorders. *Journal of the American Academy of Child & Adolescent Psychiatry* 26 (4), 546–553. https://doi.org/10.1097/00004583-198707000-00015.

Baker, L. and Cantwell, D.P. (1987c) Factors associated with the development of psychiatric illness in children with early speech/language problems. *Journal of Autism and Developmental Disorders* 17 (4), 499–510. https://doi.org/10.1007/BF01486966.

Baker, S.C. and MacIntyre, P.D. (2000) The role of gender and immersion in communication and second language orientations. *Language Learning* 50 (2), 311–341. https://doi.org/10.1111/0023-8333.00224.

Baran-Łucarz, M. (2013) Perfectionism and language anxiety. *Anglica Wratislaviensia* 51, 107–120.

Barcroft, J. (2002) Semantic and structural elaboration in L2 lexical acquisition. *Language Learning* 52 (2), 323–363. https://doi.org/10.1111/0023-8333.00186.

Beilock, S.L., Gunderson, E.A., Ramirez, G. and Levine, S.C. (2010) Female teachers' math anxiety affects girls' math achievement. *Proceedings of the National Academy of Sciences* 107 (5), 1860–1863.

Beitchman, J.H., Hood, J., Rochon, J., Peterson, M., Mantini, T. and Majumdar, S. (1989) Empirical classification of speech/language impairment in children: I. Identification of speech/language categories. *Journal of the American Academy of Child & Adolescent Psychiatry* 28 (1), 112–117. http://dx.doi.org/10.1097/00004583-198901000-00021.

Beitchman, J.H., Peterson, M. and Clegg, M. (1988) Speech and language impairment and psychiatric disorder: The relevance of family demographic variables. *Child Psychiatry and Human Development* 18 (4), 191–207.

Beitchman, J., Wilson, B., Johnson, C., Atkinson, L., Young, A., Adlaf, E., Escobar, M. and Douglas, L. (2001) Fourteen-year follow-up of speech/language-impaired and control children: Psychiatric outcome. *Journal of the American Academy of Child and Adolescent Psychiatry* 40 (1), 75–82. https://doi.org/10.1097/00004583-200101000-00019.

Bergman, C.R. (1976) Interference vs independent development in infant bilingualism. In G.D. Keller, R.V. Teschner and S. Viera (eds) *Bilingualism in the Bicentennial and Beyond* (pp. 86–96). New York: Bilingual Press.

Beschorner, B. and Hutchison, A. (2013) iPads as a literacy teaching tool in early childhood. *International Journal of Education in Mathematics, Science and Technology* 1 (1), 16–24.

Bhatia, M.S. and Goyal, A. (2018) Anxiety disorders in children and adolescents: Need for early detection. *Journal of Postgraduate Medicine* 64 (2), 75–76.

Bialystok, E. and Hakuta, K. (1994) *In Other Words: The Science and Psychology Acquisition*. New York: Basic Books.

Biggs, J. (1996) Academic development in Confucian heritage culture. Paper presented at *The International Symposium on Child Development*. Hong Kong.

Biggs, J.B. and Watkins, D.A. (1996) *The Chinese Learner: Cultural, Psychological, and Contextual Influences*. Hong Kong: CERC and ACER.

Bloom, B.S. (1956) *Taxonomy of Educational Objectives, Handbook: Cognitive Domain*. New York: David McKay.

Bongaerts, T., van Summeren, C., Planken, B. and Schils, E. (1997) Age and ultimate attainment in the pronunciation of a foreign language. *Studies in Second Language Acquisition* 19 (4), 447–465.

Boudreau, C., MacIntyre, P.D. and Dewaele, J.M. (2018) Enjoyment and anxiety in second language communication: An idiodynamic approach. *Studies in Second Language Learning and Teaching* 8 (1), 149–170.

Brophy, J. (1999) *Working with Perfectionist Students* (Report No. 4). Urbana, IL: ERIC Clearinghouse on Elementary and Early Childhood Education.

Brown, H.D. (2000) *Principles of Language Learning and Teaching* (4th edn). New York: Longman.
Bruck, M. (1978) The suitability of early French immersion programs for the language disabled child. *Canadian Journal of Education* 3, 51–72.
Bruck, M. (1982) Language impaired children's performance in an additive bilingual education program. *Applied Psycholinguistics* 3 (1), 45–60. https://doi.org/10.1017/S014271640000415X.
Bryman, A. (2012) *Social Research Methods* (4th edn). Oxford: Oxford University Press.
Burden, T. (2016) A career in child and adolescent psychiatry. *BMJ* 354, i4983.
Burghy, C., Stodola, D., Ruttle, P., Molloy, E., Armstrong, J., Oler, J., Fox, M., Hayes, A., Kalin, N., Essex, M., Davidson, R. and Birn, R. (2012) Developmental pathways to amygdala-prefrontal function and internalizing symptoms in adolescence. *Nature Neuroscience* 15 (12), 1736–1741. https://doi.org/10.1038/nn.3257.
Butler, Y.G. (2014) Current issues in English education for young learners in East Asia. *English Teaching* 69 (4), 3–25.
Bygate, M., Skehan, P. and Swain, M. (2001) Introduction. In M. Bygate, P. Skehan and M. Swain (eds) *Researching Pedagogic Tasks: Second Language Learning, Teaching and Testing* (pp. 1–20). New York: Pearson Education Limited.
Camarata, S.M., Hughes, C.A. and Ruhl, H.K. (1988) Mild/moderate behaviorally disordered students. *Language, Speech, and Hearing Services in Schools* 19 (2), 191–200. https://doi.org/10.1044/0161-1461.1902.191.
Casey, B.J., Giedd, J.N. and Thomas, K.M. (2000) Structural and functional brain development and its relation to cognitive development. *Biological Psychology* 54 (1–3), 241–257. http://dx.doi.org/10.1016/S0301-0511(00)00058-2.
Chalmers, H. (2019) *The Role of the First Language in English Medium Instruction*. Oxford: Oxford University Press.
Chan, S. (1999) The Chinese learner-a question of style. *Education and Training* 41 (6/7), 294–304.
Chang, H. and Holt, R. (1994) A Chinese perspective on face as inter-relational concern. In S. Ting-Toomey (ed.) *The Challenge of Framework* (pp. 95–132). Albany, NY: State University of New York Press.
Chao, R.K. (1995) Beyond Authoritarianism: A Cultural Perspective on Asian American Parenting Practices. Paper presented at the Annual Meeting of the American Psychological Association, New York.
Chastain, K. (1975) Affective and ability factors in second-language acquisition. *Language Learning* 25 (1), 153–161. https://doi.org/10.1111/j.1467-1770.1975.tb00115.x.
Cho, J. (2015) Sleepless in Seoul: Neoliberalism, English fever, and linguistic insecurity among Korean interpreters. *Multilingua* 34 (5), 687–710.
Choi, H.J. (2015) Mental health and early childhood education. Proceedings from *Influence of Early Education on Mental Health of Young Children and Ways to Prevent*, 1–42. Seoul: OAPE.
Choi, N.Y., Cho, H.J., Kang, S. and Sheo, J.Y. (2019a) Development of young children's English learning interest and anxiety rating scale. *Journal of Early Childhood Education & Educare Welfare* 23 (3), 7–38.
Choi, N.Y., Kang, S., Cho, H.J. and Sheo, J. (2019b) Promoting young children's interest in learning English in EFL context: The role of mothers. *Education Sciences* 9 (1), 46. https://doi.org/10.3390/educsci9010046.
Chorpita, B.F. and Barlow, D.H. (1998) The development of anxiety: The role of control in the early environment. *Psychological Bulletin* 124 (1), 3. https://doi.org/10.1037/0033-2909.124.1.3.
Clément, R. (1980) Ethnicity, contact and communicative competence in a second language. In H. Giles, W.P. Robinson and P. Smith (eds) *Language: Social Psychological Perspectives* (pp. 147–154). Oxford: Pergamon Press.
Clément, R., Dörnyei, Z and Noels, K.A. (1994) Motivation, self-confidence, and group cohesion in the foreign language classroom. *Language Learning* 44 (3), 417–448.

Cohen, A. and Robbins, M. (1976) Towards assessing interlanguage performance: The relationship between selected errors, learner's characteristics, and learner's explanations. *Language Learning* 26, 45–66. https://doi.org/10.1111/j.1467-1770.1976.tb00259.x.

Cohen, N.J., Davine, M. and Meloche-Kelly, M. (1989) Prevalence of unsuspected language disorders in a child psychiatric population. *Journal of the American Academy of Child & Adolescent Psychiatry* 28 (1), 107–111. http://dx.doi.org/10.1097/00004583-198901000-00020.

Cohen, N.J., Davine, M., Horodezky, N., Lipsett, L. and Isaacson, L. (1993) Unsuspected language impairment in psychiatrically disturbed children: Prevalence and language and behavioral characteristics. *Journal of the American Academy of Child & Adolescent Psychiatry* 32 (3), 595–603. http://dx.doi.org/10.1097/00004583-199305000-00016.

Colombo, J. (1982) The critical period concept: Research, methodology, and theoretical issues. *Psychological Bulletin* 91 (2), 260.

Conboy, B.T., Brooks, R., Meltzoff, A.N. and Kuhl, P.K. (2015) Social interaction in infants' learning of second-language phonetics: An exploration of brain–behavior relations. *Developmental Neuropsychology* 40 (4), 216–229. https://doi.org/10.1080/87565641.2015.1014487.

Cook, V.J. (1991) The poverty-of-the-stimulus argument and multi-competence. *Second Language Research* 7, 103–117.

Cook, V.J. (1997) Monolingual bias in second language acquisition research. *Revista canaria de estudios ingleses* 34, 35–50.

Cook, V.J. (1999) Going beyond the native speaker in language teaching. *TESOL Quarterly* 33 (2), 185–209. https://doi.org/10.2307/3587717.

Cook, V.J. (2001) Using the first language in the classroom. *The Canadian Modern Language Review* 57 (3), 402–423. https://doi.org/10.3138/cmlr.57.3.402.

Cook, V.J. (2016) Where is the native speaker now? *TESOL Quarterly* 50 (1), 186–189.

Cortazzi, M. and Jin, L. (2001) Large classes in China: Good teachers and interaction. In D.A. Watkins and J.B. Biggs (eds) *Teaching the Chinese Learner: Psychological and Pedagogical Perspectives* (pp. 115–134). Hong Kong/Melbourne: CERC & ACER.

Creswell, J.W. and Plano Clark, V.L. (2011) *Designing and Conducting Mixed Methods Research* (2nd edn). Los Angeles: Sage Publications.

Cummins, J. (1998) Immersion education for the millennium: What we have learned from 30 years of research on second language immersion. In M.R. Childs and R.M. Bostwick (eds) *Learning Through Two Languages: Research and Practice. Second Katoh Gakuen International Symposium on Immersion and Bilingual Education.* (pp. 34–47). Katoh Gakuen, Japan.

Cummins, J. (2000) *Language, Power and Pegagogy*. Clevedon: Multilingual Matters.

Cummins, J. and Swain, M. (1986) *Bilingualism in Education: Aspects of Theory, Research and Practice*. New York: Longman.

Curtiss, S. (1977) *Genie: A Psycholinguistic Study of a Modern Day 'Wild-Child'*. New York: Academic Press.

Curtiss, S. (1989) The independence and task-specificity of language. In M. Bornstein and J. Bruner (eds) *Interaction in Human Development* (pp. 105–137). Hillsdale, NJ: Erlbaum.

Dadds, M.R., Spence, S.H., Holland, D.E., Barrett, P.M. and Laurens, K.R. (1997) Prevention and early intervention for anxiety disorders: A controlled trial. *Journal of Consulting and Clinical Psychology* 65 (4).

Dahl, K. (1998) Why cooking in the curriculum? *Young Children* 53 (1), 81–83.

David, S. (1985) The acquisition of the phonological features of a second dialect. Unpublished master's thesis, University of South Carolina, Columbia.

Dawe, C. (2014) Native speaking English teachers as perceived by South Korean elementary and middle school students. *Journal of Shinawatra University* 1 (1), 42–58.

DCSF (2007) New arrivals in excellence programme guidance. Primary and secondary national strategies. See https://ealresources.bell-foundation.org.uk/sites/default/files/document-files/New%20Arrivals%20Guidance.pdf (accessed September 2020).

Deb, S., Strodl, E. and Sun, J. (2015) Academic stress, parental pressure, anxiety and mental health among Indian high school students. *International Journal of Psychology and Behavioral Sciences* 5 (1), 26–34.

DeKeyser, R. (2003) Implicit and explicit learning. In C. Doughty and M. Long (eds) *Handbook of Second Language Acquisition* (pp. 313–348). Oxford: Blackwell.

Demick, B. (2002) Some in S. Korea opt for a trim when English trips the tongue. *Los Angeles Times*. See https://www.latimes.com/archives/la-xpm-2002-mar-31-mn-35590-story.html.

Denham, S.A. (2003) Social and emotional learning, early childhood. In *Encyclopedia of Primary Prevention and Health Promotion* (pp. 1009–1018). Boston, MA: Springer.

Dewaele, J.M. (2010) Multilingualism and affordances: Variation in self-perceived communicative competence and communicative anxiety in French L1, L2, L3 and L4. *International Review of Applied Linguistics in Language Teaching* 48 (2), 105–129. https://doi.org/10.1515/iral.2010.006.

Dewaele, J.M. (2017) Psychological dimensions and foreign language anxiety. In S. Loewen and M. Sato (eds) *The Routledge Handbook of Instructed Second Language Acquisition* (pp. 433–450). Abingdon: Routledge.

Dewaele, J.M. (2018) Why the dichotomy 'L1 versus LX user' is better than 'native versus non-native speaker'. *Applied Linguistics* 39 (2), 236–240. https://doi.org/10.1093/applin/amw055.

Dewaele, J.M. and Dewaele, L. (2020) Are foreign language learners' enjoyment and anxiety specific to the teacher? An investigation into the dynamics of learners' classroom emotions. *Studies in Second Language Learning and Teaching* 10 (1), 45–65.

Dewaele, J.M. and MacIntyre, P. (2014) The two faces of Janus? Anxiety and enjoyment in the foreign language classroom. *Studies in Second Language Learning and Teaching* 4 (2), 237–274. https://doi.org/10.14746/ssllt.2014.4.2.5.

Dewaele, J.M. and MacIntyre, P. (2016) Foreign language enjoyment and foreign language classroom anxiety. The right and left feet of the language learner? In P. MacIntyre, T. Gregersen and S. Mercer (eds) *Positive Psychology in SLA* (pp. 215–236). Bristol: Multilingual Matters.

Dewaele, J.M., Chen, X., Padilla, A.M. and Lake, J. (2019) The flowering of positive psychology in foreign/second language teaching and acquisition research. *Frontiers in Psychology* 10, 2128.

Dewaele, J.M., Witney, J., Saito, K. and Dewaele, L. (2018) Foreign language enjoyment and anxiety: The effect of teacher and learner variables. *Language Teaching Research* 22 (6), 676–697. https://doi.org/10.1177/1362168817692161.

Didi-Ogren, H.H. (2020) Sociocultural linguistic approaches to code switching in Japanese women's talk in interaction: Region, gender, and language. *Multilingua* 1 (ahead-of-print).

Dörnyei, Z. (2005) *The Psychology of the Language Learner: Individual Differences in Second Language Acquisition*. Mahwah, NJ: Lawrence Erlbaum Associates Publishers.

Doughty, C.J. and Long, M.H. (2003) Optimal psycholinguistic environments for distance foreign language learning. *Language Learning & Technology* 7 (3), 50–80.

Drury, E. (2013) Beginners' guide to using technology in language lessons. *The Guardian*. See https://www.theguardian.com/teacher-network/teacher-blog/2013/may/18/language-lessons-technology-beginners-guide.

Dulay, H. and Burt, M. (1977) Remarks on creativity in language acquisition. In M. Burt, H. Dulay and M. Finocchiaro (eds) *Viewpoints on English as a Second Language* (pp. 95–126). New York: Regents.

Dumais, T. (2016) Can apps really help children learn languages? British Council Website. See https://www.britishcouncil.org/voices-magazine/can-apps-really-help-children-learn-languages.

Duquette, L. and Painchaud, G. (1996) A comparison of vocabulary acquisition in audio and video contexts. *The Canadian Modern Language Review* 53 (1), 143–172. https://doi.org/10.3138/cmlr.53.1.143.

Dweck, C.S. (2008) *Mindset: The New Psychology of Success*. London: Random House Digital, Inc.
Eisenberg, N., Valiente, C., Spinrad, T.L., Cumberland, A., Liew, J., Reiser, M., Zhou, Q. and Losoya, S.A. (2009) Longitudinal relations of children's effortful control, impulsiveness, and negative emotionality to their externalizing, internalizing, and co-occurring behavior problems. *Developmental Psychology* 45 (4), 988–1008. https://doi.apa.org/doi/10.1037/a0016213.
Elkhafaifi, H. (2005) Listening comprehension and anxiety in the Arabic language classroom. *The Modern Langauge Journal* 89 (2), 206–220. https://doi.org/10.1111/j.1540-4781.2005.00275.x.
Ellis, N. and Beaton, A. (1993) Factors affecting the learning of foreign language vocabulary: Imagery keyword mediators and phonological short-term memory. *The Quarterly Journal of Experimental Psychology A: Human Experimental Psychology* 46A (3), 533–558.
Ellis, R. (2003) *Task-based Language Learning and Teaching*. Oxford: University of Oxford Press.
Ellis, R. (2009) Implicit and explicit learning, knowledge, and instruction. In R. Ellis, S. Loewen, C. Elder, R. Erlam, J. Philp and H. Reinder (eds) *Implicit and Explicit Knowledge in Second Language Learning, Testing, and Teaching* (pp. 3–26). Bristol: Multilingual Matters.
ETS TOEFL (2018) *Test and Score Data Summary for TOEFL iBT Tests*. Princeton, NJ: ETS TOEFL. http://www.ets.org/toefl.
Fathman, A.K. (1975) The relationship between age and second language learning ability. *Language Learning* 25, 245–253.
Fillmore, L.W. (1991) When learning a second language means losing the first. *Early Childhood Research Quarterly* 6 (3), 323–346. https://doi.org/10.1016/S0885-2006(05)80059-6.
Firth, A. and Wagner, J. (1997) On discourse, communication, and (some) fundamental concepts in SLA research. *Modern Language Journal* 81 (3), 285–300. https://doi.org/10.1111/j.1540-4781.1997.tb05480.x.
Fortune, T.W. (2011) Struggling learners and the language immersion classroom. In D.J. Tedick, D. Christian and T.W. Fortune (eds) *Immersion Education: Practices, Policies, Possibilities*. Bristol: Multilingual Matters.
Fredrickson, B.L. (2003) The value of positive emotions. *American Scientist* 91 (4), 330–335.
Fredrickson, B.L. (2004) The broaden-and-build theory of positive emotions. *Philosophical Transactions of the Royal Society of London Series B: Biological Sciences* 359, 1367–1377.
Furner, J.M. and Berman, B.T. (2003) Review of research: math anxiety: Overcoming a major obstacle to the improvement of student math performance. *Childhood Education* 79 (3), 170–174.
Gadye, L. (2018) What part of the brain deals with anxiety? What can brains affected by anxiety tell us? Ask an Expert: Brain Facts.org. See https://www.brainfacts.org/diseases-and-disorders/mental-health/2018/what-part-of-the-brain-deals-with-anxiety-what-can-brains-affected-by-anxiety-tell-us-062918.
García, O. (2009) Education, multilingualism and translanguaging in the 21st century. In M.A. Mohanty (ed.) *Multilingual Education for Social Justice: Globalising the Local* (pp. 128–145). New Delhi: Orient Blackswan.
García, O. and Li Wei (2014) *Translanguaging: Language, Bilingualism and Education*. London: Palgrave Macmillan.
Gardner, R.C. (1985) *Social Psychology and Second Language Learning: The Role of Attitude and Motivation*. Baltimore, MD: Edward Arnold.
Gardner, R.C. and MacIntyre, P.D. (1991) An instrumental motivation in language study: Who says it isn't effective. *Studies in Second Language Acquisition* 13 (1), 57–72. https://doi.org/10.1017/S0272263100009724.
Gardner, R.C., Smythe, P.C. and Brunet, G.R. (1977) Intensive second language study: Effects on attitudes, motivation and French achievement. *Language Learning* 27, 243–261.

Gardner, R.C., Smythe, P.C. and Clément, R. (1979) Intensive second language study in a bicultural milieu: An investigation of attitudes, motivation and language proficiency. *Language Learning* 29, 305–320.

Gayton, A. (2010) Socioeconomic status and language-learning motivation: To what extent does the former influence the latter? *Scottish Languages Review* 22, 17–28.

Gebauer, S., Zaunbauer, A. and Moller, J. (2013) Cross-language transfer in English immersion programs in Germany: Reading comprehension and reading fluency. *Contemporary Educational Psychology* 38 (1), 64–74. https://doi.org/10.1016/j.cedpsych.2012.09.002.

Geist, E. (2010) The anti-anxiety curriculum: Combating math anxiety in the classroom. *Journal of Instructional Psychology* 37 (1), 24–31.

Genesee, F. (1978) Second language learning and language attitudes. *Working Papers on Bilingualism* 16, 19–42.

Genesee, F. (1987) *Learning Through Two Languages: Studies of Immersion and Bilingual Education.* Cambridge, MA: Newbury House.

Genesee, F. (2011) Reflecting on possibilities for immersion. In D.J. Tedick, D. Christian and T.W. Fortune (eds) *Immersion Education: Practices, Policies, Possibilities* (pp. 271–279). Bristol: Multilingual Matters.

Gervain, J. (2018) The role of prenatal experience in language development. *Current Opinion in Behavioral Sciences* 21, 62–67. https://doi.org/10.1016/j.cobeha.2018.02.004.

Ginsborg, H. (2006) Empirical concepts and the content of experience. *European Journal of Philosophy* 14 (3), 349–372. http://dx.doi.org/ 10.1111/j.1468-0378.2006.00230.x.

Go, Y.J. and Go, Y.H. (2013) Staus quo of English education in Japan: With a special reference to early child English education. *Journal of Linguistic Studies* 18 (1), 1–23.

Goth, K., Cloninger, C.R. and Schmerck, K. (2003) *Das Junior Temperament and Charakter Inventar fur das Kindergartenalter – JTCI/3-6.* Göttingen: Testzentrale.

Grandgeorge, M., Hausberger, M., Tordjman, S., Deleau, M., Lazartigues, A. and Lemonnier, E. (2009) Environmental factors influence language development in children with autism spectrum disorders. *PloS One* 4 (4), e4683.

Greene, J.C. (2007) *Mixed Methods in Social Inquiry* (Vol. 9). John Wiley & Sons.

Gregersen, T. and Horwitz, E.K. (2002) Language learning and perfectionism: Anxious and non-anxious language learners' reactions to their own oral performance. *The Modern Language Journal* 86 (4), 562–570.

Griskevicius, V. and Kenrick, D. (2013) Fundamental motives: How evolutionary needs influence consumer behaviour. *Journal of Consumer Psychology* 23 (3), 372–386. http://dx.doi.org/10.1016/j.jcps.2013.03.003.

Griskevicius, V., Tybur, J.M., Delton, A.W. and Robertson, T.E. (2011) The influence of mortality and socioeconomic status on risk and delayed rewards: A life history theory approach. *Journal of Personality and Social Psychology* 100 (6), 1015–1026. http://dx.doi.org/10.1037/a0022403.

Griva, E. and Sivropoulou, R. (2009) Implementation and evaluation of an early foreign language learning project in kindergarten. *Early Childhood Education Journal* 37 (1), 79–87. https://doi.org/10.1007/s10643-009-0314-3.

Grosjean, F. (2009) What parents want to know about bilingualism. *The Bilingual Family Newsletter* 26 (4), 1–6.

Grosjean, F. (2010) *Bilingual: Life and Reality.* Cambridge, MA: Harvard University Press. http://dx.doi.org/10.4159/9780674056459.

Gu, P.Y. and Johnson, R.K. (1996) Vocabulary learning strategies and language learning outcomes. *Language Learning* 46, 643–679. http://dx.doi.org/10.1111/j.1467-1770.1996.tb01355.x.

Guía, E. d.l., Camacho, V.L., Orozco-Barbosa, L., Luján, V.M.B., Penichet, V.M.R. and Pérez, M.L. (2016) Introducing IoT and wearable technologies into task-based language learning for young children. *IEEE Transactions on Learning Technologies* 9 (4), 366–378. https://doi.org/10.1109/TLT.2016.2557333.

Guiora, A.Z., Beit-Hallahmi, B., Brannon, R.C., Dull, C.Y. and Scovel T. (1972) The effects of experimentally induced changes in ego states on pronunciation ability in a second language: An exploratory study. *Comprehensive Psychiatry* 13 (5), 421–428.

Gutteling, B.M., de Weerth, C. and Buitelaar, J.K. (2005) Prenatal stress and children's cortisol reaction to the first day of school. *Psychoneuroendocrinology* 30 (6), 541–549.

Hackman, D.A. and Farah, M.J. (2009) Socioeconomic status and the developing brain. *Trends in Cognitive Sciences* 13, 65–73. http://dx.doi.org/10.1016/j.tics.2008.11.003.

Hackman, D.A., Farah, M.J. and Meaney M.J. (2010) Socioeconomic status and the brain: Mechanistic insights from human and animal research. *Nature Reviews Neuroscience* 11 (9), 651–659. http://dx.doi.org/10.1038/nrn2897.

Han, J.-H. (2018) *Eommapyo yeongeo ije sijak hamnida – 7 se kkaji yeongeo nochul jero, 16 se e haewoe daehak iphak han bimil* [Mom's English starts now-the secret to going from no exposure at age 7 to enrolling in an overseas university at age 16]. Seoul: Cheongrim Life.

Hartley, C. and Casey, B. (2013) Risk for anxiety and implications for treatment: Developmental, environmental, and genetic factors governing fear regulation. *Annals of the New York Academy of Sciences* 1304 (1), 1–13. https://doi.org/10.1111/nyas.12287.

Heo, N.S. (2013) 20,000 more "Goose Families" a year, 500,000 families living apart for the sake of children's education, a need to combat health and depression issues. *Kyunghyang Newspaper*, 10 November, p. 14. See http://news.naver.com/main/read.nhn?mode=LSD&mid=shm&sid1=102&oid=032&aid=0002404981 (accessed December 2015).

Hirsh-Pasek, K., Golinkoff, R.M., Berk, L. and Singer, D. (2009) *A Mandate for Playful Learning in Preschool: Presenting the Evidence*. New York: Oxford University Press.

Hoare, P. (2011) Context and constraints: Immersion in Hong Kong and mainland China. In D.J. Tedick, D. Christian and T.W. Fortune (eds) *Immersion Education: Practices, Policies, Possibilities* (pp. 211–230). Bristol: Multilingual Matters.

Hofstede, G. (1980) *Culture's Consequences: International Differences in Work-Related Values*. Beverly Hills, CA: Sage.

Holliday, A. (2006) Native-speakerism. *ELT Journal* 60 (4), 385–387. https://doi.org/10.1093/elt/ccl030.

Holliday, A., Aboshiha, P. and Swan, A. (2015) *(En)Countering Native-speakerism, Global Perspectives*. London: Palgrave Macmillan.

Holtgraves, T. and Yang J.-N. (1990) Politeness as universal: Cross-cultural perceptions of request strategies and inferences based on their use. *Journal of Personality and Social Psychology* 59 (4), 719–729. doi:http://dx.doi.org.myaccess.library.utoronto.ca/10.1037/0022-3514.59.4.719.

Hong, H.-J. (2017) *Sesangeseo jeil swiun eommapyo saenghwal yeongeo – yuaeseo chodeungkkaji nae aireul wihan haru 10 bun gijeogui yeongeo!* [the easiest everyday English for moms in the world- miracle English in ten minutes a day from toddlers to elementary school]. Seoul: Dongyang Books.

Hook, C.J., Lawson, G.M. and Farah, M.J. (2013) Socioeconomic status and the development of executive function. In R.E. Tremblay, M. Boivin and R. Peters (eds) *Encyclopedia on Early Childhood Development*. Montreal, Quebec: Centre of Excellence for Early Childhood Development and Strategic Knowledge Cluster on Early Child Development.

Horwitz, E. (1992) Not for learner's only: The language anxiety of nonnative teacher trainees. Paper presented at *The Annual Meeting of the International Association of Teachers of English to Speakers of Other Languages*. Vancouver, Canada.

Horwitz, E. (1993) Foreign language anxiety and pre service language teachers. Paper presented at *Annual Meeting of the American Council of Teachers of Foreign Languages*. San Antonio, TX.

Horwitz, E. (1996) Even teachers get the blues: Recognizing and alleviating language teachers' feelings of foreign language anxiety. *Foreign Language Annals* 29 (3), 365–372. https://doi.org/10.1111/j.1944-9720.1996.tb01248.x.

Horwitz, E.K. (2010) Foreign and second language anxiety. *Language Teaching* 43 (2), 154–167. https://doi.org/10.1017/S026144480999036X.

Horwitz, E.K., Horwitz, M.B. and Cope, J. (1986) Foreign language classroom anxiety. *The Modern Language Journal* 70 (2), 125–132.

Horwitz, E.K., Tallon, M. and Luo, H. (2009) Foreign language anxiety. In J.C. Cassady (ed.) *Anxiety in Schools: The Causes, Consequences, and Solutions for Academic Anxieties* (pp. 95–118). New York: Peter Lang.

Hu, G. (2004) English language education in China: Police, progress, and problems. *Language Policy* 4, 5–24.

Hultberg, P., Calongee, D.S. and Kim, S.R. (2017) Education policy in South Korea: A contemporary model of human capital accumulation? *Cogent Economics & Finance* 5 (1). http://dx.doi.org/10.1080/23322039.2017.1389804.

Huttenlocher, P.R. (2002) *Neural Plasticity*. Harvard University Press.

Hwang, K.H. and Choi, N. (2017) Effects of mothers' perceptions about early childhood English education on preschoolers' attitudes toward learning English. *Journal of Early Childhood Education & Educare Welfare* 21 (1), 189–211.

Hyson, M. (2010) The role of play in promoting children's positive approaches to learning. See https://www.researchconnections.org/files/childcare/pdf/PlayandApproachestoLearning-MarilouHyson-1.pdf.

ICEF (2013) South Korean student mobility takes a dip. *ICEF Monitor*. See http://monitor.icef.com/2013/08/south-korean-student-mobility-takes-a-dip/.

Jang, J., Lee, S.A., Kim, W., Choi, Y. and Park, E.C. (2018) Factors associated with mental health consultation in South Korea. *BMC Psychiatry* 18 (17), 1–10. https://doi.org/10.1186/s12888-018-1592-3.

Jenkins, J. (2002) A sociolinguistically based, empirically researched pronunciation syllabus for English as an international language. *Applied Linguistics* 23 (1), 83–103. https://doi.org/10.1093/applin/23.1.83.

Jeon, J.J. (2020) AI in education: Korean startup RiiD's creative disruption with 'SANTA' TOEIC learning tool. *KoreaTechDesk*. See https://www.koreatechdesk.com/ai-in-education-korean-startup-riiids-creative-disruption-with-santa-toiec-learning-tool/.

Jeon, M. (2009) Globalisation and native English speakers in English programme in Korea. *Language, Culture and Curriculum* 22 (3), 231–243. https://doi.org/10.1080/07908310903388933.

Jeong J., Kim, C., Cho, C., Lee, J., Kim, S. and Son, T. (2019) Development of IoT language learning tool for young children. Proceedings from *The Korean Institute of Information Scientists and Engineers*, 1959–1960. Seoul: KIISE.

Jeong, T.-G. (2004) Relationship between cognitive style, academic anxiety, English and English achievement in elementary school children. *The Journal of Yeolin Education* 12 (2), 195–216.

JET (2019) Eligibility criteria. Jet Programme: United Kingdom. See https://www.jet-uk.org/eligibility-criteria.html.

Jiang, Y. and Dewaele, J.M. (2020) The predictive power of sociobiographical and language variables on foreign language anxiety of Chinese university students. *System* 89, 102207. https://doi.org/10.1016/j.system.2020.102207.

Jill, B. (1995) Lending the 'unborrowable': Spanish discourse markers in indigenous American languages. In C. Silva-Corvalan (ed.) *Spanish in Four Continents: Studies in Language Contact and Bilingualism* (pp. 132–147). Washington: Georgetown University Press.

Johnson, C., Beitchman, J.H., Young, A., Escobar, M., Atkinson, M. and Wilson, B. (1999) Fourteen year follow-up of children with and without speech/language impairments: Speech/language stability and outcomes. *Journal of Speech, Language, and Hearing Research* 42 (3), 744–760. http://dx.doi.org/10.1044/jslhr.4203.744.

Johnson, J. and Newport, E. (1989) Critical period effects in second language learning: The influence of the maturational state on the acquisition of English as a second language. *Cognitive Psychology* 21, 60–99.

Johnson, R.B., Onwuegbuzie, A.J. and Turner, L.A. (2007) Toward a definition of mixed methods research. *Journal of Mixed Methods Research* 1 (2), 129. https://doi.org/10.1177/1558689806298224.

Johnson, R.K. and Swain, M. (1997) *Immersion Education: International Perspectives.* Cambridge: Cambridge University Press.

Jun, H.J. (2009) Understanding Korean private kindergarten teachers' experiences and dilemmas regarding English education for young children. *Journal of Early Childhood Education* 29 (3), 191–213.

Kachru, B. (1985) Standards, codification, and sociolinguistic realism: The English language in the outer circle. In R. Quirk and H. Widdowson (eds) *English in the World: Teaching and Learning the Language and the Literature* (pp. 241–268). Cambridge: Cambridge University Press.

Kachru, B.B. (1994) Englishization and contact linguistics. *World Englishes* 13 (2), 135–154. https://doi.org/10.1111/j.1467-971X.1994.tb00303.x.

Kachru, Y. (1994) Monolingual bias in SLA research. *TESOL Quarterly* 28 (4), 795–800.

Kagan, J. and Snidman, N. (1999) Early childhood predictors of adult anxiety disorders. *Biological Psychiatry* 46 (11), 1536–1541. https://doi.org/10.1016/s0006-3223(99)00137-7.

Kajino, S. (2014) Sociophonetic variation at the intersection of gender, region, and style in Japanese female speech. Doctoral dissertation, Georgetown University.

Kang, M.J. and Choi, J.Y. (2010) Study on understanding of teachers on early-childhood English education and an analysis of early-childhood English education curriculum in early childhood teacher education. *Korean Journal of Children's Media* 9 (1), 309–332.

KEDI (2015) *Analyzing on the State of Academic Institute Management: Focusing on English Language Institutes for Pre-school Children.* Seoul: Kim, C.H., Park, S.W., Gu, K.H., Hwang, S.O. and Moon, S.B.

Khansir, A.A., Jafarizadegan, N. and Karampoor, F. (2016) Relation between socio-economic status and motivation of learners in learning English as a foreign language. *Theory and Practice in Language Studies* 6 (4), 742–750. http://dx.doi.org/10.17507/tpls.0604.11.

Kiaer, J. (2014) *The History of English Loanwords in Korean.* Munich: Lincom.

Kiernan, P.J. and Aizawa, K. (2004) Cell phones in task based learning – Are cell phones useful language learning tools? *ReCALL* 16 (1), 71–84.

Kim, G.H., Hong, S.O. and Tak, J.H. (2014) The kindergarten teacher's perceptions and needs on English education for children. *Korea Journal of Child Care and Education* 85, 97–116.

Kim, H.J. (2010) (The) differences in Korean vocabulary, executive function stress and problem behavior according to experiences of early English education for young children. Doctoral Dissertation, Kyungsung University.

Kim, J.H. (2019) Private education cost reaches record high. *The Korea Times.* See http://www.koreatimes.co.kr/www/nation/2019/03/181_265235.html.

Kim, J.Y. (2001) The impact of early English education on English learning among elementary students. Master thesis, Dankook University.

Kim, M.H. and Yu, Y. (2012) Actual practices of young children's English education method and English teacher in kindergartens and day care centers. The *Korean Journal of Child Education* 21 (4), 153–168.

Kim, M.N. (2008) Study on the recognition of parents, principals and teachers on the early childhood English education. Master thesis, Chung-Ang University.

Kim, N.Y., Cha, Y. and Kim, H.S. (2019) Future English learning: Chatbots and artificial intelligence. *Multimedia-Assisted Language Learning* 22 (3), 32–53.

Kim, S. and Kim, T. (2012) The influence of elementary school students' interest, language anxiety, and English learning motivation about TEE class on the students' perceived English learning achievement. *The Korea Association of Primary English Education* 18 (1), 288–307.

Kim, S.H. (2018) South Korea to review banning English education for preschoolers. *The Korea Herald.* See http://www.koreaherald.com/view.php?ud=20180925000067.

Kim, S.H. and Ko, S.Y. (2019) *Eommapyo yeongeo 100 ileui gijeok- 100 il hu eneun eommado, aido yeongeoro malhanda*! [Mom'e English 100 day miracle- after 100 days both mom and child will be speaking in English!]. Paju: Nexus.

Kim, S.Y. and Wong, V.Y. (2002) Assessing Asian and Asian American parenting: A review of the literature. In K. Kurasaki, S. Okazaki and S. Sue (eds) *Asian American Mental Health: Assessment Methods and Theories* (pp. 185–201). Boston, MA: Springer.

King, J. (2013) Silence in the second language classrooms of Japanese universities. *Applied Linguistics* 34 (3), 325–343. https://doi.org/10.1093/applin/ams043.

Kitano, K. (2001) Anxiety in the college Japanese language classroom. *The Modern Language Journal* 85 (4), 549–566. https://doi.org/10.1111/0026-7902.00125.

Kleinmann, H.H. (1977) Avoidance behavior in adult second language acquisition. *Language Learning* 27 (1), 93–107. https://doi.org/10.1111/j.1467-1770.1977.tb00294.x.

Kline, R.B. (2005) *Principles and Practice of Structural Equation Modelling* (2nd edn). New York: Guilford.

Klöter, H. (2004) Language policy in the KMT and DPP Eras. *China Perspectives* 2004 (56). http://journals.openedition.org/chinaperspectives/442.

Koch, A.S. and Terrell, T.D. (1991) Affective reactions of foreign language students to natural approach activities and teaching procedures. In E.K. Horwitz and D.J. Young (eds) *Language Anxiety* (pp. 109–125). London: Prentice Hall International.

Kormos, J. and Kiddle, T. (2013) The of socio-economic factors in motivation to learn English as a foreign language. The case of Chile. *System* 41, 399–412. http://dx.doi.org/10.1016/j.system.2013.03.006.

Krashen, S.D. (1982) *Principles and Practice in Second Language Acquisition*. Oxford: Pergamon Press.

Krashen, S., Long, M. and Scarcella, R. (1979) Age, rate and eventual attainment in second language acquisition. *TESOL Quarterly* 13 (4), 573–582. doi: 10.2307/3586451. Reprinted in Scarcella R. & Higa, C (1982) Input and age differences in second language acquisition. In S. Krashen, R. Scarcella and M. Long (eds) *Child-Adult Differences in Second Language Acquisition* (pp. 161–172). Rowley, MA: Newbury House.

Kuhl, P.K., Tsao, F.M. and Liu, H.M. (2003) Foreign-language experience in infancy: Effects of short-term exposure and social interaction on phonetic learning. *Proceedings of the National Academy of Sciences* 100 (15), 9096–9101. https://doi.org/10.1073/pnas.1532872100.

Kuppens, A.H. (2010) Incidental foreign language acquisition from media exposure. *Learning, Media and Technology* 35 (1), 65–85. https://doi.org/10.1080/17439880903561876.

Kurhila, S.K. and Kotilainen, L.P. (2017) Cooking, interaction and learning: The Finnish digital kitchen as a language learning environment. In P. Seedhouse (ed.) *Task-Based Language Learning in a Real-World Digital Environment* (pp. 157–179). London: Bloomsbury Academic.

Kwon, S.K., Lee, M. and Shin, D. (2017) Educational assessment in the Republic of Korea: Lights and shadows of high-stake exam-based education system. *Assessment in Education: Principles, Policy & Practice* 24 (1), 60–77. https://doi.org/10.1080/0969594X.2015.1074540.

La Greca, A.M., Dandes, S.K., Wick, P., Shaw, K. and Stone, W.L. (1988) Development of the social anxiety scale for children: Reliability and concurrent validity. *Journal of Clinical Child Psychology* 17 (1), 84–91. https://doi.org/10.1207/s15374424jccp1701_11.

Lambert, W.E. and Tucker, G.R. (1972) *Bilingual Education of Children: The St. Lambert Experiment*. Rowley, MA: Newbury House.

Lawson, G.M., Duda, J.T., Avants, B.B., Wu, J. and Farah, M.J. (2013) Associations between children's socioeconomic status and prefrontal cortical thickness. *Developmental Science* 16 (5), 641–652. http://dx.doi.org/10.1111/desc.12096.

Lee J.E. (2020) Korona hollangi … jip eseo mannaneun AI yeongeo gyosu [The Corona confusion period … The AI English teacher you can meet at home]. *The Chungang Ilbo*. https://news.joins.com/article/23748307.

Lee, J.H. and Macaro, E. (2013) Investigating age in the use of L1 or english-only instruction: Vocabulary acquisition by Korean EFL learners. *The Modern Language Journal* 97 (4), 887–901. https://doi.org/10.1111/j.1540-4781.2013.12044.x.

Lee, J.Y. (2018) 160 English kindergarten centers in Seoul alone. Up to 1.76 million won per month for teaching. *Yonhap Agency News*. See https://www.yna.co.kr/view/AKR20180126140500004.

Lenneberg, E.H. (1960) Speech and brain mechanisms by Wildfer Penfield and Lamar Roberts. *Linguistic Society of America* 36 (1), 97–112.

Lenneberg, E.H. (1967) *Biological Foundations of Language*. New York: Wiley.

Leopold, W.F. (1939) *Speech Development of a Bilingual Child: A Linguist's Record* (No. 11). Northwestern University.

Leopold, W.F. (1952) *Bibliography of Child Language*. Indiana University Press.

Leopold, W.F. (1970) *Speech Development of a Bilingual Child: Vocabulary Growth in the First Two Years* (Vol. 1). AMS Press.

Letts, C., Edwards, S., Sinka, I., Schaefer, B. and Gibbons, W. (2013) Socio-economic status and language acquisition: Children's performance on the new Reynell developmental language scales. *International Journal of Language & Communication Disorders/Royal College of Speech & Language Therapists* 48, 131–43. http://dx.doi.org/10.1111/1460-6984.12004.

Lewis, G., Jones, B. and Baker, C. (2012) Translanguaging: Origins and development from school to street and beyond. *Educational Research and Evaluation* 18 (7), 641–654. https://doi.org/10.1080/13803611.2012.718488.

Li, C. (2019) A Positive Psychology perspective on Chinese EFL students' trait emotional intelligence, foreign language enjoyment and EFL learning achievement. *Journal of Multilingual and Multicultural Development* 41 (3), 246–263. https://doi.org/https://doi.org/10.1080/01434632.2019.1614187.

Li, C. and Xu, J. (2019) Trait Emotional Intelligence and classroom emotions: A positive psychology investigation ad intervention among Chinese EFL learners. *Frontiers in Psychology* 10, 2453. doi: 10.3389/fpsyg.2019.02453.

Li, C., Jiang, G. and Dewaele, J.M. (2018) Understanding Chinese high school students' foreign language enjoyment: Validation of the Chinese version of the foreign language enjoyment scale. *System* 76, 183–196.

Liu, H. and Chen, T. (2013) Foreign Language anxiety in young learners: How it relates to multiple intelligences, learner attitudes, and perceived competence. *Journal of Language Teaching and Research* 4 (5), 932–938. https://doi.org/10.4304/jltr.4.5.932-938.

Liu, M. and Jackson, J. (2008) An exploration of Chinese EFL learners' unwillingness to communicate and foreign language anxiety. *The Modern Language Journal* 92 (1), 71–86. http://dx.doi.org/10.1111/j.1540-4781.2008.00687.x.

Long, M. (1990) Maturational constraints on language development. *Studies on Second Language Acquisition* 12 (3), 251–285. https://doi.org/10.1017/S0272263100009165.

López, J.F., Akil, H. and Watson, S.J. (1999) Role of biological and psychological factors in early development and their impact on adult life: Neural circuits mediating stress. *Biological Psychiatry* 46 (11), 1461–1471.

Lui, P.P. and Rollock, D. (2013) Tiger mother: Popular and psychological scientific perspectives on Asian culture and parenting. *American Journal of Orthopsychiatry* 83 (4), 450.

Ma, S.H. (2008) A model for an integrative English education at kindergarten. *Journal of Korea Open Association for Early Childhood Education* 13 (4), 221–245.

Ma., S.H. (2007) Trends in the research of English education for young children. *Journal of Korea Open Association for Early Childhood Education* 12 (5), 185–208.

MacIntyre, P.D. (1999) Language anxiety: A review of literature for language teachers. In D. J. Young (ed.) *Affect in Foreign Language and Second Language Learning* (pp. 24–43). New York: Mc Graw Hill Companies.

MacIntyre, P.D. (2002) Motivation, anxiety and emotion in second language acquisition. In P. Robinson (ed.) *Individual Differences and Instructed Language Learning* (pp. 45–68). Amsterdam: John Benjamins Publishing.

MacIntyre, P.D. and Gardner, R.C. (1991) Language anxiety: Its relationship to other anxieties and to processing in native and second languages. *Language Learning* 41 (4), 513–534.

MacIntyre, P.D. and Gregersen, T. (2012) Emotions that facilitate language learning: The positive-broadening power of the imagination. *Studies in Second Language Learning and Teaching* 2 (2), 193–213. https://doi.org/10.14746/ssllt.2012.2.2.4.

MacIntyre, P.D. and Mercer, S. (2014) Introducing positive psychology to SLA. *Studies in Second Language Learning and Teaching* 4, 153–172. https://doi.org/10.14746/ssllt.2014.4.2.2.

MacIntyre, P.D., Gregersen, T. and Mercer, S. (2016) *Positive Psychology in SLA*. Bristol: Multilingual Matters.

MacIntyre, P.D., Baker, S., Clément, R. and Donovan, L. (2002) Sex and age effects on willingness to communicate, anxiety, perceived competence, and L2 motivation among junior high school French immersion students. *Language Learning* 53, 537–564. https://doi.org/10.1111/1467-9922.00194.

MacWhinnie, S.G. and Mitchell, C. (2017) English classroom reforms in Japan: A study of Japanese university EFL student anxiety and motivation. *Asian-Pacific Journal of Second and Foreign Language Education* 2 (1), 7.

Maloney, E.A. and Beilock, S.L. (2012) Math anxiety: Who has it, why it develops, and how to guard against it. *Trends in Cognitive Sciences* 16 (8), 404–406. https://doi.org/10.1016/j.tics.2012.06.008.

Marinova-Todd, S.H., Marshall, D.B. and Snow, C.E. (2000) Three misconceptions about age and L2 learning. *TESOL Quarterly* 34 (1), 9–34. https://doi.org/10.2307/3588095.

Master, P. (1998) Positive and negative aspects of the dominance of English. *TESOL Quarterly* 32 (4), 716–727. https://doi.org/10.2307/3588002.

Mayer, R.E. (2002) Multimedia learning. In B.H. Ross (ed.) *The Psychology of Learning and Motivation* (pp. 85–139). San Diego: Academic Press.

McEwen, B.S. (2012) Brain on stress: how the social environment gets under the skin. *Proceedings of the National Academy of Sciences* 109 (Supplement 2), 17180–17185.

McLeod, B.D., Wood, J.J. and Weisz, J.R. (2007) Examining the association between parenting and childhood anxiety: A meta-analysis. *Clinical Psychology Review* 27 (2), 155–172. https://doi.org/10.1016/j.cpr.2006.09.002.

Meisel, J. (1989) Early differentiation of languages in bilingual children. In K. Hyltenstam and L. Obler (eds) *Bilingualism Across the Lifespan: Aspects of Acquisition, Maturity and Loss* (pp. 13–40). Cambridge: Cambridge University Press. https://doi.org/10.1017/CBO9780511611780.003.

Miller, G.E., Chen, E. and Parker, K.J. (2011) Psychological stress in childhood and susceptibility to the chronic diseases of aging: Moving toward a model of behavioral and biological mechanisms. *Psychological Bulletin* 137 (6), 959.

Montague, E.K. (1953) The role of anxiety in serial rote learning. *Journal of Experimental Psychology* 45 (2), 91–96. http://dx.doi.org/10.1037/h0062644.

Montose, B. (2016) The global English language job market is changing: What this means for ESL teachers. *Medium*. See https://medium.com/accelerated/the-global-english-language-job-market-is-changing-what-this-means-for-esl-teachers-92c8d87cf8eb.

Moon, C., Lagercrantz, H. and Kuhl, P.K. (2013) Language experienced in utero affects vowel perception after birth. *Acta Paediatr* 102 (2), 156–160. https://doi.org/10.1111/apa.12098.

Morrison, F. (1981) *Longitudinal and Cross-sectional Studies of French Proficiency in Ottawa and Carlton Schools*. Ontario: Reserach Centre, The Ottawa Board of Education.

Mousavi, S.Y., Low, R. and Sweller, J. (1995) Reducing cognitive load by mixing auditory and visual presentation modes. *Journal of Educational Psychology* 87 (2), 319–334. http://dx.doi.org/10.1037/0022-0663.87.2.319.

Muñoz, C. and Singleton, D. (2011) A critical review of age-related research on L2 ultimate attainment. *Language Teaching* 44 (1), 1.

Myhill, D., Jones, S. and Hopper, R. (2006) *Talking, Listening and Learning Effective Talk in the Primary Classroom*. Maidenhead: Open University Press.

Na, I. and Rhee, K. (2017) The effects of teacher's types on a learner's interest, motivation/ attitude and confidence in English education for young children. *Journal of Learner-Centered Curriculum and Instruction* 17, 1–23. http://dx.doi.org/10.22251/jlcci.2017.17.15.1.

Nam, S.J. (2016) *Eommapyo yeongeo 17 nyeon bogoseo* [17-year report on Mom's English]. Seoul: Cheongrim Life.

Nation, I.S.P. and Webb, S.A. (2011) *Researching and Analyzing Vocabulary* (1st edn). Boston, MA: Cengage Learning.

National Scientific Council on the Developing Child (2010) Persistent fear and anxiety can affect young children's learning and development: working paper no. 9. http://www.developingchild.net.

Newton, T., Asimakopoulou, K., Daly, B., Scambler, S. and Scott, S. (2012) The management of dental anxiety: Time for a sense of proportion? *British Dental Journal* 213 (6), 271–274. https://doi.org/10.1038/sj.bdj.2012.830.

Nhsinform.scot (2019) Anxiety disorders in children. See https://www.nhsinform.scot/illnesses-and-conditions/mental-health/anxiety-disorders-in-children.

Noguchi, T. (2019) The impacts of an intensive English camp on English language anxiety and perceived English competence in the Japanese EFL Context. *Journal of Pan-Pacific Association of Applied Linguistics* 23 (1), 37–58.

Nölle, J., Fusaroli, R., Mills, G.J. and Tylén, K. (2020) Language as shaped by the environment: Linguistic construal in a collaborative spatial task. *Palgrave Communications* 6 (1), 1–10.

Nunez, V. (2015) Your kids will learn Spanish with these easy tips and activities. *Popsugar Latina*. See https://www.popsugar.com/latina/Tips-Teaching-Spanish-Small-Children-38173177.

NYU Steinhardt News (2015) Literacy app improves school readiness in at-risk preschoolers. See https://research.steinhardt.nyu.edu/site/ataglance/2015/04/literacy-app-improves-school-readiness-in-at-risk-preschoolers-finds-study-by-steinhardt-researchers.html (accessed November 2019).

OAPE (2014a) Jogiyeongeogyyoyuk e daehan siltae mit insikjosa [A report on the reality and perceptions of early English education]. See https://data.noworry.kr/101 (accessed September 2020).

OAPE (2014b) Eorinijib teukbyeolhwaldong siltae [The real situation of daycare's special activities]. See https://data.noworry.kr/120?category=444370 (accessed September 2020).

OAPE (2015) Yuadaesang yeongeohagwon 57.1%, deungrokhajianheun gwajeongunyeong [57.1% of English kindergartens offer unregistered curriculum]. See https://data.noworry.kr/186 (accessed September 2020).

OAPE and Yu, E.H. (2014) *A Report on the Actual Condition and Recognition of Early English Education for 8,617 Parents in Seoul and Gyeonggi Province*. Seoul: OAPE.

Ock, H.J. (2016) Korea sends fourth most students abroad. *Korea Herald*. See http://www.koreaherald.com/view.php?%20ud=20160918000267.

OECD (2017) *Education at a Glance 2017: OECD Indicators*. Paris: OECD Publishing. http://dx.doi.org/10.1787/eag-2017-en.

Oh, H. and Min, B.B. (2007) *Junior Temperament and Character Inventory 3-6 (JTCI 3-6)*. Seoul: Maumsarang.

Oh, J. (1992) The effects of L2 reading assessment methods on anxiety level. *TESOL Quarterly* 26 (1), 172–176.

Oller, D.K. and Eilers, R.E. (2002) *Language and Literacy in Bilingual Children*. Clevedon: Multilingual Matters.

Onwuegbuzie, A.J., Bailey, P. and Daley, C.E. (1999) Factors associated with foreign language anxiety. *Applied Psycholinguistics* 20 (2), 217–239. https://doi.org/10.1017/S0142716499002039.

Otheguy, R., García, O. and Reid, W. (2015) Clarifying translanguaging and deconstructing named languages: A perspective from linguistics. *Applied Linguistics Review* 6 (3), 281–307.

Oxford, R. (1999) Anxiety and the language learner: new insights. In A. Jane (ed.) *Affect in Language Learning* (pp. 58–67). Cambridge: Cambridge University Press.

Pallant, J. (2013) *SPSS Survival Manual*. London: McGraw-Hill Education.

Pallotti, G., Niemants, N., Seedhouse, P. and Preston, A. (2017) Vocabulary learning in a real-world digital environment. In P. Seedhouse (ed.) *Task-based Language Learning in a Real-World Digital Environment: The European Digital Kitchen*. London: Bloomsbury.

Park, H. (2002) The effects of anxiety on Korean EFL learners' achievement. *The Linguistic Association of Korea Journal* 10 (3), 171–191.

Park, H. and Song, S. (2008) The effects of early English learning on elementary school learners' affective characteristics. *Journal of Modern British & American Language & Literature* 26 (1), 187–214.

Park, J.A. and Chung, M.J. (2007) Moderating effects of mothers' parenting behaviors on the relationship between temperament of preschoolers with anxiety disorders and their dysfunctional emotion regulation. *Korean J Couns Psychother* 19 (2), 273–295.

Park, J. and Seedhouse, P. (2017) Sight and touch in vocabulary learning: The Korean digital kitchen. In P. Seedhouse (ed.) *Task-based Language Learning in a Real-World Digital Environment: The European Digital Kitchen. Advances in Digital Language Learning and Teaching* (pp. 231–257). London: Bloomsbury Academic.

Park, J. and Shin, N. (2017) Students' perceptions of artificial intelligence technology and artificial intelligence teachers. *The Journal of Korean Teacher Education* 34 (2), 169–192.

Park, J.K. (2007) Korean parents in 'English fever' and their 'early study-abroad' children in the U.S.: Parents beliefs and practices concerning first language peers. Doctoral dissertation, ProQuest Dissertations Publishing.

Park, J.K. (2009a) Korea secondary teachers' perception of teaching English pronunciation for international communication. *Studies in English Studies* 4 (2), 30–53.

Park, J.K. (2009b) 'English fever' in South Korea: Its history and symptoms. *English Today* 25 (1), 50–57. doi:10.1017/S026607840900008X.

Park, J., Choi, N., Kiaer, J. and Seedhouse, P. (2019) Young children's L2 vocabulary learning through cooking: The case of Korean EFL children. *The Asian EFL* 21 (1), 109–138.

Park, S.J. (2012) The identity of 'English kindergarten', recognized by directors of institutes who runs 'English kindergarten'. Master thesis, Sookmyung Women's University.

Park, S.Y. (2014) (A) Comparative analysis of the curriculums of English kindergartens in the Bundang area. Master thesis, Dankook University.

Park, S.Y. (2015) An Analysis of the current status of the early English education and parent's perception in Ulsan. Master thesis, Kyungnam University.

Park, Y.S. (2010) The rise in private education costs, which is a big problem. *Yonhap News Agency*. See https://www.yna.co.kr/view/AKR20100223157700004.

Park, Y.S., Kim, B.S., Chiang, J. and Ju, C.M. (2010) Acculturation, enculturation, parental adherence to Asian cultural values, parenting styles, and family conflict among Asian American college students. *Asian American Journal of Psychology* 1 (1), 67.

Park, Y. and Song, J.M. (2002) A research survey on the actual condition of kindergarten English education. *Foreign Languages Education* 7 (2), 139–161.

Parry, R.L. (2002) Koreans take a short cut on the road to English. *Independent*. See https://www.independent.co.uk/news/world/asia/koreans-take-a-short-cut-on-the-road-to-english-5361932.html.

Paterson, A. and Willis, J. (2008) *English Through Music*. Oxford: Oxford University Press.

Pearson, B.Z. (1998) Assessing lexical development in bilingual babies and toddlers. *International Journal of Bilingualism* 2 (3), 347–372. https://doi.org/10.1177% 2F136700699800200305.

Pemba, D., Mann, V. and Azertash, K. (2016) New technology for teaching spoken English to native speakers of mandarin Chinese. *Open Journal of Social Sciences* 4, 85–91.

Penfield, W. and Roberts, L. (1959) *Speech and Brain Mechanisms*. Princeton, NJ: Princeton University Press.

Peterson, D.J. and Mulligan, N. (2012) The negative testing effect and multifactor account. *Journal of Experimental Psychology Learning Memory and Cognition* 39 (4), 1287–1293. https://psycnet.apa.org/doi/10.1037/a0031337.

Pfenninger, S.E. and Singleton, D. (2016) Affect trumps age: A person-in-context relational view of age and motivation in SLA. *Second Language Research* 32 (3), 311–345.

Pfenninger, S.E. and Singleton, D. (2017) *Beyond Age Effects in Instructional L2 Learning: Revisiting the Age Factor*. Bristol: Multilingual Matters.

Pfenninger, S.E. and Singleton, D. (2019) Starting age overshadowed: The primacy of differential environmental and family support effects on second language attainment in an instructional context. *Language Learning* 69 (S1), 207–234.

Pichette, F. (2009) Second language anxiety and distance language learning. *Foreign Language Annals* 42 (1), 77–93. https://doi.org/10.1111/j.1944-9720.2009.01009.x.

Pishghadam, R. and Akhondpoor, F. (2011) Learner perfectionism and its role in foreign language learning success, academic achievement, and learner anxiety. *Journal of Language Teaching & Research* 2 (2), 432–440.

Pollak, S.D., Cicchetti, D., Hornung, K. and Reed, A. (2000) Recognizing emotion in faces: Developmental effects of child abuse and neglect. *Developmental Psychology* 36 (5), 679.

Pong, S.L., Johnston, J. and Chen, V. (2010) Authoritarian parenting and Asian adolescent school performance: Insights from the US and Taiwan. *International Journal of Behavioral Development* 34 (1), 62–72.

Post, R.M., Weiss, S.R.B., Li, H., Smith, M.A., Zhang, L.X., Xing, G. and McCann, U.D. (1998) Neural plasticity and emotional memory. *Development and Psychopathology* 10 (4), 829–855.

Proposition 227 (1998) English Language in Public Schools. Initiative Statute. State of California. See https://web.archive.org/web/20100618094226/http://primary98.sos.ca.gov/ VoterGuide/Propositions/227text.htm.

Raizada, R.D.S. and Kishiyama, M.M. (2010) Effects of socioeconomic status on brain development, and how cognitive neuroscience may contribute to levelling the playing field. *Frontiers in Human Neuroscience* 4, Article ID 3.

Ramirez, G., Gunderson, E.A., Levine, S.C. and Beilock, S.L. (2013) Math anxiety, working memory, and math achievement in early elementary school. *Journal of Cognition and Development* 14 (2), 187–202. https://doi.org/10.1080/15248372.2012.664593.

Raymond, L.C. and Choon, T.T. (2017) Understanding Asian students learning styles, cultural influence and learning strategies. *Journal of Education & Social Policy* 7 (1), 194–210.

Revet, A., Hebebrand, J. and Bhide, S. (2018) Dual training as clinician-scientist in child and adolescent psychiatry: Are we there yet? *European Child & Adolescent Psychiatry* 27 (3), 263–265. https://doi.org/10.1007/s00787-017-1104-x.

Reynolds, C.R. and Richmond, B.O. (1978) What I think and feel: A revised measure of children's manifest anxiety. *Journal of Abnormal Psychology* 6 (2), 271–280.

Rivera, N.F. (1998) Effecto de la edad de inicio de aprendizaje de la lengua extranjera (ingls) y cantidad de exposici6n a la LE en la percepcion de las fonemas del ingls por hablantes de espanol y catalan [Effect of age at starting to learn English as a foreign language and amount of exposure on perception of English phonemes for speakers of Spanish and Catalan]. Paper presented at *Il Encuentro Interacional sobre Adquisici6n de las Lenguas del Estado*. Barcelona, Spain.

Rockhill, C., Kodish, I., DiBattisto, C., Macias, M., Varley, C. and Ryan, S. (2010) Anxiety disorders in children and adolescents. *Current Problems in Pediatric and Adolescent Health Care* 40 (4), 66–99.

Romer D., Betancourt, L., Giannetta, J.M., Brodsky, N.L., Farah, M. and Hurt, H. (2009) Executive cognitive functions and impulsivity as correlates of risk taking and problem behavior in preadolescents. *Neuropsychologia* 47 (13), 2916–2926. http://dx.doi.org/10.1016/j.neuropsychologia.2009.06.019.

Rumbold, A.R., Giles, L.C., Whitrow, M.J., Steele, E.J., Davies, C.E., Davies, M.J. and Moore, V.M. (2012) The effects of house moves during early childhood on child mental health at age 9 years. *BMC Public Health* 12 (1), 583.

Russet, F., Humbertclaude, V., Dieleman, G., Dodig-Ćurković, K., Hendrickx, G., Kovač, V. and Schulze, U.M. (2019) Training of adult psychiatrists and child and adolescent psychiatrists in Europe: A systematic review of training characteristics and transition from child/adolescent to adult mental health services. *BMC Medical Education* 19 (1), 204.

Saito, Y. and Samimy, K. (1996) Foreign language anxiety and language performance: A study of learner anxiety in beginning, intermediate, and advanced-level college students of Japanese. *Foreign Language Annals* 29 (2), 239–249. https://doi.org/10.1111/j.1944-9720.1996.tb02330.x.

Salisch, M.V. (2001) Children's emotional development: Challenges in their relationships to parents, peers, and friends. *International Journal of Behavioral Development* 25 (4), 310–319.

Sanaoui, R. (1995) Adult learners' approaches to learning vocabulary in second languages. *The Modern Language Journal* 79 (1), 15–28. https://doi.org/10.1111/j.1540-4781.1995.tb05410.x.

Sandvik, M., Smørdal, O. and Østerud, S. (2012) Exploring iPads in practitioners' repertoires for language learning and literacy practices in kindergarten. *Nordic Journal of Digital Literacy* 7 (03), 204–221.

Savignon, S.J. (2018) Communicative competence. *The TESOL Encyclopedia of English Language Teaching.* https://doi.org/10.1002/9781118784235.eelt0047.

Saville-Troike, M. (1984) What really matters in second language learning for academic achievement? *TESOL Quarterly* 18 (2), 199–219. https://doi.org/10.2307/3586690.

Schmidt, L.A., Polak, C.P. and Spooner, A.L. (2005) Biological and environmental contributions to childhood shyness: a diathesis-stress model. In W.R. Crozier and L.E. Alden (eds) *The Essential Handbook of Social Anxiety for Clinicians* (pp. 33–55). Chichester: John Wiley and Sons.

Schuele, M. (2001) Socioeconomic influences on children's language acquisition. *Journal of Speech-Language Pathology and Audiology* 25 (2), 77–88.

Schwab, J.F. and Lew-Williams, C. (2016) Repetition across successive sentences facilitates young children's word learning. *Developmental Psychology* 52 (6), 879–86. https://doi.org/10.1037/dev0000125.

Scollon, R. (1985) The machine stops: Silence in the metaphor of malfunction. In D. Tanne and M. Saville-Troike (eds) *Perspective on Silence* (pp. 21–30). Norwood, NJ: Ablex.

Scovel, T. (1978) The effect of affect on foreign language learning: A review of the anxiety research. *Language Learning* 28 (1), 129–142. https://doi.org/10.1111/j.1467-1770.1978.tb00309.x.

Scovel, T. (2001) *Learning New Languages: A Guide to Second Language Acquisition.* Boston: Heinle & Heinle.

Seedhouse, P. (2017) *Task-based Language Learning in a Real-World Digital Environment: The European Digital Kitchen.* London: Bloomsbury Academic.

Seo, J., Goh, R., Goh, E., Lee, E., Rho, S. and Chin, S. (2015) AR-based language learning apps for infants and toddlers. Conference proceedings from *The Institute of Electronics and Information Engineers*, 717–718. Seoul: IEEE.

Seoul National University (2019) Information on tuition payment for the first semester of the 2019. Seoul National University. See http://www.snu.ac.kr/notice?bm=v&bbsidx=125909.

Shapley, K.S., Sheehan, D., Maloney, C. and Caranikas-Walker, F. (2010) Evaluating the implementation fidelity of technology immersion and its relationship with student achievement. *The Journal of Technology, Learning and Assessment* 9 (4).

Sheo, J., Choi, N. and Kang, S. (2019) Individual and parental factors associated with young children's foreign language anxiety in an EFL setting. Paper presented at *International Conference on Early Childhood Development: Fostering an Effective Early Childhood Development*, Malaysia. Malaysia: MNNF network.

Shields, G., Ng, R., Ventriglio, A., Castaldelli-Maia, J., Torales, J. and Bhugra, D. (2017) WPA Position Statement on Recruitment in Psychiatry. *World Psychiatry: Official Journal of The World Psychiatric Association (WPA)* 16 (1), 113–114. https://doi.org/10.1002/wps.20392.

Shim, D. and Park, J.Y. (2008) The language politics of 'English fever' in South Korea. *Korea Journal* 48 (2), 136–159. https://doi.org/10.25024/kj.2008.48.2.136.

Shin, S.J. (2005) *Developing in Two Languages: Korean Children in America*. Clevedon: Multilingual Matters.

Shin, Y.J. (2002) Early education and developmental problems. Proceedings from *Korean Association of Child Studies Fall Conference: Current Status and Tasks of Early Education in Korea* 29–42. Seoul: Korean Association of Child Studies.

Shonkoff, J.P., Garner, A.S., Siegel, B.S., Dobbins, M.I., Earls, M.F., McGuinn, L. and Committee on Early Childhood, Adoption, and Dependent Care (2012) The lifelong effects of early childhood adversity and toxic stress. *Pediatrics* 129 (1), e232–e246. https://doi.org/10.1542/peds.2011-2663.

Sims, M., Guilfoyle, A. and Parry, T. (2005) What children's cortisol levels tell us about quality in childcare centres. *Australasian Journal of Early Childhood* 30 (2), 29–39.

Sims, M., Guilfoyle, A. and Parry, T.S. (2006) Children's cortisol levels and quality of child care provision. *Child: Care, Health and Development* 32 (4), 453–466.

Singleton, D. and Muñoz, C. (2011) Around and beyond the critical period hypothesis. In E. Hinkel (ed.) *Handbook of Research in Second Language Teaching and Learning* 2 (pp. 407–425).

Skehan, P. (1998) *A Cognitive Approach to Language Learning*. Oxford: Oxford University Press.

Skehan, P. (2003) Task-Based Instruction. *Language Teaching* 36 (1), 1–14.

Smits, J., Huisman, J. and Kruijff, K. (2008) Home language and education in the developing world. *Commissioned Study for EFA Global Monitoring Report 2009*. Nijmegen, The Netherlands: Radboud University Nijmegen.

Snow, C.E. and Hoefnagel-Höhle, M. (1978) The critical period for language acquisition: Evidence from second language learning. *Child Development* 49 (4), 1114–1128. http://dx.doi.org/10.2307/1128751.

Song, M.S., Park, H.J. and Kim, J.J. (2011) An analysis of research results on parents perception in early childhood English education. *Korean Journal of Children's Media* 10 (3), 115–134.

Song, S. (2014) Politeness in Korea and America: A comparative analysis of request strategy in English communication. *Korea Journal* 54 (1), 60–84.

Sonstroem, R.J. and Bernardo, P. (1982) Intraindividual pregame state anxiety and basketball performance: A re-examination of the inverted–U curve. *Journal of Sport Psychology* 4 (3), 235–245. https://doi.org/10.1123/jsp.4.3.235.

Sparks, R. and Ganschow, L. (2007) Is the foreign language classroom anxiety scale measuring anxiety or language skills? *Foreign Language Annals* 40 (2), 260–287. https://doi.org/10.1111/j.1944-9720.2007.tb03201.x.

Sparks, R. and Young, D.J. (2009) Language learning and disabilities, anxiety, and special needs. *Foreign Language Annals* 42 (1).

Spitalli, E.J. (2000) The relationship between foreign language anxiety and attitudes toward multiculturalism in high-school students. Unpublished master's thesis, Benedictine University.

Sreetharan, C.S. (2004) Students, sarariiman (pl.), and seniors: Japanese men's use of 'manly' speech register. *Language in Society* 33 (1), 81–107.

Sreetharan, C.S. (2006) Gentlemanly gender? Japanese men's use of clause-final politeness in casual conversations. *Journal of Sociolinguistics* 10 (1), 70–92.

Stanford Alumni [username] (2014) Developing a growth mindset with Carol Dweck. See https://www.youtube.com/watch?v=hiiEeMN7vbQ (accessed April 2020).

Steele, J.L., Slater, R.O., Zamarro, G., Miller, T., Li, J., Burkhauser, S. and Bacon, M. (2017) Effects of dual-language immersion programs on student achievement: Evidence from lottery data. *American Educational Research Journal* 54 (1_suppl), 282S–306S. https://doi.org/10.3102/0002831216634463.

Stern, H.H. (1967) *Foreign Languages in Primary Education*. Oxford: Oxford University Press.

Stern, H.H. (1976) Optimum age: Myth or reality? *Canadian Modern Language Review* 32 (2), 283–294. https://doi.org/10.3138/cmlr.32.3.283.

Steven, H.W. and Stigler, J.W. (1992) *The Learning Gap*. New York: Simon & Schuster.

Stone, J. (2016) London children whose first language isn't English are doing better at school than native speakers. *Independent*. See https://www.independent.co.uk/news/uk/politics/children-whose-first-language-isn-t-english-are-doing-better-at-school-than-native-speakers-a6827631.html.

Suinn, R.M., Taylor, S. and Edwards, R.W. (1988) Suinn mathematics anxiety rating scale for elementary school students (MARS-E): Psychometric and normative data. *Educational and Psychological Measurement* 48 (4), 979–986. https://doi.org/10.1177/0013164488484013.

Sundqvist, P. (2009) Extramural English matters: Out-of-school English and its impact on Swedish ninth graders' oral proficiency and vocabulary. Doctoral dissertation, Karlstad University.

Sundqvist, P. and Olin-Scheller, C. (2013) Classroom vs. extramural English: Teachers dealing with demotivation. *Language and Linguistics Compass* 7 (6), 329–338.

Swain, M. and Lapkin, S. (1982) *Evaluating Bilingual Education: A Canadian Case Study*. Clevedon: Multicultural Matters.

Tahta, S., Wood, M. and Lowenthal, K. (1981) Age changes in the ability to replicate foreign pronunciation and intonation. *Language and Speech* 24, 363–372.

Tanaka, K. and Ellis, R. (2003) Study abroad, language proficiency, and learner beliefs about language learning. *JALT Journal* 25, 63–85.

Thomson, R.I. and Derwing, T.M. (2014) The effectiveness of L2 pronunciation instruction: A narrative review. *Applied Linguistics* 36 (3), 326–344.

Trubek, A.B. and Belliveau, C. (2009) Cooking as pedagogy: Engaging the senses through experiential learning. *Anthropology News* 50 (4), 16–16. https://doi.org/10.1111/j.1556-3502.2009.50416.x.

Trudell, B. (2016) *The Impact of Language Policy and Practice on Children's Learning: Evidence from Eastern and Southern Africa*. Nairobi: UNICEF.

UNESCO/UNICEF (2007) *A Human Rights-based approach to education for all: A framework for the realization of children's right to education and rights within education*. United Nations Children's Fund/United Nations Educational, Scientific and Cultural Organization.

Utako, M., Gustafson, K., Fiorentino, R., Jongman, A. and Sereno, J. (2017) Fetal rhythm-based language discrimination. *Neuroreport* 28 (10), 561–564. https://doi.org/10.1097/WNR.0000000000000794.

van der Merwe, B., Robb, M.P., Lewis, J.G. and Ormond, T. (2011) Anxiety measures and salivary cortisol responses in preschool children who stutter. *Contemporary Issues in Communication Science and Disorders* 38 (Spring), 1–10.

van Gelderen, A., Schoonen, R., Stoel, R. and Hulstijn, J. (2007) Development of adolescent reading comprehension in language 1 and language 2: A longitudinal analysis of constituent components. *Journal of Educational Psychology* 99 (3), 477–491. http://dx.doi.org/10.1037/0022-0663.99.3.477.

Vanderplank, R. (2008) The significance of first language development in five to nine year old children for second and foreign language learning. *Applied Linguistics* 29 (4), 717–722. https://doi.org/10.1093/applin/amn040.

Vermeer, H.J. and van IJzendoorn, M.H. (2006) Children's elevated cortisol levels at daycare: A review and meta-analysis. *Early Childhood Research Quarterly* 21 (3), 390–401.

Vliegenthart, J., Noppe, G., Van Rossum, E.F.C., Koper, J.W., Raat, H. and Van den Akker, E.L.T. (2016) Socioeconomic status in children is associated with hair cortisol levels as a biological measure of chronic stress. *Psychoneuroendocrinology* 65, 9–14.

Wang, L. (2011) Foreign English teachers in the Chinese classroom: Focus on teacher-student interaction. *The Journal of Asia TEFL* 8 (2), 73–93.

Woolf, B., Lane, H., Chaudhri, V. and Kolodner, J. (2013) AI grand challenges for education. *AI Magazine* 34, 66–84.

World Health Organization (2017) *Depression and Other Common Mental Disorders: Global Health Estimate* (WHO Reference No. WHO/MSD/MER/2017.2). Geneva: World Health Organization.

Wren, D.G. and Benson, J. (2004) Measuring test anxiety in children: Scale development and internal construct validation. *Anxiety, Stress & Coping* 17 (3), 227–240. http://dx.doi.org/10.1080/10615800412331292606.

Wu, N.H., Baek, H.J. and Kim, H,S. (2005) The cognitive, emotional, and social characteristics of preschoolers in early childhood private education as perceived by private kindergarten headmasters. *Journal of Early Childhood Education* 25 (1), 5–24.

Wu, N.H., Seo, Y.H. and Kang, Y.E. (2002) *A Report on the Adequacy of Early English Education for Young Children*. Seoul: Ministry of Education, Science and Technology.

Xinhua (2018) China tightens supervision over after-school institutions. Ministry of Education-The People's Republic of China. See http://en.moe.gov.cn/News/Top_News/201811/t20181126_361462.html (accessed October 2020).

Yamada, J., Takatsuka, S., Kotabe, N. and Kuruse, J. (1980) On the optimum age for teaching foreign vocabulary to children. *International Review of Applied Linguistics* 28, 245–247.

Yan, J. and Dewaele, J.M. (2018) Language anxiety in Chinese dialects and Putonghua among college students in mainland China: The effects of sociobiographical and linguistic variables. *Journal of Multilingual and Multicultural Development* 40 (4), 289–303. https://doi.org/10.1080/01434632.2018.1515213.

Yan, J. and Dewaele, J.M. (2020) The predictive power of sociobiographical and language variables on foreign language anxiety of Chinese university students. *System* 89, 102–207.

Yang, C.C.R. (2010) Teacher questions in second language classrooms: An investigation of three case studies. *Asian EFL Journal* 12 (1), 181–201.

Yashima, T. (2002) Willingness to communicate in a second language: The Japanese EFL context. *The Modern Language Journal* 86 (1), 54–66.

Yi, B.C. (2009) Comparative study on kindergarten and elementary English curriculum. *Modern Studies in English Language & Literature* 53 (4), 89–115.

Yi, C.C. (ed.) (2013) *The Psychological Well-being of East Asian Youth* (Vol. 2). Cham: Springer Science & Business Media.

Yi, S.G. and Yi, J.H. (2015) A study of the parents' view on English education for early childhood. *Studies in Modern Grammar* 84, 115–140.

Yi, S.O. (2002) Ch'odeunghakgyo 3haknyeon yeongeo kyoyuk-e natanan jogi yeongeo kyoyuk-eui yeonghyang [The effects of early childhood English education that appear in third year primary school English education]. Master thesis, Cheongju National University of Education.

Young, D.J. (1990) An investigation of students' perspectives on anxiety and speaking. *Foreign Language Annals* 23 (6), 539–553.

Young, D.J. (1991) Creating a low-anxiety classroom environment: What does language anxiety research suggest? *Modern Language Journal* 75 (4), 426–439. http://dx.doi.org/10.2307/329492.

Young, D.J. (1999) *Affect in Foreign Language and Second Language Learning*. New York: Mc Graw Hill Companies.

Yu Chang, J.-F. (2007) The role of children's literature in the teaching of English to young learners in Taiwan. Doctorial dissertation, University of Waikato.

Zheng, Y. (2008) Anxiety and second/foreign language learning revisited. *Canadian Journal for New Scholars in Education* 1 (1), 1–12.

Zhou, Y.R., Knoke D. and Sakamoto, I. (2005) Rethinking silence in the classroom: Chinese students' experiences of sharing indigenous knowledge. *International Journal of Inclusive Education* 9 (3), 287–311. https://doi.org/10.1080/13603110500075180.

Zosh, J.M., Hirsh-Pasek, K., Golinkoff, R.M. and Dore, R.A. (2016) Where learning meets creativity: The promise of guided play. In R. Beghetto and B. Sriraman (eds) *Creative Contradictions in Education: Cross Disciplinary Paradoxes and Perspectives* (pp. 165–180). New York, NY: Springer International Publishing.

Index

affective filters 4, 7, 38–9, 47–8, 58, 122, 125, 127
age 5, 17, 23, 30, 33, 43, 53, 61, 63–4, 69–70, 88, 93
anticipatory worry 64–5, 69–71, 78–9, 82. *See also* anxiety; fear; stress; mental health
anxiety 1–22, 24–9, 37–41, 44, 46–8, 50, 56–7, 59, 62–3, 77–9, 83, 86–9, 91, 106–7, 109–17, 119–20, 124–6, 128–35, 137–40, 144
  general 10, 15–16, 18, 20
  math 15–17, 20–2, 112–13, 140
  situation-specific 10
  state 6, 10, 15–16, 20
  trait 6, 10, 15, 18. *See also* anticipatory worry; fear; stress; mental health
apps 88–90, 123
Artificial Intelligence (AI) 89, 93, 135

bilingual 4, 24, 36, 45–6, 48–9, 52, 109, 120–1, 129, 133–4, 143

childhood 2–4, 10–12, 16, 18–19, 21–2, 24, 26–30, 32–7, 39, 41, 61, 84, 88, 109, 112–16, 119–20, 122, 124–6, 129–30, 134
China 1, 7–8, 34, 41–4, 47, 50, 55–7, 59, 88, 125
classroom 2–13, 15–22, 24, 28, 37–40, 43–50, 53–9, 61–2, 67–8, 81, 83–5, 87–9, 91–2, 96–7, 99, 105–16, 118–23, 125–36
Cognitive Behavioural Therapy (CBT) 117–19
competence 14, 21, 42, 47, 50, 52–3, 58–9, 114, 128, 132
cooking 87, 91–4, 96–9, 102–7, 126, 131
Cope, Joann 5–6, 10, 16–17, 25, 67
cram schools. *See* hagwon
Critical Period Hypothesis (CPH) 22–4, 51–4, 124
culture 28, 30, 37, 40, 43, 51, 54–9, 61–2, 86, 115–16, 122, 127–9, 143–8

Dewaele, Jean-Marc 3, 5, 7–9, 13, 19, 40, 48, 53, 108, 115, 125–6, 130

East Asia 1–2, 7–8, 13, 21, 24, 28–30, 34, 40–44, 47, 50, 54–9, 61, 88, 125, 128–9, 132–3, 135. *See also* China, Japan, South Korea, Taiwan
education 1–4, 7, 10–20, 24, 27–62, 65, 69–75, 79–90, 95, 106–109, 115–16, 119–24, 126–135
  early childhood English education 2–4, 10, 12, 16, 18–22, 24, 28, 32–7, 39, 41, 84, 88, 109, 112–16, 119–20, 122, 124, 126, 129–30, 134
  prenatal 1, 29
English
  immersion institution 63–85, 127, 131
  language ability 64, 66, 69–72, 78–84
  language acquisition 2, 14, 29, 32, 35, 41, 54, 58–61, 124, 129
  See also kindergarten, English
'English Fever' 1, 3, 24, 28–30, 41, 44, 86–7, 106–7, 128–9, 132
English as a Foreign Language (EFL) 52, 54, 57, 84, 87–8, 93, 106–7, 131–2
English as the medium of instruction (EMI) 30, 56
Extramural English (EE) 88–9
'Expanding Circle' 1, 14, 42, 45

family 11, 18, 61, 63, 65–6, 68–74, 79–80, 82, 84–5, 114, 119, 129. *See also* father; grandparents; mother; parents
father 29, 34, 62, 69–70, 72, 80, 142
fear 10, 13, 16, 19, 25–6, 28, 31, 40, 48, 56, 112, 117, 120, 135. *See also* anxiety; anticipatory worry; stress; mental health
Fear of Negative Evaluation (FNE) 10, 13, 16, 19, 28, 56, 112, 135
first language (L1) 12, 22–4, 39, 45, 49, 53, 83, 85, 121. *See also* second language (L2)

foreign language
Foreign Language Anxiety (FLA) 1–18, 20–25, 28–9, 37–9, 44, 46–8, 51, 53, 55–9, 61–3, 67–70, 77–93, 105, 107, 109–10, 112, 114–16, 118–35
Foreign Language Classroom Anxiety (FLCA) 3, 6–10, 16–17, 87, 108
Foreign Language Classroom Anxiety Scale (FLCAS) 6, 10, 16–17
Foreign Language Enjoyment (FLE) 3, 7–10, 12, 28, 37, 40, 44–6, 48, 51, 56, 59, 61, 86–9, 103, 105, 107–9, 113, 116, 122–3, 125–6, 128, 130–6
foreign language learning 87, 91–3, 106–7, 125

gender 8, 21, 58, 64, 69–71, 78–9
government 1, 4, 29–32, 36, 42–4, 47, 51–2, 116, 121, 123, 130
grandparents 29, 35, 61

hagwon 31, 34
Horwitz, Elaine K. 3, 5–6, 9–10, 13, 16–17, 21, 25, 67

immersion 1, 4, 24, 29, 34, 37–9, 44–9, 63–5, 67–8, 70–2, 74–86, 121, 126–7, 129, 131
impulsiveness 64–5, 69–71, 78–9, 82–85

Japan 1, 30, 41–3, 57–8, 125

kinaesthetic 93, 113, 122
kindergarten 1, 32–8, 40, 44, 49, 63–5, 67–9, 71–2, 74–85, 87, 95, 127, 129–131
  English 1, 32–8, 40, 44, 49, 63, 65, 67–85, 87, 95, 127, 129–31
  regular 63–4, 71–2, 75–9, 81, 83–5, 127, 131
  See also nursery
Korea. *See* South Korea
Korean Education Development Institute (KEDI) 34–7

language attainment 7, 12, 107
learning 1–13, 15–17, 19–26, 28–35, 37–42, 44–51, 53–63, 78–9, 81, 83–128, 130–6
  a language 1–10, 16, 19, 21–4, 29, 35, 37–40, 45–50, 54, 56–7, 59–61, 83, 85–93, 105–7, 110, 112, 114–16, 119–127, 130–6
  environment 3–4, 9, 34, 47, 61, 92–3, 106, 109, 114, 116, 120, 122–5, 132–6

by rote 4, 14, 24, 46, 50, 58–9, 114, 126, 133
successful language learning 9, 24, 39, 44, 46–7, 50, 116, 126, 135
Likert scale 6, 60, 64–5, 68
Lingua Franca 1, 10, 42, 51–2, 128
lingual frenectomy 42

MacIntyre, Peter D. 3, 5, 7–10, 19, 46–8, 87, 108, 115, 130
memorization 14, 50, 86, 104, 126
memory 16–17, 20–2, 25, 40, 90, 103–4, 119
mental health 26, 28, 62, 117, 125
monolingual 36–8, 48–9, 53, 121. *See also* multilingual
mother 1, 22, 29, 34–5, 59–61, 63–6, 68–70, 72, 80, 84, 119, 123, 134
  tongue 1, 8, 33
  language 33
motivation
  instrumental 19, 60, 127–8
  integrative 19, 60–1, 127
multi-sensory 92, 105–6
multilingual 53, 89, 121. *See also* monolingual

native speaker (NS) 24, 36–7, 43, 46, 49, 51–3, 66, 88–9, 114–15, 128–9, 143. *See also* native speakerism
native speakerism 51–3, 115, 128
Negative Evaluation (NE) 10, 13, 16, 19, 28, 56, 112, 135. *See also* Fear of Negative Evaluation (FNE)
neural plasticity 26–7, 53–4
North America 30, 33, 36, 38, 44, 49, 51–3, 96, 110, 115, 127–9
nursery 33, 36, 49, 142, 146–8. *See also* kindergarten

Organization Against Private-sector Education (OAPE) 32–4
'One Language at a Time (OLAT)' 86

parents 1–5, 12, 15, 17–19, 22, 24, 26, 28–36, 40–4, 46–9, 51–4, 59–66, 72, 79–80, 82, 84–5, 88–9, 103, 109–12, 114–15, 117–20, 123–5, 127–9, 131, 134–5. *See also* mother; father
perfectionism 12–5, 28, 52–3, 62, 114, 128–9, 144
phonology 35, 42, 51, 102, 124
proficiency 8–10, 23, 30, 38, 45, 49, 53, 64, 66, 86, 88, 145
pronunciation 4, 24, 35–7, 40, 42, 51–3, 58, 64, 88, 115, 143–5

psychology 3, 5–7, 9–10, 24, 28, 115, 118
  positive 3, 7, 9–10, 20, 115

question 17, 55–9, 67–8, 98, 103, 110, 115, 130
questionnaire 17, 63–6, 85, 140

repetition 90, 96, 105–7
rote learning. *See* learning, by rote

second language (L2) 5–7, 10, 18, 22–4, 35, 42, 48, 53–4, 57–8, 60, 86–7, 90, 120. *See also* first language (L1)
Second Language Acquisition (SLA) 5, 22–4, 35, 46, 53–4, 86, 120, 124
Social Avoidance and Distress (SAD) 16, 19, 56, 138
Socioeconomic Status (SES)
South America 27
South Korea 2–3, 8, 14, 22, 28–39, 41–5, 49, 51–2, 54, 63, 86–7, 89, 95, 106–7, 115, 122, 126, 129, 132–4
Standard Deviation (SD) 68–72, 74–5, 77, 95, 99–102
stress 1, 7, 9, 11–12, 15–17, 19, 24–5, 27, 40, 59, 61–2, 86, 111, 113, 144, 146. *See also* anticipatory worry; anxiety; fear; mental health
study abroad 12, 29, 34, 129
Suneung 14, 30–1

Taiwan 42, 44
Target Language (TL) 8–9, 21, 24, 56–7, 59–60, 90, 110, 114, 123, 127
Task-based Language Learning (TBLL) 108, 122, 126, 128
Task-based Language Teaching (TBLT) 4, 86, 91–3, 106, 128, 131
teacher 3, 13, 18–19, 21–2, 24–5, 28, 31–2, 34, 36–7, 39, 43, 46, 48–52, 54–9, 62–4, 67–70, 74–6, 81–4, 89–90, 96–7, 99, 102, 105–6, 109–20, 122–5, 127–30, 132, 134–6
Teaching English as a Foreign Language (TEFL) 43, 116
Teaching English to Speakers of Other Languages (TESOL) 43, 56, 116
technology 16–17, 88–91, 93, 110–1, 122–3, 126, 134–5
Test of English as a Foreign Language (TOEFL) 14, 31, 42, 132
Test of English Proficiency (TEPS) 66
translanguaging 4, 9, 44, 49, 53, 109, 120–3, 127–9, 131, 133–4, 136

vocabulary 4, 13, 35–6, 38, 50–2, 58, 64, 87–8, 90–4, 96–107, 115, 144–5

Young Language Learners (YLLs) 4, 9–10, 16, 18, 28, 40, 45, 88, 107–9, 116, 120, 123, 125, 127–31, 133–4

For Product Safety Concerns and Information please contact our EU Authorised Representative:

Easy Access System Europe

Mustamäe tee 50

10621 Tallinn

Estonia

gpsr.requests@easproject.com

www.ingramcontent.com/pod-product-compliance
Lightning Source LLC
Chambersburg PA
CBHW070615300426
44113CB00010B/1541